C000095972

It's My Party

It's My Party

Reading Twentieth-century Women's Writing

Edited by **Gina Wisker**

Pluto Press

LONDON • BOULDER, COLORADO

First published 1994 by Pluto Press
345 Archway Road, London N6 5AA
and 5500 Central Avenue
Boulder, Colorado 80301, USA

Collection and introduction copyright © Gina Wisker, 1994

The right of the contributors to be identified as the authors of
their work has been asserted by them in accordance with the
Copyright, Designs and Patents Act 1988

British Library Cataloguing in Publication Data
A catalogue record for this book is available from
the British Library

Library of Congress Cataloging in Publication Data
It's my party: reading twentieth-century women's writing
/ edited by Gina Wisker
215pp. 22cm.
Includes bibliographical references and index.
ISBN 0-7453-0679-9
1. English literature–Women authors–History and criticism.
2. Women and literature–Great Britain–History–20th century.
3. Women and literature–United States–History–20th century.
4. American literature–Women authors–History and criticism.
5. American literature–20th century–History and criticism.
6. English literature–20th century–History and criticism.
I. Wisker, Gina, 1951–
PR116.I8   1994
820.9'9287'0904–dc20   93–45416
                                                        CIP
ISBN 0 7453 0679 9 hbk.

Designed, typeset and produced for Pluto Press by
Chase Production Services, Chipping Norton, OX7 5QR
Printed in Finland by WSOY

Contents

Notes on Contributors

Sue Anderson teaches at Anglia Polytechnic University part time, and at Harlow College. She is currently studying for the MA in Women's Studies at Anglia.

Marilyn Brooks teaches for the Open University, Cambridge University Board of Continuing Education and Anglia Polytechnic University. She is currently completing her PhD.

Sally Brown is the Enterprise Director at the University of Northumbria at Newcastle, and used to be an Open University literature tutor for many years. She has co-written (with Phil Race) *500 Tips for Students* and *500 Tips for Tutors*, and edits and writes for publications on teaching and learning, and on women in higher education.

Odette l'Henry Evans is a Principal Lecturer in Comparative Literature at the University of North London. Her specialism is modern poetry but, as a murder mystery buff, she has published numerous articles on detective fiction writers, including Mickey Spillane, Patricia Highsmith and Georges Simenon. She is currently completing a full-length study of tales of the supernatural.

Gabriele Griffin lectures in English at Nene College. Her recent publications include *Lesbian Images in Twentieth-Century Women's Writing* (1991) and with E.A. Aston *Stage Left: Women's Theatre Groups in Interview* (1991). She and Dr Aston are also editing plays for the Women's Theatre Group for Sheffield Academic Press.

Maggie Humm is Senior Lecturer and Co-ordinator of Women's Studies at the University of Westminster. She has contributed widely to such journals as *Women's Studies International Quarterly*, *Feminist Teacher* and *Canadian Women's Studies*, and has published several books including *Feminist Criticism* (1986).

Stuart Laing is Assistant Director at the University of Brighton. His previous publications include *Representations of Working Class Life 1957–64* (1986) and the co-authored *Disorder and Discipline: Popular Culture 1550 to the Present* (1988).

Maria Lauret lectures in English at the University of Southampton. She has published widely on twentieth-century women's writing.

Gina Wisker is Principal Lecturer working in English, Staff Development and Women's Studies at Anglia Polytechnic University. She also teaches for the Cambridge University Board of Continuing Education and the Open University. She edited and contributed to *Insights into Black Women's Writing* (1993), *What's So Special About Women in Higher Education?* Vols 1 and 2, and has contributed essays on contemporary women's writing to *Over Here, Wasafiri, Literature Teaching Politics, Ideas and Production* and *Million* and on both poetry and fiction to various *Insights* volumes, on horror fiction to *Creepers* (1993). Gina has had poems published in *Poetry Now: Women* (1993/4), *Private View Amaryllis*, etc.

Bruce Woodcock is a Lecturer in English at the University of Hull. His published works include *Male Mythologies: John Fowles and Masculinity* (Harvester, 1984) as well as articles on Tony Harrison, Thom Gunn and other contemporary British poets.

Introduction

Gina Wisker

The idea for this book grew out of excitement at becoming aware of the variety and vitality of writing by twentieth-century women writers whose work skirted the mainstream, who were not the alternative canon, the greats, Virginia Woolf, Iris Murdoch, ensconced safely and influentially now on literature syllabuses. The women discussed here are experimental, critical products of their cultural context, who are kicking over the traces of the forms and values of popular writing developed by male writers, producing critiques, new angles, new emphases, new representations. Their work is both *popular* in that it often grows directly out of popular fictional genres dominated by male writers, such as science fiction, detective fiction, realism, soft-core porn masquerading as romantic fiction, and/or it is *popular* in so far as it is widely read, influential, even televised. In the works discussed here received forms as well as received representations are deconstructed, focused on with an ironic, askance viewpoint. The writers discussed in this collection question, displace, they mock and they celebrate difference, scuffing and reshaping established forms, established clues and readings, and leaving new, fresh prints.

This collection of essays concentrates on twentieth-century writing by women in popular fictional modes, and writing by women whose work has been widely read and which presents a critical position on what is termed 'popular'. Several of the essays focus on a female/feminist intervention in *popular fictional* fields traditionally dominated by male writers which commonly present reductive, stereotyped versions of women's roles. Others concentrate on writing by women whose work is widely read, work which transcends any divisions of the 'popular' and the 'great'. Several of the women writers here ask questions about the popularity of women's writing and reading, about magazine fictions, books for girls and serialised TV versions of novels. Those whose work and reception are considered here all engage with and cast a critical, deconstructive eye on established myths, representations and values whether writing as Winifred Holtby at the beginning of the century, as Erica Jong at its initial feminist zenith, as Jean Rhys at a strange cultural conjunction of race, time, and rereadings, or as Angela Carter, soaring sceptically and magically free towards the end of the century. They re-vision, de- and remythologise, reinscribe women centre text, differently valued.

Popular fiction/writing by women has traditionally been carica-
tured and characterised as the formulaic Mills and Boon story for
the tired housewife seeking escapism. Elitist literary critics found
no room for the discussion of such trivia. With the advent of the
'crisis in English studies' in the 1970s and 1980s an exciting new
revaluation of texts in their cultural and historical context, and in
terms of psychoanalytic, semiotic, Marxist, feminist, structuralist
and post-structuralist readings blew wide open the canon of
'acceptable' reading and study matter. Theoretical work by
Macherey, Gramsci, Derrida and Bakhtin caused a critical
refocus: the popular text could be read for its absences and
silences, for its covert and overt reinforcement, or subversion, of
dominant ideology and cultural practices, not merely for its
resemblance or otherwise to writing by Lawrence, Joyce and
George Eliot.

There is a strong argument that writing from a position of
social subordination or marginality results inevitably in an askance
view of culture and ideology. Women's writing and particularly
women's popular writing/fiction is seen by many contemporary
feminists such as Kristeva, Cixous, and Irigaray as *necessarily*
subversive and liberating, *necessarily* analytical and critical.

Here we investigate some of the range of popular writing by
women, or writing by women whose work is widely read and has
in some cases been converted to the visual media of film or TV.
One main aim is to open up the variety of readings of these
texts, seeing them as sites for debate about the constrictions and
deconstructions of gendered subjectivities. Several of the essays
explore the sources of power, fantasy and the myths which lie
behind social conditioning and the representation or misrepresentation of gender roles. All enable us as readers to reopen discussions as to the meanings and the effects of popular writing by
women, often with a view of these works as subversive, critical,
celebratory, rather than merely aimed at reinforcing gender role
constrictions and the status quo.

The collection is roughly divided in two main parts, though
individual essays might sit happily in both. The first part concentrates on sexuality and representation, on context, constriction, and
deconstruction. The second offers a critical celebration of women's
reappropriation of hitherto male-defined popular fictional genres.

I chose Stuart Laing's essay to begin with because it raises
questions central to the collection concerning the uneasy relationship between 'high' and 'popular' fiction, and considers the interaction between context and text in the treatment and reception of
representations of women and women's sexuality. Pornography,
popularity and potential sexual freedoms in the context of historical changes in women's lives are the metatext of novels con-

sidered later on in the collection by Maria Lauret. They are issues fascinatingly central to Stuart Laing's discussion of that marvellously inaccurate period piece of soft-core porn, *Lady Chatterley's Daughter*. Stuart Laing considers the instability of the romantic fiction genre. His essay focuses both on women's writing and on the popular genre of romantic fiction. *Jane Eyre*, one of the novels, like *Wuthering Heights*, which leaves its traces in so much romantic fiction, crops up here when he notes how Lawrence's *Lady Chatterley's Lover* grows out of this nineteenth-century seminal work, and the furore of the pornography trial comes into sharper focus as a result; it exposed a historically contextualised set of conflicts of sexual ideologies. *Lady Chatterley's Daughter*, a vastly less notable piece of romantic fiction than the mother text, is seen to renegotiate the narrative and thematic structures of Lawrence's novel, and consideration of this twentieth-century piece of popular romantic fiction in this context adds here to debates running throughout this collection of essays about representations of sexuality and gender roles in relation to 'norms' encoded in fiction.

Lady Chatterley's Daughter returns a notion of Englishness even as it returns Clare, the daughter, to a traditional 'balanced', 'normal' sexual relationship devoid of the excesses of her parents and their selfish romantic extremism. *Lady Chatterley's Lover* is recognised for the truly revolutionary way *it* rewrote romantic fiction, subverting the national, familial and sexual myths underlying traditional romantic fictions, myths which ensured the stability of the status quo. Ironically, given its radical predecessor, *Lady Chatterley's Daughter*, the product of quite a traditionalist woman writer, restores these familiar comforts and so plays the traditionally supportive role of romantic fictions; it is sexually titillating, inexplicit, and it bolsters up ideas about male power and female submission, ultimately reinforcing sexual and gender 'norms'.

Maria Lauret rereads the novels of the heyday of 'sexual liberation', finding this liberated lust more a rather shallow parallel to the established soft-core pornography of Henry Miller and others than a really satisfying, genuinely new representation of women's sexuality and freedoms. Historically contextualising Jong, Alther, Alix Kates Shulman and Rita Mae Brown, Maria Lauret rediscovers the ostensible fun and promises on which these books reneged, their rather 'ambivalent and alienated representations of femininity' sitting uncomfortably with the newly raised feminist consciousness, providing confusing, ultimately oddly collusive messages to questioning women readers. They might have given us all a sense of freedom at the time, but their forms were far from radical. Moving on, Maria Lauret contextualises our reading of these novels in the continuing debate about sexuality, and lesbian or heterosexual relationships, particularly now in the era of AIDS. The rather antagonistic, even bruising sexual debates engendered by radical lesbian feminists of the 1980s have continued the concern with sexuality and sexual relations but, she argues, heterosexual women, feeling perhaps apologetic about their non-radical sexual stance, are floundering again in terms of how to articulate sexual freedoms now, and how to discover any possibility of sexual self-definition. The 'liberated' novels of the 1970s mark a transitional period, and although, she argues, they fail as novels of real sexual freedoms, establishing new responses and new expressions, their failure is an index of transition and we are all still searching!

Maggie Humm's essay on Jean Rhys, which follows, is central to the collection as a whole because it confronts so many of the issues of representation, and of writing and reading which the book seeks to address. Focusing on a range of Jean Rhys's writing, from *Good Morning Midnight* and *Voyage in the Dark* to the autobiographical *Smile Please* and Rhys's letters, but most specifically on that most complex novel of 'border crossing', *Wide Sargasso Sea*, Maggie Humm shows how Rhys constructs a feminist anticolonialism. The novel subverts colonialism, the appropriation of what is different, other; it subverts colonial romance, and turns over and refertilises the psychologically and sociopolitically rich romantic fictional soil of *Jane Eyre*.

Maggie Humm shows how Rhys uses the historical referent of the border to signal her exposure and violation of configurations of power relations premised upon difference: racial, gendered, class differences. She examines how Rhys, by crossing these boundaries of difference and crossing also the discursive boundaries between the fictional and the autobiographical, the original fiction and its origin in a prior fiction, enables us to question the sources of representation and the sources of gendered power relations.

The margins are written in and of; they cast light on and refocus what has been considered *the centre*, i.e. male representations of women, commonly held beliefs about women of different races and backgrounds. Rhys enables us to celebrate differences. Her work also provides a paradigm for the textual and symbolic changes that grow from the work of these popular and widely read women writers, their changes and developments of position and of expression. Her work is textually innovative, enabling exploration of the relationship between the paternal symbolic and the maternal semiotic, negotiating expression for the semiotic against a background of established forms, established representations, established discourses, established texts (*Jane Eyre*).

As such, then, we can see Rhys, and Maggie Humm's discussion of her work here, as a central focus in the collection's examination of how women writers of popular fiction/widely read women writers negotiate new representations, new ways of writing, new readings out of the familial background of received versions of women, their sexuality and identities, their potential and their writing forms, and out of the particular patriarchal dominance of the family of established popular fictional forms.

Acts of defiance are the focus of Gabriele Griffin's consideration of popular lesbian heroes in Jeanette Winterson's *Oranges Are Not the Only Fruit*, Alice Walker's *The Color Purple* and Rita Mae Brown's *Rubyfruit Jungle*. Gabriele analyses the construction of these lesbian protagonists as one of affirmation of the positive value of their difference. They choose relationships with women on the basis of *informed* choice, and each can be seen celebrating lesbianism as an expression of female sexuality, a commitment and a positive, rewarding move. In the context of western literature's history of popular 'deviant' characters who react against a moral authority, the attraction, accessibility and popularity for a wide audience of the lesbian protagonists and their sexual choices are explored and explained.

Part of the attraction and popularity of *Oranges Are Not the Only Fruit*, *The Color Purple* and *Rubyfruit Jungle* lies in their celebration of deviant, defiant heroes whose quest for and discovery of sexual identity appeals to readers' desire for the affirmation of certain positive myths and configurations. That these heroes fly in the face of 'sexual norms' in their sexual choices firmly establishes their appeal with a lesbian readership as well. These are some of the readers who appreciate the development of a positive alternative mythology with which to represent women's sexuality. Myths, stereotypes and culturally conditioned representations are, however, sadly, more frequently agents for repression and constraint than they are for liberation and it is with these particular straightjacketing denigrations of women that I take issue, and engage in battle, in Chapter 5.

Battle is an image, because the bad press Medusa has had is central to arguments about demythologising and remythologising, and restoring the vitality and value of women's magical vision. Snakey-haired, sexually liberated, Medusa emerges constantly surrounded by images and connotations of the destructive powers of forbidden knowledge, of comparisons with Eve and with a palpable sense of the attractions and dangers of a rejection of patriarchal power. Medusa becomes the object of male hate because of the threat she represents as a sexually lively, self-aware woman.

She has to be beheaded to prove male power, and establish the viability and sense of safety of the male-originated myths

which place women firmly in subordinate positions. Examining
feminist rewriting and re-visioning of myths and their cultural
sources, I side with Cixous in celebrating the powers of theft –
developments of different forms from a base 'stolen' from male-
defined genres and expressions – and of flight – creativity, the
assertion of the magical and the imaginative alongside the
rational.

Looking at the use of magic realism in works by Angela
Carter, Emma Tennant, Toni Morrison, Suniti Namjoshi, Sarah
Maitland, Fay Weldon, Michèle Roberts, Grace Nichols and Alice
Walker, I consider how a feminist deconstruction and reconstruction of alternative myths can be a mere overturning of the tables,
a reinforcement of the mythic con trick, or liberating for women's
consciousness, for the potentiality of a female erotic, and for our
sense of our own gender conditioning and roles. Open-ended and
highly imaginative, these texts are subversive in their critique and
in the alternatives suggested by their use of spirituality, the
supernatural and magic. Women's writing here is seen as offering
a flexible, creative and celebratory view of women's potential.

Debate about the extent to which popular forms and genres
reinforce the dominant, patriarchally defined ideology of women's
subservience, and how far they actually subvert and interrogate it,
continues in Marilyn Brooks's essay on televising provocative and
popular women's fiction. Marilyn Brooks argues that the production of radical texts in televised and film format, although reaching a wider audience, seems inevitably to defuse their radical
nature, rendering them more palatable and less challenging. The
contradictory changes undergone by Ruth in Fay Weldon's *The
Life and Loves of a She-Devil* which question the value of her
revenge if it merely encourages her to turn into a female
stereotype are watered down in the TV version and entirely
dissolved into soap drama in the American film version of the
novel. Similarly, Jeanette Winterson's *Oranges Are Not the Only
Fruit* appears much less challenging and radical when televised,
the lesbian element seen as one example of a tomboyish rebellion
motif. Television in particular, reaching a very large, home-based
audience, is clearly in need of some radicalising if stereotypical
representations of women and defused versions of alternatives are
not to continue to dominate the popular consciousness.

The second section of the book focuses more intently on the
issue of women's writing in popular genres. Sally Brown's companion piece to Stuart Laing's earlier essay on romantic fiction
considers the historically innovatory work of Winifred Holtby who
problematised both romantic love and the myth of the happy, all
satisfying marriage. Sally Brown contextualises Holtby's work of
the 1920s and 1930s in questions surrounding the role and

proper place of women in the home, ensconced in domesticity and married bliss, in a period when the Great War had rendered this myth even more unrealisable than usual. Holtby negotiates an uneasy path between the familiar purplish passages of romantic fiction and plots, characters and considerations which question the basis in marriage and the sexual role status quo which underpin such romantic fiction. She casts a questioning eye on a society which blithely reinforces cant about marriage and romance, and highlights the entrapment and constriction of women's roles within and without the married state. While the ostensible familiarity of her realistic, romantic model attracts readers, Sally Brown argues, Holtby offers a scepticism about the sexual politics between men and women, and a historically viable, new model of resourceful, resolute womanhood.

Much has been written about women's detective fiction, probably the most popular male-established fictional genre to appeal to women writers and feminist critics alike. Ruth Rendell and P.D. James are familiar figures for critical appreciation, and their works carry some fascinating comments about women's roles, lesbianism and possibilities for alternative representations and relationships. Less familiar a focus for the feminist critic, however, is the less feminist Agatha Christie, the grand old lady of murder mysteries. Agatha Christie's particular brand of detective novel writing is the subject of Odette l'Henry Evans's essay which looks at the formulaic trajectory of the novels but goes on to analyse the ways in which Christie's language reveals the psychological traps and tricks of her characters. She particularly concentrates on the convolutions of Christie's murderesses' minds, topical today in the light of recent interest in women who kill. Odette l'Henry Evans also looks at Christie's Miss Marple. Here she aligns herself with other feminist critics examining the work of women detective novel writers, women who write within or against the rules of a male-dominated genre, their work undercutting stereotyped roles, diverting the power of unravelling the mystery from its traditional residence in the male, particularly the male detective, and developing a new sort of investigative procedure, a new role for the woman detective, a new power.

Detectives traditionally collect clues and Christie's, too, rely on realistic details, a manageable and solvable world, the world of realism upset by minds which follow their own logic. Concern with the detective novel in Odette l'Henry Evans's chapter relates closely to the concerns of Sue Anderson who, in her work on Pat Barker and realist women writers, reinvests the realist text with its value as socially/historically/politically engaged representation of the constrictions of working-class women's lives in regional contexts. The grimly realist text is all too often the forum of the male writer such as Stan Barstow, Alan Sillitoe, writers who position women as the fag-smoking, maternal, frying-pan wielding Mam, or the floosie tarted up in her high heels and lipstick, ripe for a bit of a fling. Women figure as sexual objects on the route to male sexual liberation and assertion of a world dominated by materialism and small-town, grimy gasworks machismo. Pat Barker's texts reposition women centre stage, although they avoid any sentimentalising, even of the notions of the 'community of women', and Barker's version of 'writing the body' seems confined glue-like to excesses of bodily fluids. Sue Anderson looks at the immediacy and grim honesty of Barker's writing but recognises the more subtle, underlying myths and fairytales that Barker examines and debunks/demythologisesin her work.

The final essay in the collection is one which looks at women's revitalising of an established genre of popular fiction in a way which provides positive models and asks fundamental questions. Bruce Woodcock's essay on Ursula Le Guin's radical Taoism explores her relationship with recent feminist developments in science fiction – a landscape of imagination found to be particularly fertile and promising for contemporary women writers eager to explore dystopias, to deconstruct versions of contemporary relations and the potential for alternative worlds and representations. Doris Lessing's own series of explorations in the *Canopus in Argus* series, Margaret Atwood's *The Handmaid's Tale*, Angela Carter's *The Passion of New Eve* are similar explorations, Carter's novel being particularly relevant to our discussions of the popular as it juxtaposes the representational lies of romantic fictions purveyed by Hollywood against a landscape of the sexually experimental and deconstructive.

Le Guin allies the science fictional with the spiritual, relating her to the novelists explored in my own chapter, where the revaluation of the magical is based upon a philosophy of difference, equality, flexibility, imagination given as much space as reason. Bruce Woodcock explores women's science fiction, focusing on Le Guin's work as a site for investigation and interrogation of gendered roles of power. Le Guin's Taoism and mysticism ally with her science fictional techniques and her feminism and political concerns to urge more equable future relations between the sexes. For left critics Le Guin provides an interesting example of marriage between radical, feminist politics and the spiritual, the magical, with popular sci-fi forms. In Le Guin's rejection of binary oppositions and her androgynous vision she comes close to the radical, poetic, philosophical arguments of Cixous, Kristeva and Irigaray, and uses a popular fictional form to posit and dramatise an alternative vision, perhaps the most radical of all the writers considered here.

PART ONE

SEXUALITY AND REPRESENTATION

CHAPTER 1

Authenticating Romantic Fiction: *Lady Chatterley's Daughter*

Stuart Laing

A central issue in any attempt to understand popular fiction is that of the relationship between genre and individual text. Where should analysis focus? On similarities or differences between particular examples? This problem is made more difficult still when a historical perspective is introduced. Any particular genre must then be recognised as itself never stable – the rules and conventions of popular fictional forms (whether thrillers, westerns or SF) being always in the process of transformation. In the case of romantic fiction this issue has an especial significance since, as Jean Radford has recently argued, we must also 'give some weight to the claim that romance is one of the oldest and most enduring of literary modes which survives today'.[1] Patterns of stability and change within this mode are then likely to throw some light on more general questions of cultural continuity and transformation.

In the same essay Radford points to a further defining element of the romantic fiction genre in noting that romantic narrative conventions have never remained confined to popular or subordinate literary material – that, for example, within nineteenth-century literature, 'they remained alive and well not only on the margins but in the heartland of the realist novel'.[2] Indeed, even if a deliberately simplified definition of 'romance elements' is used (plots in which the whole emphasis tends towards a resolution through the marriage of a single hero and heroine) then the main line of the English novel between 1750 and 1900 (as constructed through the academic syllabus) is composed within this form. Fielding, Austen, the Brontës, Dickens, Thackeray, Eliot, Hardy and Lawrence are all subscribers to the genre. One way of defining the modernist break in English fiction (Conrad, Forster, Woolf, Joyce) is precisely the refusal to work within these conventions – the conventions about which Forster complained in *Aspects of the Novel*:

> Love, like death, is congenial to a novelist because it ends a book conveniently. He can make it a permanency, and his readers easily acquiesce, because one of the illusions attached to love is that it will be permanent. Not has been – will be. All history, all our experience, teaches us that no human relation-

ship is constant, it is as unstable as the living beings who
compose it, and they must balance like jugglers if it is to
remain; if it is constant it is no longer a human relationship
but a social habit, the emphasis in it has passed from love to
marriage.[3]

A different way of registering the same difficulty comes through
in the later fiction of Hardy and, more self-consciously, in Lawrence. In his essay on Hardy, Lawrence spends a lot of time
trying to come to terms with Hardy's last novel, *Jude the Obscure*,
and the variety of ideas on marriage contained within it. According to Lawrence a central aspect of Hardy's philosophy was that
'the convention of the community is a prison to [man's] natural,
individual desire, a desire that compels him, whether he feels
justified or not, to break the bounds of the community ...'.[4] This
opposition between 'community convention' and 'natural desire'
parallels that between Forster's 'social habit' and 'human relationship', but with the crucial difference that while Forster consigns
marriage to the realm of 'social habit', Lawrence's fiction dedi-
cates itself to rescuing it for 'natural desire'. It is, in fact,
generally characteristic that when a particular cultural convention
or fictional genre falls into crisis, its unconscious assumptions, its
structural rules are laid bare, are interrogated, refused, redefined
or explicitly reaffirmed; they themselves become the subject
matter of fiction, rather than constituting the given basis on
which narratives are constructed. Lawrence's novels of love, marriage and the impossibility of social integration are clear examples
of this process.

Lady Chatterley's Lover,[5] for instance, effects a recomposition
of the elements of *Jane Eyre*, a novel which Lawrence, in his
essay 'Pornography and Obscenity', uses as an example of great
literature with unconscious 'sex appeal'. In both texts a central
woman character (Jane/Connie) chooses between two men – one
cerebral, cold and sexless (St John Rivers/Clifford), the other
passionate and physical (Rochester/Mellors, both of whom are
given an excessively passionate first wife called Bertha).
Lawrence's transference of the physical disability from Rochester/
Mellors to St John/Clifford and the total social isolation of the
concluding 'marriage' mark a conscious restructuring of the received conventions of the comic romance form. In Northrop
Frye's terms, *Lady Chatterley's Lover* belongs to 'the phase of the
collapse and disintegration of the comic society ... the social units
of comedy become small and esoteric ... secret and sheltered
places, forests in the moonlight ... become more prominent'.[6]

Lawrence's novel is, for literary history, the terminal point of a
tradition in the English novel with roots in the mid-eighteenth
century. Its place within contemporary cultural history is,

however, rather more complex. *Lady Chatterley's Lover* here must be seen in terms not of its textual integrity but of its processes of production, reproduction and consumption. The key moment here is no longer that of the late 1920s (its moment of authorial origin) but rather that of the early 1960s – the Penguin paperback edition, the 'Trial of Lady Chatterley' and its aftermath. The significant context of this cultural moment is then not Lawrence's relation to the 'Great Tradition', but the consequences (both potential and actual) of the insertion of *Lady Chatterley's Lover* into the domain of popular culture.

The Trial of Lady Chatterley

A detailed examination of the complex of reasons determining the occurrence of the Chatterley trial in London in autumn 1960 falls outside the brief of this essay. Only an abbreviated account is possible. For Penguin Books the year 1960 was an important milestone in their longstanding project of publishing a complete paperback edition of Lawrence's major works. It was simultaneously the thirtieth anniversary of Lawrence's death and the twenty-fifth of Penguin's foundation; a major publishing event marking both was required. During the previous year both the arrival on the statutes of a new British Obscene Publications Act (which now allowed defence against obscenity on the grounds of literary merit) and the legal publication in America of an unexpurgated edition suggested a favourable climate to test the general consensus (held since Lawrence's death) that the whole novel could not legally be sold or published in Britain.

The trial itself covered a two-week period and involved '35 distinguished men and women of letters, moral theologians, teachers, publishers, editors and critics'[7] as defence witnesses, including E.M. Forster, C. Day Lewis, Richard Hoggart, Raymond Williams, Roy Jenkins (the author of the 1959 Act under which the trial was being conducted) and the Bishop of Woolwich. The acquittal of 'Lady Chatterley' or, rather, Penguin Books, led to sales (in Britain alone) of up to two million within a year and up to four million by the end of the 1960s.

The full text of the Chatterley trial remains a rich seam for any analyst of sexual ideologies in mid-twentieth-century Britain. Both Griffith-Jones's extraordinarily snobbish prosecutor's question – 'Is it a book you would even wish your wife or your servants to read?'[8] – and the various defence witnesses' almost religious accounts of the spiritual connotations of Lawrence's attitude to sexual relations have occasioned a good deal of comment. As has been pointed out the core of the prosecution case at times seemed to lie in the moral reprehensibility of the fact of adultery rather than the particularities of how the book might 'deprave or corrupt'. However, towards the end of the proceedings Griffith-Jones did become relatively specific as to the moral damage that would be done. The central issue was specified as *restraint*. When refused leave to read out details of sexual offences from the *Criminal Statistics of 1959* he commented:

> one has only got to read one's daily papers to see the kind of thing that is happening, and it is all that type of offence, it is all through lack of standards, lack of restraint, lack of discipline – mental, moral discipline.[9]

More particularly, at the very end of his closing speech, he summed up the prosecution case by claiming that the effect of reading the novel 'must be to deprave and corrupt, must be to lower the general standards of thought, conduct and decency, and must be the very opposite to encouraging that restraint in sexual matters which is so all-important at the present time'.[10] An implicit equation was made between openness of expression (lack of linguistic 'restraint') and unregulated sexual behaviour. In Lawrence's terms the prosecution was arguing for the value of 'secrecy' in sexual matters – a secrecy which, so Lawrence had claimed in the 1920s, was itself liable to impair 'the nervous and psychic health of the individual'.[11] While the prosecution lost the case, the debate continued, although in a new cultural and legal context. A new agenda had been set concerning the possibilities for the treatment of romance and sexuality in legitimate fiction. It was in this context that *Lady Chatterley's Daughter*[12] was written and read.

Lady Chatterley's Daughter

The novel *Lady Chatterley's Daughter* was published by Consul Books in the early months of 1961. It had the same price, 3/6d (17½p), as the Penguin edition of Lawrence's novel. Prior to the book's publication it had been serialised in an abridged form in the *Sunday Pictorial*, a popular national newspaper (the forerunner of the present *Sunday Mirror* into which it was converted during the early 1960s), with a circulation of over five million. This figure suggests that the claim made on the front cover of the Consul edition – 'Six million readers thrilled to the serial ...' – may have been an underestimate (since most copies would have two or more readers). The author Patricia Robins (daughter of Denise Robins) had already published at least 20 novels, whose general character may be reasonably inferred from such representative titles as *Awake My Heart, So This is Love, Where Duty Lies, He is Mine* and *Love Must Wait* (more recently she has published a number of family saga novels under the pseudonym of Clare Lorrimer). The first edition of *Lady Chatterley's Daughter* carried a front cover illustration of a young woman with long brown hair lying in bed alone with a somewhat pensive, vacant expression – with the captioned question, 'What was the guilty secret which held her on the edge of a surging passion?' and immediately below the implicit answer, in three-quarter inch capitals, 'Lady Chatterley's Daughter'.

The novel itself is narrated in the third person, although predominantly following the perspective and fortunes of the eponymous daughter, Clare Mellors. The action is set in World War Two Britain (roughly 1942–5). At the novel's opening Clare (aged 20) is a VAD nurse in a London hospital awaiting the return of her fiancé (Robin) from the North African front. Marriage is imminent, however Robin's attempts (while drunk) to consummate the marriage before the ceremony are rejected in a way which indicates not only moral disapproval but, even more, strong physical distaste. Clare breaks off the engagement, while Robin complains to a friend that 'she oughtn't to be so frigid. God knows her mother wasn't'.[13]

The main narrative then traces Clare's subsequent misfortunes in her relationships with men. She rejects the too-casual attitude to sexual matters of 'Ham' Craig, the young CO of an American airbase. She is almost physically assaulted by 'Cas' Binelli ('Cas' being short, presumably, for Casanova rather then 'Casandra' as the novel itself improbably suggests), a naturalised Italian whose father 'ran a big restaurant in the West End'.[14] On the rebound from this display of machismo, Clare runs (literally) into the arms of Jo Albiss, a woman of 'about thirty ... rather handsome in a boyish way'.[15] An alliance is formed, but proves short-lived when Clare realises that Jo's 'thoughtful care sprang not from the normal desire for friendship but from perversion'.[16] Rejecting lesbianism, Clare is then attracted by Jacques, a Free French officer. Jacques is a connoisseur of food, wine and music (he plays Chopin and Debussy to Clare on a 'glorious Bechstein' in a house in Chelsea) and, 'like all Frenchmen', he possesses 'that natural ability to make a woman feel she was the most beautiful, the most wonderful in the world'.[17] Clare's inability to respond physically even to Jacques precipitates a major crisis – a nervous breakdown in which she reveals that the source of her problem lies in her own childhood and, particularly, in her perspective on her own parents' sexuality.

Following her psychiatrist's advice Clare stops her active search for personal romantic fulfilment and resolves to 'wait' for 'Nature' to send her the right man. She becomes instead increasingly involved in trying to help a former patient (Colin) and his

wife (Eve). Colin appears at the beginning of the novel as one of
the few officer-patients whom Clare likes, because 'he never made
a pass at her';[18] his subsequent marriage to Eve falters, however,
when he is rehospitalised with severe facial burns. Eve proves too
weak and 'superficial' to cope (despite Clare's steady support)
and, to escape, she accepts a posting in Malta. Her ship is
torpedoed en route. Following Eve's death Colin and Clare
remain friends, although it is only after Colin's partial recovery
(and after VE Day) that they admit their love. Their post-marriage
sexual consummation takes time, but is the final vindication of
the psychiatrist's advice.

This summarises the main outlines of the narrative, but there
are two significant subplots interwoven – both of which result in
a firm cementing of *Lady Chatterley's Daughter* into the issues
raised both by Lawrence's original text and by the trial.
Periodically throughout the novel Clare returns (both in memory
and actuality) to her parents at their new home, Swanningdean
Farm, just north of Brighton. The quality and character of the
continuing relationship between Connie and Mellors forms both a
backcloth to Clare's problems and a source of interest in itself for
the text's exploration of different models of heterosexual relationship. A further parallel is provided by the arrival at the farm of
Mellors's other daughter (by his first marriage) in a state of
advanced pregnancy. An unknown American soldier is the prob-
able father. Having given birth and proving utterly unable to cope
(despite every kind attention from Mellors and Connie), Gloria
absconds, leaving baby Johnnie to his grandfather's care. The
reappearance of Connie and Mellors in this sequel novel is, of
course, essential if only to authenticate fully Clare's identity.
However, secondly, and more daringly, the reader is also reintro-
duced to Clifford Chatterley. After her breakdown Clare recuperates with a friend who lives only five miles from Wragby Hall.
During a social call Clare reveals her identity to Clifford and,
after initial shock, the two prove to be generally like-minded
about life, love and art. Clifford, admitting his own past mistakes,
advises Clare on her problems and subsequently (his death following shortly after Clare's marriage) leaves Wragby Hall to Clare
and Colin, whence they are bound at the end of the novel – in
effect a reborn Clifford and Connie out to atone for the mistakes
of their predecessors.

As this plot summary suggests, particularly when full weight is
given to the subplots and the roles played by the three resurrected Lawrence characters, *Lady Chatterley's Daughter* can be
read as an explicit renegotiation of the narrative and thematic
structures of *Lady Chatterley's Lover*, occurring especially around
two closely interwoven (although, below, analytically separated)

issues – those of English national identity and direction and, predominantly, of the nature of normal sexuality and its place as a form of social conduct.

Sexuality, Normality and Restraint

In *Lady Chatterley's Daughter* Clare's character development is towards the achievement of a properly balanced sexuality – one that can be integrated within the perfect marriage (which is itself defined as requiring adherence to a particular set of wider social values). This development proves, however, extremely difficult because of her conflict of values with her parents. The major differences between Clare's views and those of her mother are expressed in terms that directly resume debates heard during the trial. Connie is the idealistic progressive parent – 'Both your father and I wanted you to develop in your own way without prejudice or undue restraint ... You were the child of our love.' [19] Against this Clare demands from her parents precisely the kind of exercise of (self-) discipline which they are presented as opposing:

> if you'd had the smallest understanding, the least you and Father could have done was to reserve exhibiting your great passion for each other until you were in your own bedroom ... I think you might have tried a little harder to control yourself in front of me ...[20]

Here 'reserve' and 'control' stand as synonyms for restraint in a debate which is about style of behaviour as much as substance of emotion. When, later, Clare visits Wragby Hall she finds support for her views in Clifford's preservation of traditional values – 'At Wragby she found the strength, the vision and above all the restraint which appealed to everything fundamental in her.' [21]

In more specifically sexual matters the issue of restraint is debated throughout. Clare rejects Robin's advances as those of 'an animal that couldn't wait',[22] a response whose terms are subsequently shown to be too extreme. Clare herself is advised (by her woman psychiatrist) to 'wait' rather than actively search for the right man, but particularly crucial in the text's formulation of positions is the post-marriage behaviour of Colin. Prior to marriage he restrains his own sexual desire – 'it was essential for him to deal with all her complexities with the utmost tact and patience'.[23] But also, after marriage, he 'battles' with his desires: 'He could not have said why such restraint was necessary but sensed deep down within him that if he could only be patient, she would in time find her own way to him.' [24]

Such need for restraint is partly justified by the general assumptions about male sexuality which run through the text.

Male sexual passion is seen (especially by Clare herself) as a
violent uncontrollable urge likely to break through at any moment
of a romantic relationship. Robin is like an 'animal', Ham (she
fears) will become 'harsh', fiercer', 'more relentless'[25] Binelli
physically assaults her, and even Colin comes to feel 'an almost
uncontrollable passion'.[26] Equally, however, Clare's lack of sexual
responsiveness is portrayed as considerably in excess of that
restraint required to control such male sexual aggression; it is
rooted rather in uncertainties about her own sexuality and female
sexuality in general. In particular this issue is posed in terms of
the difference between Clare and Connie.

Two childhood memories are invoked (by Clare herself) to
explain her excessive 'restraint' (her 'frigidity'). Aged twelve she
came across a farm girl and a farm labourer making love in a
hayfield – 'I was frightened. I imagined it might be a murderer.' [27]
Connie's reaction to her daughter's fears is, however, to assure
her that the sex act is 'perfectly natural and even beautiful'. More
disturbingly (a memory retold twice), shortly after the hayfield
incident, Clare enters her parents' bedroom in the afternoon to
find her father naked and her mother in bed. She associates this
directly with the hayfield scene – 'I hated him for doing this thing
to Mother and hated her for wanting him to do it.' [28] This 'primal
scene' theory of sexual disturbance (mobilised by the text in a
particularly blatant and literalist way) is seen as a central and
integral part of Clare's general discomfort with her parents' lack
of concern for social etiquette in the way they behave and display
their mutual feelings.

Lady Chatterley's Daughter does not, however, simply endorse
Clare's rejection of her parents' life- (and love-) style. Indeed it
could hardly have remained faithful to the norms of romantic
fiction by doing so. For if *Lady Chatterley's Lover* is a novel
which seeks to undermine many social and sexual conventions (in
literature and life), it also constitutes the apotheosis of a major
ideal of romantic fiction. No romantic fiction text could be wholly
critical of that supreme celebration of heterosexual passion (and,
ultimately, fidelity) represented by the Connie/Mellors relationship. *Lady Chatterley's Daughter* contains scenes in which Connie
and Mellors are seen on their own, and on their own terms (not
just through Clare's eyes), and their characteristic discourse is a
recognisable mixture of debased Lawrentian rhetoric and the
conventional language of popular romantic fiction:

> she decided long ago that the most important thing in life was
> to be true to oneself ... it was far more honest for a girl to go
> to bed with a boy she loved and who loved her, than to stick
> to her virginity and then to sell it to some young man with
> money or a title.[29]

Lady Chatterley's Daughter does not, then, present Connie and Mellors as the grossly immoral pair of adulterers described by the trial prosecutor. The quality of their internal relationship is reaffirmed. However, they are seen as extreme and excessive precisely in the degree of their mutual self-enclosure. Selfishness is suggested both implicitly – through Mellors's comment, 'If a man and woman are as we are, and have always been, they have no need for all the others. Sometimes I don't even like that lass of ours to come down and interrupt us' [30] – and explicitly, through Clare's reflections from the comparative perspective of Wragby Hall, 'her mother and father lived in the little snug farmhouse more or less in each other's arms ... Only the present mattered to them, within the confines of their egotistical passion.' [31]

Lawrence's sexual ethic in *Lady Chatterley's Lover* is, then, implicitly criticised through the valuing of the Connie/Mellors relationship as unbalanced in its total exclusion of the concerns (and conventions) of a wider society. At the same time, despite the key role played by Clifford in Clare's psychological rehabilitation, this does not lead to a complete reversal of (what are presented as) Lawrentian values. Clifford is himself shown to be a man who has moderated his views – 'Your mother wasn't altogether wrong, you know – about the need of men and women for love .... Wait for the right man by all means – but don't put the possibility of marriage right out of your life.' [32]

Just as Clifford's advice is the prelude to Clare's romantic relationship with Colin, so those aspects of Connie's position which the text wishes to legitimise are reflected in her advice to Clare on her marriage: 'there is only one way in which a woman can really be happy – A subjugation of self. A one hundred per cent surrender.' [33] The adoption of this attitude by Clare proves the key to her final breakthrough to sexual fulfilment with Colin. The route to Clare's achievement of sexual 'normality' lies, then, in the selection and combination of advice and values derived from both her mother and her (spiritual) father, Clifford. She becomes, in fact, the vehicle for a reconnection of the personal and the social – worlds which *Lady Chatterley's Lover* so radically splits apart.

Healing the Nation

Restoration and reunification are also the aims of *Lady Chatterley's Daughter* in its consideration of the 'condition of England'. Most obviously the novel proposes that the national disruption caused by World War One ('We've got to live, no matter how many skies have fallen ... The war brought down the roof over her head', claims the opening of *Lady Chatterley's Lover*) has now been followed by another period of social disturbance (World War Two, conveniently occurring one generation on) leading to a jolting of affairs back into frame, a recomposition of disrupted elements back into normality. In this respect much of Clare's dissatisfaction with her parents (and her discovery of a kindred spirit in Clifford) can be read at the level of issues to do with class and culture as much as with sexual behaviour.

From the novel's opening Clare is represented as a displaced daughter of the aristocracy. Despite her love for her father she is ashamed of his background and feels an instinctive revulsion at any acknowledgement of her relationship to her half-sister. By contrast Wragby Hall and Sir Clifford come to represent (she feels) a true mirroring of her identity; even before they meet Connie suggests 'In a curious way you're like each other even though there's no relationship.' [34] This is confirmed by Clifford's comparison of Connie to Clare:

> It had been the most appalling shock to him to realise that she had chosen for her lover a low common fellow.
> But there were no signs of 'commonness' about *Clare*. She looked more of a thoroughbred than her mother.[35]

Clare's 'class' is demonstrated especially by her aesthetic taste. She enjoys 'books, poetry and music' [36] and is herself twice likened to a Rossetti painting. Art by itself is, however, not enough. Francis Peverel, a painter, is another of Clare's failed suitors. Too 'pale and delicate-looking' for Clare, his feebleness is subsequently revealed to be a symptom of leukaemia – 'It seemed awful' (thinks Clare) 'that Francis had to die without even the glory of being killed in defence of his country'. [37]

It is rather precisely the kind of art which *is* implicated in the defence of national values that Clare endorses most strongly. If on the one hand she is twice likened to a Rossetti heroine (by Jacques and Francis), she is also twice compared (by Colin and by herself) to Florence Nightingale. The quintessence of Englishness is further invoked through the figure of Shakespeare. Colin's character, as simultaneously a brave officer and a man of culture, is established in the first chapter through the reporting of his ambition, after the war, 'to go on to the production side of Drama. He was particularly interested in Shakespeare.' [38] A love of Shakespeare is also used to signal the commonality of view between Clare and Clifford when they attend a film show for the wounded officers in the convalescent home to which part of Wragby Hall has been converted:

> The film was an old favourite – Lawrence Olivier's Henry V – the only sort of film to appeal to Sir Clifford. It appealed equally to Clare. She had been much younger when she first

saw it but she enjoyed it more now and gave a little exclama-
tion of pleasure when they reached that particular point in the
film when the archers in a long line let loose their arrows from
their upraised bows. It was flawless artistry. Superb!

Clifford from his wheel-chair smiled as he heard Clare's
little cry and in the dimness saw the rapt expression on the
young girl's face.

How sensitive she was to art and all things beautiful ...39

This passage is worth examining in detail, and not just for its
historical inaccuracy. Since the Olivier film of *Henry V* was not
released until mid-1944 it could not have been already well known
to either Clare or Clifford (the film was, of course, made as a
contribution to wartime propaganda). However, if this is a minor
and excusable error by an author writing some 16 years later, it is
also highly functional for the signifying work of the text by
connoting the film as itself part of a tradition of already established and entrenched values ('an *old* favourite', '*much* younger')
represented, at root, by Shakespeare. Further, this form of art is
active in its defence of English values. The 'flawless artistry' is
simultaneously that of the art form (the naturalistic representation
of war) and of *the archers themselves*. Finally this passage illustrates Clifford's mutation, in *Lady Chatterley's Daughter*, into a
guardian of traditional values and perspectives. This rather drasti-
cally contrasts with Lawrence's Clifford who, by turns, is an
admirer of Proust, a successful modern(ist) short-story writer and
a man determined to 'capture the bitch-goddess (of success) by
means of industrial production.' 40 There is no trace of any of
these in the Clifford of the later book, now reborn as the
embodiment of stable English tradition.

This new role for Clifford is clearly established by Clare's
responses to Wragby Hall. Its parkland and 'grand old trees' are
'symbolic of an England untouched by war – unchanged by time.
They had been here when her mother was a young girl. They were
still here. They were wise, almost human.'41 The hall itself combines
life, art and English character in much the same way as *Henry V*.
Clare is 'fascinated' by the portraits of Elizabethan, Stuart and
eighteenth-century Chatterleys (with 'a definite likeness to Sir
Clifford'). Despite having no heir of his own, Clifford maintains
family traditions:

> She had caught a glimpse of the massive silver, still to be seen
> in the dining-room. War or no war, Sir Clifford would not
> have it put away. Bound by the golden cord of English
> tradition, he would not depart from its demands upon his time
> or his pocket, and continued to preserve it.42

Wragby Hall is in fact already a stately home awaiting its post-

war surge of visitors. If, like Evelyn Waugh's Brideshead, it is
partly devoted in wartime to other uses, then (from the perspective of a decade and a half later) it is also possible to project
forward from 1944–5 to suggest the future significance of what is
being preserved. Writing in 1945 Waugh seemed both elegiac
about the glory that was gone and pessimistic as to its chances of
revival; by 1959 (in his preface to the revised edition of *Brideshead Revisited*) he could note his own mistake:

> Brideshead today would be open to trippers, its treasures
> rearranged by expert hands and the fabric better maintained
> by Lord Marchmain. And the English aristocracy has main-
> tained its identity to a degree that then seemed impossible.[43]

Lady Chatterley's Daughter is written with the benefit of such
hindsight, evident not only in the handling of the character of
Clifford but, even more, in the style and implied trajectory of
Clare and Colin's married life. The honeymoon is spent at Strat-
ford, in a hotel overlooking the Shakespeare Memorial Theatre,
while their projected future, as the new owners of Wragby Hall,
lies in becoming upper-class theatrical impresarios. It is in fact
Colin's suggestion to Clifford that he (Clifford) should turn
Wragby into 'the Glyndebourne of the North' which both gives
him 'one of the most exciting moments of his life'[44] and apparently motivates his decision to leave Wragby to Clare. This is a
quite brilliant touch by the author to close the novel. Glyndebourne, founded in the early 1930s as a country-house open-air
opera house, had become a national, 'traditional', institution by
the late 1950s. Its combination of upper-class style, country-
house setting, commitment to 'serious' art and manifest success
represented precisely that amalgam of old values in a new form
which the marriage of Colin and Clare was to represent.

The novel's conclusion in fact effects a double displacement in
order to undertake its task of rebalancing social and sexual norms.
Colin and Clare (both as surrogate children of Clifford) inherit
Wragby Hall; as a further confirmation that Clare has now found
the security which she previously lacked, the reader may recall the
opening pages of the novel where Clare confesses that Colin is 'the
sort of man I'd like to have had for a father'.[45] Clare is then lost to
Connie and Mellors by entering into her deserved aristocratic
inheritance (which Connie herself had previously disowned). As a
consolation, and as a confirmation of their rather different social
position, Connie and Mellors are awarded Johnnie, a child of
dubious lower-class origins, who realigns Mellors with the lineage of
his first marriage. The 'tragic age' of the opening of *Lady Chatterley's Lover* is then redeemed, brought full circle to (in the structural
sense) a suitably 'comic', a popular romantic, conclusion.

Stabilising the Culture

It would require a detailed account of the social and political character of Britain in the 1950s and 60s to situate the precise ideological and cultural interventions made by the Penguin *Lady Chatterley's Lover* and Patricia Robins's sequel. Only a few points can be touched on here; these will concern particularly questions of cultural levels and cultural standards.

In her history of women in post-war Britain, *Only Halfway to Paradise*, Elizabeth Wilson suggests the significance that Lawrence, in the 1950s, held for 'the educated young':

> Lawrence in his novels not only offered men a justification for their sexual drive, he offered girls and women a richer female nature, and a sexuality that was neither vulgar nor aseptically repressed.[46]

While this suggests gender-specific readings of Lawrence which might, in terms of sexual politics, be diametrically opposed in their implications, both positions were seen as equally dangerous by the trial prosecutor. They were, however, infinitely more dangerous if the *uneducated* young were also involved. The question of what different types of reader might make of Lawrence was one that was of considerable significance for the prosecution case (although predominantly in terms of class, rather than gender, difference). The judge, in his summing-up, also repeatedly returned to the social implications of the proposed price:

> In these days when not only high wages but shall I say high pocket-money to younger members of the community are the order of the day, 3s.6d., you might think, would be putting this book within the grasp of a vast mass of the population.[47]

> It finds its way into the bookshops and on to the bookstalls, at 3s.6d. a time, into public libraries, where it is available for all and sundry to read.[48]

This point (which followed closely the prosecutor's own formulations) was not, in fact, as legally irrelevant as some accounts of the case have suggested since the Act did specifically require a consideration, in coming to judgment, of who would be 'likely, having regard to all relevant circumstances ... to read ... the matter ...'.[49] The general reader, it was suggested, would be more likely (without the benefit of educational guidance or an educated sensibility) to read the book as a direct endorsement of unregulated sexual activity. The proposed *general* availability (in court Penguin reported in initial print run of 200,000 copies) was then a central part of the prosecution case.

It was this fact of mass circulation that constituted the seriousness of the challenge of *Lady Chatterley's Lover* to existing popular fictional norms and, more generally, threatened to undermine the stability of the boundaries between high and popular culture by directly infusing the ideas of a major twentieth-century 'high' literary figure into the minds of millions of uneducated readers. The period of the early 1960s constituted a particularly unstable cultural moment in this respect. Paperback editions and film versions of texts such as *Room at the Top* and *Saturday Night and Sunday Morning* were already in wide circulation, suggesting that apparently 'serious' novels could also head best-seller lists and be a box-office success. Many cultural distinctions (high/low, mass/minority, popular/serious) were being put in question, as new hybrid and transgressive forms appeared, with television entertainment and drama in the forefront.

In the midst of this cultural anarchy *Lady Chatterley's Daughter* offered a reasoned position of reassurance and stability. In matters of sexual relations it took account of Lawrence's position, neither endorsing nor wholly rejecting it; rather it offered the 'vast mass of the population' and 'the younger members of the community' a more acceptably restrained view of the place of sexual activity. It repositioned high and popular culture in their proper spheres. Art was realigned with an appropriate class position and lifestyle (Wragby/Glyndebourne/Shakespeare),and as a spectacle to be viewed from afar. Almost incidentally *Jane Eyre* was vindicated as Colin paralleled Rochester by being burned and disfigured into an acceptable match for the heroine (Connie's rejection of the disabled Clifford being revalued as Eve's personal weakness and failure to cope). Finally there was a revaluation of the achievements of the whole nation. Britain at war and victorious redeemed the failures and conflicts of the Lawrentian 1920s. Implicitly, if by 1960 problems of lack of 'restraint' had again developed, then the wartime values of duty and endurance gave a benchmark by which to live; as Mr Griffith-Jones put it: 'when one sees what is happening today and has been happening, perhaps all the more since the war, restraint becomes all the more essential, does it not ...'.[50]

Whatever depredations *Lady Chatterley's Lover* might be wreaking on the culture as a whole, *Lady Chatterley's Daughter* sought to defuse and answer its challenge to the continuing successful operation of popular fiction.

In Conclusion – Still Harping on Daughters

Lady Chatterley's Daughter, then, reauthenticates the narrative conventions of popular romantic fiction (and those of a whole tradition of 'serious' realist English fiction) by its reversal and recomposition of its parent text. One aspect of this process may be worth discussing further, by way of conclusion. One of the more puzzling aspects of *Lady Chatterley's Daughter* is the degree of emphasis laid on Clare's 'frigidity' being caused by direct observation of sexual encounters at too young an age – this leading her to view sex as 'a dark and frightening tunnel at the end of which outrage rather than passionate satisfaction waited for her'.[51] As already suggested, one interpretation of this is to note the use of a vulgar Freudianism in which a simplified notion of the observation of the 'primal scene' as a cause of neurosis is appropriated wholesale. However, a return once more to the text of the trial suggests that something rather more complex may also be at stake here.

Griffiths-Jones's notorious 'wife/servant' gaffe has already been mentioned, but the immediately preceding passage in his opening speech makes a more substantive point:

would you approve of your young sons, young daughters – because girls can read as well as boys – reading this book? Is it a book you would have lying around in your own house? [52]

Leaving aside for a moment the ludicrous (but very telling) parenthesis, this passage provides an important clue to the narrative treatment of Clare's sexual problems. In *Lady Chatterley's Lover* Lawrence's linguistic frankness and commitment to the (repeated) description of the sexual act itself (rather than just to the infinite variety of public and private preliminaries to it) cuts the ground from under the rationale for the characteristic language and plot manoeuvres of popular romantic fiction. *Lady Chatterley's Daughter* replies to this challenge by accepting the prosecution case that direct contact with sexual explicitness *is* harmful and also by taking further the (undeveloped) prosecution suggestion that 'sons' and 'daughters' need to be considered differently. The issue as regards males was, of course, fairly simple – would reading *Lady Chatterley's Lover* encourage them to go on the sexual rampage? This could be asked of the effect on girls too (Connie as adulteress and role model), but *Lady Chatterley's Daughter* pursued a line of argument both more subtle and more in line with dominant conceptions of femininity. It did so by a process of narrative substitution. The presumed effect on the young female reader of *Lady Chatterley's Lover*, incurred in the act of reading, is transferred to Clare in the act of directly observing. What is 'lying around the house' in Swanningdean Farm is not Lawrence's novel but *Connie and Mellors themselves* caught (more or less) in the act. Further, Clare's restoration to psychic health and social normality is itself achieved by her consciously subscribing to those very linguistic and narrative conventions of romantic fiction (the need for restraint, deferral of gratification through the 'jamming' of the narrative progression) with which *Lady Chatterley's Lover* proposed to dispense. *Lady Chatterley's Daughter* then does not merely offer a direct critique of the selfishness and romantic extremism of the Connie/Mellors relationship, it also refutes Lawrence's case for the value of frankness and explicitness in language and literature. It is this doubly articulated reinscription of the values and practices of popular romantic fiction that marks *Lady Chatterley's Daughter* as an unusually complex, self-regarding and, therefore, highly instructive instance of the genre.

Notes and References

1. Jean Radford ed. *The Progress of Romance* London: Routledge and Kegan Paul 1986 p. 8.
2. Ibid. p. 12.
3. E.M. Forster *Aspects of the Novel* London: Edward Arnold 1969 p. 54.
4. D.H. Lawrence *Study of Thomas Hardy and Other Essays* Cambridge: Cambridge University Press 1985 p. 21.
5. D.H. Lawrence *Lady Chatterley's Lover* Harmondsworth: Penguin 1961.
6. Northrop Frye *The Anatomy of Criticism* Princeton: Princeton University Press 1957 p. 185.
7. C.H. Rolph *The Trial of Lady Chatterley* Harmondsworth: Penguin 1961 p. 5.
8. Ibid. p. 17.
9. Ibid. p. 211.
10. Ibid. p. 225.
11. D. H. Lawrence *Pornography and So On* London: Faber 1939 p. 30.
12. Pauline Robins *Lady Chatterley's Daughter* London: Consul Books 1961.
13. Ibid. p. 28.
14. Ibid. p. 12.
15. Ibid. p. 119.
16. Ibid. p. 134.
17. Ibid. p. 142.
18. Ibid. p. 9.
19. Ibid. p. 100.
20. Ibid. pp. 101–2.
21. Ibid. p. 188.
22. Ibid. p. 27.
23. Ibid. p. 242.
24. Ibid. p. 251.
25. Ibid. p. 58.
26. Ibid. p. 242.
27. Ibid. p. 151.

28. Ibid. p. 153.
29. Ibid. p. 38.
30. Ibid. p. 79.
31. Ibid. p. 188.
32. Ibid. pp. 201–2.
33. Ibid. p. 250.
34. Ibid. p. 170.
35. Ibid. p. 182.
36. Ibid. p. 9.
37. Ibid. p. 216.
38. Ibid. p. 9.
39. Ibid. p. 200.
40. D.H. Lawrence *Lady Chatterley's Lover* Harmondsworth: Penguin 1961 p. 111.
41. Robins *Lady Chatterley's Daughter* 1961 p. 187.
42. Ibid. p. 187.
43. Evelyn Waugh *Brideshead Revisited* (revised) London: Chapman and Hall 1960.
44. Robins *Lady Chatterley's Daughter* 1961 p. 254.
45. Ibid. p. 17.
46. Elizabeth Wilson *Only Halfway to Paradise* London: Tavistock 1980 p. 134–5.
47. Rolph *The Trial of Lady Chatterley* 1961 p. 228.
48. Ibid. p. 230.
49. Ibid. p. 10.
50. Robins *Lady Chatterley's Daughter* 1961 p. 210.
51. Ibid. p. 8.
52. Rolph *The Trial of Lady Chatterley* 1961 p. 17.

CHAPTER 2

It's My Party: American Bestsellers of the 1970s

Maria Lauret

Junk shops are treasure-troves of discarded dreams and dejected aspirations, of objects waiting like old love-lorn mistresses to be rediscovered. There is a certain brand of novel that you find in these shops: the so-called Women's Lib bestsellers of the American 1970s. So-called, because they belong to the sexual revolution rather than to women's liberation, and to the 1960s rather than the 1970s. Once well read, passed on to mothers and friends while the excitement lasted, they ended up in the box-for-charity, cast out with the flares and the peasant blouses of those days. They are always there, the copies of *The Women's Room*, *Kinflicks*, *Fear of Flying*, *Original Sins*, *How to Save Your Own Life*. Their covers look up at you, wrinkled and stained like the face of an ageing beauty, undistinguished among the Jilly Coopers, the Ken Folletts and the Harold Robbinses.

I always feel sorry for these books, indifferently thrown together with that other kind, the sort you only read once, on holiday. It seems that the novels of the sexual revolution have had their day now – heady days, of which their readers do not want to be reminded, perhaps. Days when women – budding feminists – convinced they could not learn anything they wanted to know from their mothers, turned to sex and drugs and rock'n'roll for their kicks, and found that they hurt. Women read these novels in the 1970s to understand what was happening to them, or to get a glimpse of what a more exciting life might look like. Novels like *Kinflicks*, *Fear of Flying* and *Rubyfruit Jungle* were hot stuff then: controversial, sexy, and if the publishers were to be believed, even liberating: American women's answer to Norman Mailer and Philip Roth. Erica Jong, Lisa Alther and Rita Mae Brown provided a good laugh, and their heroines were role models, for once, of wit and nerve rather than sense and sensibility. The blurbs on their alluring covers promised the insights into the female condition that women readers were looking for – answers to the question of how to live as a woman in a world of choices, a sexual world, a world in which marriage

and childbearing were no longer every woman's plotted
destiny, a world completely different from the one their
mothers had prepared them for.

> I was furious with my mother for not teaching me how to be a
> woman, for not teaching me how to make peace between the
> raging hunger in my cunt and the hunger in my head. So I
> learned about women from men. I saw them through the eyes
> of male writers. Of course, I didn't think of them as *male*
> writers. I thought of them as *writers*, as authorities, as gods
> who knew and were to be trusted completely.[1]

Writers like Erica Jong were among the first to 'write back', to
represent men in their fiction the same way that women were
being treated in American literature: on their backs, with their
sexual equipment exposed for the world to see, all hairless balls
and missionary delusions, not to mention the shit marks on the
sheets. In *Kinflicks* the feel of the male member is described as
the trunk of a 'recalcitrant baby elephant'.[2] The heroine of *Rubyfruit Jungle*, Molly Bolt, by contrast coolly strips a little boy of his
illusions of impending manhood by describing his penis as just 'a
wad of pink wrinkles', 'ugly'.[3]

Yet despite such attempts at demystifying the phallus along
with dethroning the god of male authorship, these women's texts
in the end did not satisfy for long. Rereading them now, they
seem curiously inhibited, marred by an undertow of defeat belying
their surface exuberance. Isadora (White Stollerman) Wing, Ginny
(Babcock) Bliss, Molly Bolt and Sasha Burke (formerly Raybel,
née Davis) don't actually learn anything very much from their
exploits in the wide wide world. By the end of their stories the
cunt is still as hungry as the head, despite multiple orgasms and
countless seminars in the history of philosophy 101.

No wonder, perhaps, that women readers, having consumed
large quantities of rampant sexuality and textuality in the pages of
these blockbusting novels, all but lost their appetite for lust: it all
seemed too complicated.

In real life, of course, it was the women's liberation movement which came up with the answers to how to save your
own life, answers which were so glaringly lacking – promises,
promises – in the fictions of the sexual revolution. If these
fictions raised the question of what the search for knowledge
might have to do with the quest for the zipless fuck (or
suck), and suggested the idea that 'one's body is intimately
related to one's writing',[4] the question was left hanging and
the idea remained an idea. For women readers the novel's
ambivalent and alienated representation of femininity and its
discontents could not sit comfortably with a recently raised

feminist consciousness. Thus the books that changed lives in due course had to make room for lives that changed books, and the seriously feminist text made its entry into the literary arena.

The novels I want to discuss here – Lisa Alther's *Kinflicks*, Erica Jong's *Fear of Flying*, Alix Kates Shulman's *Memoirs of an Ex-Prom Queen* and Rita Mae Brown's *Rubyfruit Jungle* – were all published in America in the early to mid-1970s. Packaged as a mass-market product by publishers keen to cash in on the interest that the women's liberation movement was generating in the popular media, these novels found a wide readership – among men as well as women. For readers like myself, they were the first point of contact with feminism. If I mistrusted or disbelieved the mainstream press in its reporting of what women's liberation was all about, at least here I could 'see for myself', or so I thought. It was only later that I, like many others, realised that these fictions did not speak *for* the women's movement, even if some of them spoke *of* it. Their relationship to feminism was, at best, tenuous and at worst trivialising.

It is not at all surprising that Brown, Shulman, Jong and Alther have not been treated favourably by feminist critics, who have found them lacking in seriousness, too market oriented or simply not feminist enough. Yet often it is precisely the unsuccessful work that is interesting: the subgenre, the hybrid form, the semi-literary. It is here, in the failed experiment, that we can see contradictory cultural currents at work, on the cusp of political confusion and formal conventionality.

What I want to do here is to speculate on other factors which may modify or complicate that judgement. For one, I think the feminists' harsh view is partly a result of a historical misrecognition: these novels belong, as I see it, to the late 1960s' stage of the sexual revolution rather than to feminism, and they are better read in that light. Secondly, in popular parlance of the time the sexual revolution shaded into women's liberation by a confusion of terms. The title of Kate Millett's landmark study of women's oppression, *Sexual Politics*, highlights this habitual blurring of sex and gender, of sexual and sociopolitical issues (which of course for women's liberation were intertwined, but not coextensive). Hence both the cultural climate in which these novels were received, when the women's struggle was still regarded a titillating novelty, and the confusion over what a 'sexual politics' actually was, created inflated or misguided expectations of new women's fiction. Thirdly, I think that we should be aware, in our critical engagement with them, that *Rubyfruit Jungle*, *Kinflicks*, *Memoirs of an Ex-Prom Queen* and *Fear of Flying* are not the readily consumable reads that they purport to be. Twenty-odd years later (and they were odd years, as I shall show later on) these texts seem awkward and uncomfortable, with themselves and with their readership. Like their heroines, they can't quite make up their minds what they want to be: novels of development, post-modern pastiches of the Great American Novel, female picaresque, or the portrait of the artist as a young gal. Most of all, they want to project a self-determining female sexuality, but in each case that projection is an act of faith, and faith, for the unfaithful, is inevitably betrayed. All four protagonists are convinced that 'I can be more than the breeder of the next generation' [5] but by the end of *Memoirs of an Ex-Prom Queen* even that conviction crumbles. Sasha Davis, the heroine in this novel, once so ravenous and relentless in the pursuit of pleasure, is infantilised by marriage and childbearing in the end, waiting for hubby to come home:

> Our island life was hard for him to adapt to. We talked baby talk and read picture books, by common standards primitive. We cried unpredictably and often, stifling him. We had tantrums and provoked wrath. We lacked spontaneity ... We bugged him, we bored him, we were united against him.[6]

Sasha sides with the babies in the end, and although there clearly is a political analysis in evidence here which puts the blame fair and square on the institution of the family and the sexual division of labour, there is for Sasha no alternative but a new haircut to unleash domestic revolution. Prom Queen becomes ex Prom Queen – and a radical haircut is a big deal for one who has lived by her looks thus far, but it is hardly a stab in the heart of patriarchy.

In *Fear of Flying*, and this has been much commented upon, the heroine tries to convince herself on the final page that she has learnt something, that things are different: 'The cold stone I had worn inside my chest for twenty nine years was gone. Not suddenly. And maybe not for good. But it was gone.' [7] Yet at the very end, after a series of metafictional musings on plots and endings, husband comes back and we all know what that means: the hunt for the elusive zipless fuck is off and marriage rules OK, temporarily, until the whole cycle starts again.

Even in Rita Mae Brown's lesbian novel *Rubyfruit Jungle*, which stands the test of time much better than the others can, the ending is ambivalent in terms of lessons learnt or radiant futures ahead. Molly Bolt, just graduated *cum laude* from filmschool, reflects on the state of the world, rebellion in the streets:

> But somehow I knew my rage wasn't their rage and they'd have run me out of their movement for being a lesbian anyway. I read somewhere too that women's groups were starting but they'd trash me just the same. What the hell ... I

wish I could get up in the morning and look at the day the
way I used to when I was a child.[8]

Girls, grown up to be women, will be girls again – and girls alone.

Of the four, the only one who *does* learn something is
Ginny Babcock in *Kinflicks*, but paradoxically her learning
process is one of unlearning, of shedding (as in the title of
Verena Stefan's contemporaneous novel *Shedding*). Ginny's
story is told alternately by herself and in the third person,
partly from her mother's point of view. The mother is dying,
and the narrative traces the mother's last week of life in
episodes scattered among those charting Ginny's whirlwind
existence. Becoming a person in this novel, according to
Patricia Waugh, is to throw off internalised roles; other feminist critics have pointed to the significance of the mother's
death in giving birth to the daughter's identity.[9]

Before her mother's death, Ginny still wonders 'If she was no
longer Ira's wife, Wendy's mother, her mother's daughter, who was
she?' [10] But afterwards Ginny, having shed her various roles,
changes and comes to understand a more complex notion of self:
'She wrapped her mother's clock in her faded Sisterhood Is Powerful T-shirt and packed it in Hawk's knapsack with her other scant
belongings. She left the cabin, to go where she had no idea.' [11]

In this apparent reversal of the traditional Bildungsroman
(where the hero sets out on his adventures at the beginning with
a knapsack on his back) the mother's measured time (the clock)
and the daughter's passing time (faded sisterhood) are wrapped
up together in the container of 60s counter-cultural consciousness
(Hawk being a Vietnam deserter who teaches Ginny to meditate).
Together they make up the luggage she will take into the world –
her life is just beginning, *after* all she has been through. The
romps through adolescent sexual experiment, lesbian relationships, communal living and marriage have yielded no insight. And
while a biology textbook can explain the phenomenon of 'blue
balls' to Ginny, giving her 'access to her experience', just as
medical science can explain the mother's illness, such knowledge
is only partial. When the mother on her deathbed finally finishes
reading through the entire encyclopaedia, she cannot give Ginny
any advice on how to live. What the mother does give her is
abdication of maternal responsibility, the admission that she
knows nothing that can be of use to Ginny. The latter then
moves from a known quantity of roles and identifications to an
unknown destiny. This radically open future – not a *tabular rasa*
but a scarred surface – can be seen as a recognition of the
complexity of female subjectivity and a positive evaluation of its
fragmented status. What such a reading would leave out of

account though is that Ginny repeats her mother's abdication in leaving her own daughter behind, too. Curiously, nothing is made of that desertion in the novel – one of many instances in *Kinflicks* where pain cannot be spoken of, and questions raised are questions quickly buried, or laughed off.

In rescuing these four novels from the junkshop of feminist rejects what I am trying to do is give them a new lease of life as fictions of the sexual revolution, fictions of sexual transgression in search of a new definition of femininity. Even as such, they remain tattered, damaged by the passage of time which has changed not only our thinking about women's sexuality but also our sexual practices. From the vantage point of the 1990s sexuality is one area where feminist space has contracted rather than expanded by comparison with 20 years ago, partly as a result of media scare-tactics and moral crusades (so well documented by Susan Faludi recently in *Backlash*), partly also because of age, because of AIDS, and because of what I see as a long-standing refusal on the part of heterosexual feminists to continue the debate on sexual pleasure which had its origins in the sexual revolution but was stifled subsequently in the women's movement.

Fiction has always been important to feminism, from Wollstonecraft onwards, and some of the most innovative scholarship the movement has generated has come from feminist literary criticism, precisely because it can address questions of fantasy and desire as well as social and political issues. I think that *Kinflicks*, *Fear of Flying*, *Rubyfruit Jungle* and *Memoirs of an Ex-Prom Queen* are still of interest to feminists today because they are crucially concerned with women's changing sexual behaviour and wants at a time when their social position was changing too. Isadora Wing and Molly Bolt are adamant that they are going to make a success of themselves as poet and film maker, respectively, even if they lack positive role models: 'Where were the women who were *really* free, who didn't spend their lives bouncing from man to man, who felt complete with or without a man?' [12] sighs Isadora Wing, thinking of Anna Wulf in Lessing's *The Golden Notebook*. And Virginia Woolf, Sylvia Plath, Georgia O'Keeffe, the Brontës and Lillian Hellmann are no help either: 'What a strange group! Severe, suicidal, strange.' [13]

Although Isadora cannot think of heterosexuality in terms other than either celibacy or enslavement to men, she can at least refuse childbearing in favour of writing, just as Molly Bolt can choose to make movies in defiance of a world which has forced her on to the margins. Contrary to popular feminist opinion I think the refusal of childbearing (in both cases) is important here and positive, rather than evidence of an old double standard in which women have to choose be-

tween children and work while men do not. That Isadora's
choice might be taken as an admission of defeat, or even as
selfish indulgence (plenty of evidence for that in the rest of
the novel, after all, hedonist that she is) is a measure of how
far thinking about femininity has shifted in the past two
decades back to a pro-natalist position. 'Having it all' now
means work and partner and children, as if having all you
want without children (or, indeed, partner) could not mean
having it all at all.

Apart from articulating radical changes in sexual mores,
these novels are interesting too because they were among the
first adamantly written by women *as* women (rather than by
writers who 'happened to be women' as the Alison Luries and
Mary McCarthys would have it at the time), and before a
literary domain-of-their-own had been carved out by women's
movement writers and feminist literary historians. Although, as
I mentioned before, these texts were received into a politi-
cised space of women's writing, the gap (both ideological and
historical) between the discourses of sexual revolution and
those of women's liberation may account for their problematic
status. I believe that as literary productions they lack confi-
dence in their audience. It is as if they don't quite know
who might be listening; they are written *by* women but not
yet quite *for* women – hence the almost hysterical tendency,
in *Kinflicks* and *Fear of Flying* in particular, to 'play for
laughs' as Rosalind Coward[14] has pointed out.

The laughs are not all satirical jibes at men; they are also
self-conscious and quite literally betray an inability on the part of
the women to take themselves seriously. They represent the
wisecracking wit of the insecure loudmouth who talks too much
for fear of exposing herself. This phenomenon is the most problematic and disturbing in *Kinflicks* and *Rubyfruit Jungle*, both of
which are violent novels, painful to read between the lines. Yet
that is where their serious and protopolitical messages (about
class, race and sexual orientation in *Rubyfruit*, and about grief
and loss in *Kinflicks*) are located.

I see these novels, then, as looking for a new form in textuality as well as sexuality and failing to find it. What they end up
with instead is not just disillusionment about a free-floating
female sexual agency, but also a peculiarly hybrid literary form in
which ribald comedy is at odds with an underlying sense of pain
and violence (*Kinflicks*, *Rubyfruit Jungle*) or alternatively where a
concern with high culture and serious writing cannot be successfully integrated with self-parody and unexamined female fantasy
(*Fear of Flying* and *Memoirs of an Ex-Prom Queen*, respectively).

Isadora, as we have seen, is determined to be a poet and the

literary-political necessity of the female voice is stressed repeatedly: 'Until women started writing books there was only one side
of the story.' [15] But the credibility of comments such as these are
constantly undermined by the likes of this:

> I had been a feminist all my life (I date my radicalisation to
> the night in 1955 on the IRT subway when the moronic
> Horace Mann boy who was my date asked me if I planned to
> be a secretary), but the big problem was how to make your
> feminism jibe with your unappeasable hunger for male
> bodies.[16]

Feminism here is at once reduced to individual ambition and put
in opposition to female heterosexual desire, just as elsewhere in
the novel 'feminism' can only surface as rhetoric, vain talk, or
slogan (as when Isadora sees French women marching with a
banner 'Femmes, Liberons-Nous!'). Isadora's liberal, but half-
baked borrowings from women's liberation theory in the long
discursive passages at the beginning of the novel give no hint of a
women's *movement*, no sense of a social context for personal
change. Hence the judgement of feminist critics that ' ... [Writing
and sexual pleasure] are complacently offered as individual satis-
factions and silently substituted for a feminist politics'.[17]

But *Memoirs of an Ex-Prom Queen* is perhaps an even
more extreme example of the disjunctive text, one which does
not know itself and cannot bear to look in the mirror for
fear of seeing something other than the image of 'serious',
'literary' writing.` Gayle Green has written about the 'confu-
sion' that she sees in *Memoirs*, a confusion in the different
directions that the novel seems to be taking at various times
and which creates breaks in the characterisation. To put this
another way, I think that Shulman could not successfully
integrate female fantasy with what is essentially a thoroughly
realist novel, exhaustive domestic and sartorial detail and all.
Basically this is the story of a woman's progress, or, if we
take her siding-with-the-babies ending seriously, regression
through two marriages and various forms of relationship.
From pubescent puppy-love via a passion for philosophy,
which predictably ends in tacky tutor-love, to a torrid affair
in Spain, the story of Sasha Davis presents a panoply of
sexual options for the modern woman: 'Sex and the Single
Girl' as well as its sequel 'Sex and the Married Woman'. This
menu of rampant heterosex is served up with such a strange
mixture of dry matter-of-factness in some sections, acid self-
irony in others and a syrupy sweetness in the romance with
the second husband-to-be, that the novel as a whole leaves a
distinctly foul taste:

> Suddenly he jerked himself out, and pulling my head abruptly
> to his lap, came in my mouth. I considered it an honour. We
> smoked one cigarette without a word, and then we started all
> over again.[18]

This scene is reminiscent of an episode in *Kinflicks*, where one of
the women in the commune, Laverne, is being gang-banged.
When the other women want to come to her rescue it turns out
that she is enjoying it – considers it 'an honour', no doubt.

Strange phenomena – not in themselves necessarily, but because of the way they are being presented in the text, without
comment or self-reflection. Such absence of self-reflection is also
evident in the latter part of *Memoirs*, when Sasha starts her affair
with Will Burke, as romantic a romantic hero as they come. Yet
in a novel which from the very beginning signals its high literary
ambitions, the tale of hot pursuit and happy coupledom (as in
most of these novels, the affair ends in marriage) does not blend
well with the tone of worldly but resigned weariness in the
preface:

> There was once a time when I would do anything I chose for
> which I had ten good reasons, or again, anything for which I
> could not find a reason not to, a time when I would not resist
> a dare.
>   I am more cautious now. I have children and responsibili-
> ties ...
>   To share what I've learned (and to have something interest-
> ing to do now that I am past thirty and the children are in
> school) I shall compose a memoir. I shall begin my story
> neither at the beginning, moving forward as the reader
> expects, nor at the end, moving backward as the writer recalls,
> but rather somewhere in between, where the truth is said to
> lie.[19]

Truth lies indeed, in this novel, at least if it is supposed to be a
feminist truth. The novel is, after all, dedicated to the Redstock-
ings, one of the first women's liberation groups in New York. Yet
there is no evidence of a feminist critique in this text, bar the
overriding obsession with the beauty myth. Sasha is one of those
women whose success lies, as she sees it, in being attractive,
'feminine' in a stereotyped sense, and if the novel has any political message (however muffled), it is that even with beauty and
brains as assets, even with an adoring husband and children,
things still go wrong.

Memoirs of an Ex-Prom Queen is a good example of a novel
poised between sexual revolution and women's liberation, one
foot in each camp – a spreadeagled text.

I have called these novels fictions of the sexual revolution
without adequately defining what 'the sexual revolution' stands for

in this context. By way of conclusion I now want to examine very briefly the history of the sexual revolution and its continuing importance, as I see it, for feminism.

It seems as if the sexual revolution as a memory of real-life change has suffered the same fate as the junkshop novels: it has worn, not grown on feminism since the 1960s, and has ended up in the closet of outmoded ideas and concepts (along with androgyny, the productive status of housework, socialisation and sex itself, to name but a few golden oldies). Researching this essay in my library of feminist history and theory, I found few references to the sexual revolution, and those I did find were in publications dated around the late 1970s. Apart from Lillian Faderman's recent history of twentieth-century lesbian existence, *Odd Girls and Twilight Lovers*,[20] the sexual revolution seems to have disappeared as a frame of reference for feminist scholarship. I am sure that it is no accident, however, that Faderman's book does acknowledge the relevance of the sexual revolution for feminism where others do not; the sexual revolution has carried on in lesbian debates on sex, whereas it has been almost erased from the memorybanks of heterosexual feminism.

It is, now, as if it never happened, or can only be referred to in feminist discourse ironically, surrounded by quotation marks, or prefaced with 'so-called'. In the context of Susan Faludi's *Backlash*[21] and its exposure of multiple media myths which have harmed feminism's public image in the past 20 years, it would be easy enough to dismiss the sexual revolution as a media-generated backlash *avant-la-lettre*, a pre-emptive strike against women in the 1960s who were on the march for economic advancement even before women's liberation came along.

Undoubtedly at that time the media were instrumental in spreading and sensationalising the ideas and values of the sexual revolution. Undoubtedly also did media interest promote a commodified version of the sexual revolution from which women suffered in particular, seeing their image glamorised and eroticised for the purposes of advertising and pornography, signed, sealed and delivered for the delectation of men, all under the banner of a new 'sexual freedom'.

But there is another side to the sexual revolution too. What we remember is a vulgarised version in which middle-class suburbia starts to engage *en masse* in 'swinging' and 'wife-swapping' round about the turn of the decade (50s/60s). A time also when men assume that 'when a girl says no she means yes' (but she can't admit it because she is too repressed, neurotic, etc.). What we forget is that at least on the face of it there were also plenty of women who meant yes when they said yes, who welcomed the arrival of the pill because it liberated them from the fear of pregnancy, and who were glad of the opportunity it gave them for sexual exploration.

During the Vietnam War protests, for example, young women carried banners and placards promising draft resisters that 'Girls Say Yes to Guys Who Say No'. A deliberate play on the sexist cliché, but not just a play. There was something else at stake here too.

The underlying theory of a sexual revolution derived from theorists like Herbert Marcuse[22] and Wilhelm Reich[23] who combined the insights of psychoanalysis with Marxist political critique. 'Can we speak of a juncture between the erotic and political dimension?' Marcuse asks in his Preface to *Eros and Civilisation*, and answers 'Today the fight for life, the fight for Eros, is the *political* fight.' [24]

Their belief in the liberating potential of an active, genital sexuality (i.e. not fantasy or sublimation) fitted in with a much broader programme of what has since come to be known as the cultural revolution of the 1960s. That programme encompassed a critique of capitalism (more particularly that of the 'military-industrial complex') and of social conformism, and was formulated by the American new left in the early 1960s. Crucial to this new left, as distinct from the old, was a desire for 'personal authenticity' and for a transformation of society which would create the conditions for such authenticity.

Traces of the rhetoric of *this* sexual revolution are everywhere to be found in the novels by Shulman, Jong, Alther and Brown. Here, for example, is Molly Bolt, answering the question whether she is 'queer':

> I don't know what I am – polymorphous and perverse. Shit. I don't even know if I'm white. I'm me. That's all I am and all I want to be. Do I have to be something? [25]

She uses Marcuse's phrase to signal her refusal, not of lesbian identity necessarily, but of the label 'queer' as social stigma, as well as, interestingly, the notion of racial purity. *Rubyfruit Jungle* is a fiction of the sexual revolution because its discourse hovers on the brink of a proud assertion of lesbian identity, but without the collective and political dimension that Lesbian Nation was to bring to it.

Clearly writing against that other lesbian classic, Radclyffe Hall's *The Well of Loneliness* in terms of class, race and sexology, *Rubyfruit* turns the tragedy of that earlier text into comedy but nevertheless retains a tension between the positive of Molly Bolt as a role model and the negative of her marginalised status.

Whereas in the other novels mothers fail to prepare their daughters adequately for the world of adult sexual relations, Brown's heroine does not know her mother (but she was a 'filthy slut' by repute) and has to invent herself in the course of her story. It is as if Molly Bolt has landed from Mars: no precedent, no antecedent, a bolt from the blue. Yet while Molly's originality and derring-do are the by-product of her alienation from conventional femininity, that sense of alienation is not just a strength. Like Stephen in *The Well*, Molly finds herself alone at the end. 'It makes no difference where I came from. I'm here, ain't I?' [27] she asserts throughout, but the novel cannot resolve her alienation in any other way than by restating the 'personal authenticity' of the early new left, later trivialised in pop psychology: 'Damn, I wish the world would let me be myself.' [28]

In the 'Political Preface' to *Eros and Civilisation* of 1966 Marcuse looked back on the impact his book had when it was first published in the 1950s. He explains that his previous optimism regarding the possibilities of using 'the social wealth for shaping man's world in accordance with his Life Instincts' in a post-scarcity society had been unwarranted:

> Scientific management of instinctual needs has long since become a vital factor in the reproduction of the system: merchandise which has to be bought and used is made into objects of the libido and the national Enemy who has to be fought and hated is distorted and inflated to such an extent that he can activate and satisfy aggressiveness in the depth dimension of the unconscious.[29]

Although this rhetoric is now unfamiliar to us, Marcuse is here talking about familiar things: institutions (the family, education, social sciences, law and order) which delimit the expression and realisation of human needs, the Cold War, consumerism, and the Reichian idea that repressed sexuality leads to aggression. We can see, then, that the war resisters with their placards were acting in the spirit of Reich and Marcuse, seeing sex as an alternative to war (as also in the much more famous 60s slogan 'Make Love Not War'). The women who were prepared to say yes saw their sexuality in the context of a political rebellion and not – as women's liberationists were to do later – as self-prostitution under the duress of a sexist society.

The ground of female sexuality, of 'what women want', has shifted considerably in the past three decades. First of all, the sexual revolution opened up monogamous marriage along with the closet and butch/femme roles and made sure that these were no longer the only sites of female sexual pleasure. The sexual revolution furthermore sanctioned sex before marriage and regarded promiscuity as a means of gaining sexual experience, rather than as moral failure. Thirdly, it fostered a culture of androgyny in appearance and modes of behaviour which began to break down the rigid binaries of previous cultural definitions of masculine and feminine. And finally the sexual revolution for women highlighted very clearly connections between sex and social power relations. It was because of the sexual revolution, perhaps because of social pressure on women to engage in sexual experimentation, that women became less, not more, tolerant of the sexual double standard. They made more demands of men in their sexual relationships. And while monogamy may still have been a preferred option for some, others benefited from a multiplicity of sexual partners, female as well as male.

Although none of these gains has quite been undone, the culture of experimentation and sexual adventure has decidedly passed, and not just because of AIDS. I think that in part the women's liberation movement must be held responsible, in so far as it sought to analyse and redress what it saw as the bad effects of the sexual revolution for women without perhaps duly stressing and developing the gains. 1960s libertarianism, hand in hand with mass marketing of the pill, so the women's liberation argument went, made women more available for sex than they had been in the past. Women were victimised by male-defined ideas of sexual innovation (promiscuity, group sex, public sex) which suit neither women's needs nor their 'socialisation'. Furthermore, the sexual researches of the 1950s and 60s were used to support the idea of women's capacity for sexual pleasure. Ehrenreich and English write that Masters and Johnson:

> emerged convinced of [the clitoris's] exhaustive powers (which now made the penis seem feeble in comparison) and gave their scientific imprimatur to a new era of female sexuality – in which pleasure could potentially be divorced from its last ties to marriage, babies, and even men themselves.[30]

Women's liberation concluded that the sexual revolution had been part of the problem of the oppression of women rather than offering a solution to it (as Reich had believed). It developed a thoroughgoing critique not just of male sexuality as a site of power but of heterosexuality itself. Enter the familiar debates about pornography and sexual violence, about lesbianism as a political choice, about the woman-identified woman and politically acceptable sexual practices.

But this critique of sex-and-power, necessary as it was, resulted in effect in an anti-sexual/pro-love position within a women's movement that had in part developed out of and in conjunction with the sexual radicalism of the 1960s. There is nothing wrong with love, but it is questionable whether this emphasis on sex-in-the-context-of-a-loving-relationship (preferably between women) did not return women to where they came from: the private domain, where we dream of true love rather than true sex.

Fought out in the midst of a general rightward swing in American politics and culture, the new puritanism debate played right into the hands of the moral majority and other crusaders for the sanctity of motherhood and the nuclear family. Nor was this puritanism confined to the 'problem' of heterosexuality. First the heterosexual feminist came to be defined as a contradiction in terms by those who strictly applied the notion that the personal is political ('sleeping with the enemy'). But with the prohibition on inequality in sexual relations, lesbian practices soon came under scrutiny also. Butch and femme role play was out and the policing of 'male-identified' sexual behaviours began – soon, only touchy-feely 'vanilla sex' was seen as politically correct.

Lillian Faderman shows that, while the heterosexuality debate quickly reached a dead-end, the rhetoric of the sexual revolution of the 1960s was revived by sexually radical lesbians in the 1980s. Advocating such controversial practices as sado-masochism, pornography for women and cruising (hitherto associated with gay (male) sexuality), the sexual radicals:

> wished their own sexual revolution to be by and truly for women. They wanted to convince lesbians of the importance of enjoying the most imaginative and exciting sex their minds and bodies could construct ... They saw lust as a positive virtue, an appreciation of one's own and others' sexual dynamism.[31]

But the intense, important, and often bruising discussions which took place among lesbians in the late 1980s were not taken up by heterosexual feminists. The silence endures, despite the prurient public interest that the researches of Shere Hite and Nancy Friday have generated. Susan Ardill and Sue O'Sullivan posed the question in *Feminist Review*:

> In some ways our lesbianism does set us apart from 'women', whoever they are. It makes us different and forces us to reflect on our sexuality ... But we're still waiting for individual heterosexual socialist-feminists to come out of the closet and discuss and reveal the intricacies of their sexuality ... Do heterosexual feminists have thoughts on SM? Has anyone sighted a butch het woman and a femme het man together? [32]

The issues of dominance and submission in heterosexual relations, female promiscuity, sex without love (but with friendship, or – if

pushed – with a stranger) are, I think, still pertinent ones for
feminists. But perhaps, paradoxically, they are more of a taboo
now than they were in the days of *Fear of Flying* and *Memoirs of
an Ex-Prom Queen*. Somehow true heterosex got lost. That must
be because as long as feminists had to apologise for also being
heterosexuals any true discussion was impossible. But it is also,
and crucially, because heterosexuality has traditionally always
been associated with powerful socioeconomic institutions and
ideologies such as those of marriage and the nuclear family. In
the fictions of the sexual revolution, any true daring in the realm
of female sexual exploration is always temporary and provisional,
because circumscribed by the option – almost the inevitability –
of 'going legit' in the end.

Perhaps now that women have moved on to different modes
of living, far more diverse than marriage and nuclear family-
in-financial-dependency, it is a good time to reopen the question
of sex and power in hetero as well as lesbian relations.

Arguably the sexual revolution did little to change men's
sexual self-definition (apart from the gay movement, of course); it
merely expanded the playing field. For women it marked the
difference between their own generation and that of their
mothers, but also between the ideal and the real in sexual
pleasure, the theory and the practice of self-determination, the
desirable and the possible in a misogynist culture.

I think that the fictions of the sexual revolution such as
Memoirs of an Ex-Prom Queen, *Kinflicks*, *Fear of Flying* and
Rubyfruit Jungle articulate in however inchoate a fashion that
experience of a feminine sexuality in transition. They certainly
embody the gap between the old and the new in the disjunctive
forms they all employ. They fail as texts of female sexual adventure and enlightment, but they fail – as I hope to have shown –
interestingly. If feminism was and is about finding a voice, then
the vocal chords of these novels are stretched to breaking point:
they are the voices of girls straining to be women. They sing: 'It's
my party and I cry if I want to.'

Notes and References

1. Erica Jong *Fear of Flying* London: Granada 1974 p. 145.
2. Lisa Alther *Kinflicks* Harmondsworth: Penguin 1977 p. 69.
3. Rita Mae Brown *Rubyfruit Jungle* London: Corgi 1978 p. 4.
4. Jong *Fear of Flying* 1974 p. 257.
5. Brown *Rubyfruit Jungle* 1978 p. 221.
6. Alix Kates Shulman *Memoirs of an Ex-Prom Queen* Chicago:
   Cassandra 1985 p. 273.
7. Jong *Fear of Flying* 1974 p. 277.

8. Brown *Rubyfruit Jungle* 1978 p. 246.
9. Patricia Waugh *Feminine Fictions: Revisiting the Postmodern* London: Routledge 1989 p. 25; Mary Anne Ferguson 'The Female Novel of Development and the Myth of Psyche' in E. Abel et al eds *The Voyage In: Fictions of Female Development* London: University of New England Press 1983 p. 246; Judith Kegan Gardiner 'The Heroine as Her Author's Own Daughter' in C. Brown and K. Olson eds *Feminist Criticism* p. 244.
10. Alther *Kinflicks* 1977 p. 562.
11. Ibid. p. 568.
12. Jong *Fear of Flying* 1974 p. 97.
13. Ibid. p. 98.
14. Rosalind Coward 'The True Story of How I Became My Own Person' in C. Belsey and T. Moore eds *The Feminist Reader* 1989 p. 41.
15. Jong *Fear of Flying* 1974 p. 30.
16. Ibid. p. 88.
17. Elizabeth Cowie et al 'Representation vs. Communication' in Feminist Anthology Collective eds *No Turning Back: Writings from the Women's Liberation Movement 1975-80* London: The Women's Press 1981 pp. 238–45.
18. Shulman *Memoirs of an Ex-Prom Queen* 1985 p. 149.
19. Ibid. p. 3.
20. Lillian Faderman *Odd Girls and Twilight Lovers: A History of Lesbian Lives in the Twentieth Century* Harmondsworth: Penguin 1992.
21. Susan Faludi *Backlash: The Undeclared War Against Women* London: Chatto and Windus 1992.
22. Herbert Marcuse *Eros and Civilisation* London: Abacus 1972 (1956).
23. Wilhelm Reich *The Sexual Revolution* London: Peter Nevill, Vision Press 1952.
24. Marcuse *Eros and Civilisation* 1972 pp. 16, 19.
25. Brown *Rubyfruit Jungle* 1978 p. 107.
26. Radclyffe Hall *The Well of Loneliness* London: Virago 1982 (1928).
27. Brown *Rubyfruit Jungle* 1978 p. 7.
28. Ibid. p. 118.
29. Marcuse *Eros and Civilisation* 1972 p. 11.
30. Barbara Ehrenreich and Deirdre English *For Her Own Good: 150 Years of Experts' Advice to Women* London: Pluto Press 1979.
31. Faderman *Odd Girls and Twilight Lovers* 1992 pp. 253–4.
32. Susan Ardill and Sue O'Sullivan 'Sex in the Summer of 88' *Feminist Review* 31 Spring 1989 pp. 126–34.

CHAPTER 3

Jean Rhys: Race, Gender and History

Maggie Humm

Anthropology names the first border crossing the rite of passage. This is the moment when boys become men in a journey across the border of the wilderness, or girls become women crossing the threshold into a menses hut. Border crossing signifies the detachment of an individual from the one set of fixed gender categories in any given social structure and a celebrated movement into another.[1] Yet to be a coloured woman, a Creole, or a mulatto is to be a visual signifier of *permanent* border. Neither white self nor Black other, the Creole can only be manumitted across the boundary of colonial difference.[2]

Wide Sargasso Sea[3] is Jean Rhys's most complex novel of border crossing in relation to colour. It is not her only writing to chart that passage. Indeed the most consistent note in all her work is exactly the explicitly thematised interrogation of racial categories. *Voyage in the Dark*,[4] *Good Morning Midnight*,[5] her letters[6] and her autobiography *Smile Please*[7] all explore the moves women characters make to rewrite the colonial script, and navigate their way through the consolidated limits of imperialism. In 1907, at 16 years of age, Jean Rhys left her own colonial 'home' for Britain, the mother country. Yet 'home' and 'mother' are ambivalent, paradoxical terms for a writer of the colonial race and class whose allegiance is to the 'mothering' experience of Caribbean culture. The Creole Antoinette and the Black Christophine struggle together in *Wide Sargasso Sea*, through complex discursive negotiations, to cross the border between them. It is Jean Rhys's particular relation to 'desire' and 'difference' that dinomic of the colonial world which gives marginalised women a hearing.

Wide Sargasso Sea lies between Rochester's England and Antoinette Cosway's island, between the opposite categories of colonisers and colonised, and between the world of capitalism and the post-emancipation West Indies. Of course other Caribbean writers also refuse an island confine, but they often resolve the division of white subject from Black objects by placing the Caribbean into a myth of lost origins; or, like V.S. Naipaul, use a Europeanised character to patrol traditional culture with a baleful eye.[8] Gender as well as race is at issue here. In North American literature, for example in William Faulkner's *Absalom, Absalom!*

the West Indian woman is *the* repressed subject. For example it is Eulalia Bon's sexual as well as racial characteristics which make her the feared and different dark other. In Faulkner's novels all Caribbean Blacks, even at their best, are passive victims of sexual, economic or imperial events.

Wide Sargasso Sea rigorously refuses this reductionism. Rhys's novel subverts the conventions of colonial romance by denying the white patriarch, Rochester, his geography. It subverts colonial history by refusing linear time. It crosses the boundary of racial difference with the mirroring of Black, Creole and white women and the choice of a Black other as mother. It replaces the colonial gaze with a Black semiotic vernacular. The border between writing and reality, between languages and childhood, is a major theme that Rhys's heroines openly acknowledge and dispute.

For all their possibilities, *Wide Sargasso Sea* and Rhys's earlier writing cannot create an easy ingress into fiction for minority women. There are absences inseparable from any act of emergence, an appropriate unsaid, since Rhys writes often about absence. In a letter to Frances Wyndham, Rhys interweaves her sense of absence with race and sexual politics.

'As fas as I know I am white – but I have no country really now ... *Meek*!!! When I long to slaughter for a week or more. All over the place.' [9] Rearticulated by Antoinette in *Wide Sargasso Sea*, the letter, now dialogue, dramatises the ambivalence of racial place:

> It was a song about a white cockroach. That's me. That's what they call all of us who were here before their own people in Africa sold them to the slave trades. And I've heard English women call us white niggers. So between you I often wonder who I am and where is my country and where do I belong and why was I ever born at all.[10]

As Elizabeth Nunez-Harrell points out, the Caribbean street name for the Trinidadian woman is 'whitey cockroach', a term signifying a lack, both of colour and of social status.[11] Antoinette, like her author Jean Rhys, is unable to assert a fixed and definable racial identity. The full meaning of such an identity comes from the long historical chain of colour coding used by imperialism to void miscegenation and to negate the possibility of Black and white women's intimacy. Hence all Rhys's novels are fictions about female creativity. They are about females mercilessly experiencing the racist, financial and gendered constraints imposed by an imperialist ethic and feverishly searching for meanings to pose against monotonous masculinity. Not to enjoy the exhilaration of knowing is precisely the kind of ambivalence which is the mark of border women.

What importance does the border have as a meaningful category in Rhys's writing and in the shaping of her style? If, by nothing else, minority writers are linked by an imperative to violate, initiated by the prior violation of minority culture by the coloniser. The historical referent of the border is in Rhys's accurate evocation of gender. The alternative negotiation of borders by male and by female characters symbolises gender difference. For example, exile signifies great physical hardship for Rhys's women. In Rhys's historical reconstruction of the Caribbean and in her construction of England and Paris in the 1920s and 1930s, women like Anna in *Voyage in the Dark* cannot enjoy the detached objectivity of a masculine flaneur. Rhys's novels are boundary texts, full of signals about epistemological and ideological rupture, which group women in newly conceived differences. Rhys makes a fresh figurability of history to avoid the constraints of racial stereotype, juxtaposing her own autobiographical history with fictive moments to scan a larger horizon of literary meaning.

The question to ask of Rhys is: how does the subjective need to cross discursive boundaries become a new literary resource? What is the relation between social and literary conventions on the one hand and racial awareness, sexuality and literary innovation on the other?

> When I went into it [the Roseau Cathedral] I thought it beautiful. Instead of the Black people sitting in a different part of the church, they were all mixed up with the white and this pleased me very much.[12]

Yet, in *Wide Sargasso Sea*, Rhys's own mixture of Black and white – her attempt to write across racial boundaries – is often not 'beautiful'. The tension produces a text which awkwardly rides along the edge of many styles, sometimes sliding into a clichéd vocabulary where coffee is always 'brimming' and butter is always 'melting'; and righting itself into the veracity of Christophine's doubts about England. "'I don't say I don't *believe*, I say I don't *know*, I know what I see with my eyes and I never see it.'" [13]

In a discussion of the problem involved in dialogic fiction, Bakhtin says, in passing, that to understand another person or character at any given moment 'is to come to terms with meaning on the boundary between one's own and another's language: to translate'.[14] I want to express Bakhtin's concept applied to Rhys, as the crossing of two major boundaries.[15] First I want to analyse Rhys's writing by actively contesting academic boundaries, by leafing through the disciplinary catalogues of literary criticism, psychoanalysis, cultural theory and history. Finally, I want to move Rhys herself across the boundary of history, juxtaposing her childhood with the sexual politics of colonial history, and with the racial/sexual politics of the British healthcare Rhys experienced in the 1960s. The three histories of *Wide Sargasso Sea* are its historical setting, the history of its author and the historical moment of its composition.

This chapter has a writer, Jean Rhys, at its centre and it is about her crossing of writing boundaries and the stories she tells us in order to cross. This chapter, then, is about meanings, about the ways in which we rework what we read to give fiction meanings. It is about the kinds of stories we can tell about fiction and the contradictions between those stories. The regenerative motor of Rhys's fiction is colour. Jean Rhys writes about white, Black and Creole women and, in a quite particular way, escapes the limits of colonised colour. She escapes, I will argue, through creating a reciprocal world of mothers and daughters of different races.

In *Smile Please*, her autobiography written between 1976 and 1978, Jean Rhys describes a struggle she witnessed in the school convent between the articulation of the maternal and patriarchal law:

> 'Who made you?' It asked, and my chief memory of the catechism was a 'No, dear, that's not the answer. Now think – who made you?'
> 'My mother,' the stolid girl replied. At last the nun, exasperated, banished her from the class.[16]

An ambiguous passage in which the sense of the ferocity of the symbolic law and its consequent denial of the empirical experience of mothers and daughters is unmistakable but displaced on to another child. In the novels *Voyage in the Dark* and, especially, *Wide Sargasso Sea*, Rhys labours over the need of women to name their mothers. In Rhys's aristocracy of sensuality, there is a lyrical and careful observance of the maternal in what might be described as the makings of a female identity. Nancy Chodorow, in *The Reproduction of Mothering*,[17] argues that women's identities develop in identification with their mothers and continue in a relationship with them, real or imagined, that is interdependent and empathic. Rhys chose a particular figure – the Black woman nurse – to suggest the continuum of sensual warmth that was at least a possibility for women sharing the nurturing pre-Oedipal moment. Of course we must be cautious not to endow only women with affiliative qualities as if gender identity is not also, and equally, shaped by changing constructions of history and culture. Yet in Rhys's novels this affiliative moment is always a uniquely female ecstasy outside the understanding of men and their colonial prerogatives.

The lost mother is Rhys's organising motif. I want to read Rhys, to look at Rhys's recognition of race, gender and history in relation to the maternal, or, to use the good fairy of feminist theory, the semiotic. In telling Rhys's stories my sketches of Rhys's fiction, autobiography and history cannot in themselves constitute a closed, finished account of a writer. Neither can the point of the chapter lie only in the books Rhys wrote in the 1930s and 1960s. There is also the point that Black mothers occupy a very marginal space in white criticism. The only point for all of us lies in interpretation, in critical methods. It matters, then, for us to know that a feminist criticism of borders is likely to understand better the Black mother/nurse figure through the agencies of history, literary criticism, cultural theory or psycho-analysis by itself examining the borders and limits of those disciplines' own meaning making. Of course the stories that critics write in order to explain the writers they read are not the same. The interpretative devices of history or cultural theory are often in deep and ambiguous conflict. This chapter is placed on the border of these conflicts, taking as its starting point that no single disciplinary method, of history or of literary criticism, can deal with a 'difficult woman'.

Although Jean Rhys claimed to resent the nomenclature 'a woman writer', she addresses one of the central questions that feminist criticism seeks to answer: what is the connection between women as material objects of their own histories and the representation of women in narrative? It is Jean Rhys's place as a woman writer in modernist discourse which literary criticism appears best equipped first to handle. Certainly from *Quartet* to *Wide Sargasso Sea*, Rhys uses many interpretative devices of literature and her work is dense with allusions to contemporary and past English and French literature. In addi-tion, literary critics are now in general agreement that meanings do not lie directly in texts but in the interpretative strategies we agree to share to produce texts. Since the 1960s, with the advent of deconstructive and feminist criticism, literary studies have become aware of the issues involved in using metalan-guages to colonise figural domains.[18] In the system of classifica-tions that literary criticism relies on, imagery figures (sic) very large. Rhys's texts are littered with a residue of literary effects designed to emphasise a literary thematics of romance. Rhys's images are consistently those of journeys and consequently of borders.

Rhys began her descriptions of marginal women and their repression tentatively in her first novel *Quartet* (1928) [19] where Marya Zelli tests the bounds of femininity in the bourgeois Paris of the 1920s. Rhys doubled her literary currency in *After Leaving*

Mr Mackenzie (1931) [20] with the character Julia Martin, a similarly placed but older version of Marya. In *Voyage in the Dark* (1935) Anna's geographical journey from the Caribbean to England is replicated by her psychic return to the 'mother' world of her childhood. In *Good Morning Midnight* (1939) Sasha's rite of passage through the abnegation of Parisian poverty is into her unconscious, her only world *sans frontières*. In Rhys's final and marvellous novel *Wide Sargasso Sea*, she completes her examination of women's marginality by laying claim to the 'real' story of Bertha Rochester in *Jane Eyre*, named as Antoinette Cosway, but equally abused by the patriarchal boundaries of mid-Victorian empire.

Wide Sargasso Sea works with, and through, images and languages of borders to undermine them radically and to substitute real unities between women of different races for the smoothness of border differentiation. In the *Wide Sargasso Sea* Jean Rhys makes Black Christophine the one character who might free Creole Antoinette from the stereotypes of white settler discourse by encouraging her with songs and patois expressions.

> 'Not horse piss like the English madams drink,' she said. 'I know them. Drink their yellow horse piss, talk, talk their lying talk.' Her dress trailed and rustled as she walked to the door. There she turned. 'I send the girl to clear up the mess you make with the frangipane, it bring cockroach in the house. Take care not to slip on the flowers, young master.' She slid through the door.
> 'Her coffee is delicious but her language is horrible ...' [21]

This speech constitutes a direct and explicit representation of a Black woman's facility with the languages of race and sexuality. In defining and contrasting the cultural signifiers of 'coffee' and 'horse piss', Christophine's speech is governed by the intersection of two languages. Christophine's intercession here has an obvious effect: by switching between the syntactics of dialect 'talk their lying talk' and the orthography of standard address 'Take care not to slip ... young master', she installs difference in the discourse of the text. Christophine constantly interweaves 'standard' and non-standard English, drawing profoundly on a wide range of linguistic variation. The verbal dexterity of this passage does not bespeak merely Christophine's personal skill and authority but suggests as well that Rhys actively supports (by allowing unparaphrased 'speechifying') Christophine's understanding here that words embody rather than merely represent the racial characteristics they stand for. Rochester's stabilising displacement of Christophine's dangerous 'code-switching' as 'horrible' reveals not only that he occupies another language but that he occupies a different way of understanding the practice and meanings of languages in the colonial context. Christophine's speeches are always governed by the doubling of 'vernacular' and 'standard' English. That she constantly draws attention to the *opposition* of these codes rather than simply either appropriating received English or adhering to patois is a clear example of Rhys's faith in the Black woman/ mother as bearer of linguistic variance and as maker of a more complex dynamic of appropriation. Christophine's continuous bifurcation between the rhythms of the vernacular voice and the limited colonial language is an explicitly thematised Black verbal power.

Christophine's facility in English, French and patois, the trope of the translator, represents boundary crossing itself. Powerful women are those who can speak across linguistic boundaries. Rhys was herself a translator before she became a writer. The activity of translation has great social as well as creative potential. So in *Wide Sargasso Sea* Aunt Cora saves the family from the fire at Coulibri because she 'translates' family needs into local dialect. And it is Annette who incurs colonial incomprehension with her ability to distinguish between 'nigger', 'negro' and 'Black'. The violence of the coloniser is both linguistic and sexual. Possessing Antoinette, Rochester appropriates her 'I' by renaming Antoinette – Bertha as he textually appropriates the signifier for his own monologue by taking over the narration of the long middle section of the novel. At the end of *Wide Sargasso Sea* Antoinette triumphantly recovers her 'I' by displacing Rochester's monologue although, of course, she is unable to fight the narrative prison of Charlotte Brontë's Thornfield. Where, in her short story 'Pioneers, Oh Pioneers', Rhys created a coloured woman, Mrs Ramage, merely as a mediating plot device in order to motivate a confrontation between the white colonialists and Black others, by the time of *Wide Sargasso Sea*, Rhys allows Antoinette's 'authorship' to be empowered as a 'palimpsest' by Christophine's Black language of Hoodoo which helps Antoinette regain her voice. It is significant here that in the two sections of *Wide Sargasso Sea* which comprise Antoinette's own narrative she speaks, not of her marriage, but first of her childhood and then of her incarceration in Thornfield – those periods when her identity is consolidated by her Creole mother and by her Black servants.

Let us consider the opening of *Wide Sargasso Sea*:

They say when trouble comes close ranks, and so the white people did. But we were not in their ranks. The Jamaican ladies had never approved of my mother, because she pretty like pretty self,' Christophine said. She was my father's second wife, far too young for him they thought, and, worse still, a Martinique girl. When I asked her why so few people came to see us, she told me that the road from Spanish town to Coulibri Estate where we lived was very bad and that the road repairing was now a thing of the past. (My father, visitors, horses, feeling safe in bed all belonged to the past.) [22]

The most significant feature of this opening is the immediate positioning of Black/Creole speech as direct, authentic language dramatised in its own space (Antoinette merges her mother into Christophine with the indefinite pronoun). In addition, Rhys suggests the mirroring of Black/Creole, mother and daughter through the indeterminate use of 'she' and the eliding of Annette/ Antoinette as 'pretty selves' by Christophine. Rhys signals both the possibility of a self-expressive Black woman and the simultaneous domination of all women caught in a colonial nexus of decaying plantations and a history which places women's past, of 'feeling safe', in parenthesis. One of the remarkable aspects of Rhys's sentences are the conventional rhetorical figures they deploy yet the power they carry. Note, for example, the hidden metaphor 'a thing of the past' (road/childhood) reinforced by the use of repetition; and the choice of the ironic 'ladies' to signal class/race boundaries. The connotative effect of the passage overwhelms any trite denotative function.

The tools of literary criticism and its insistence that the subject is a discursive construct can take this issue of subjectivity into account. Certainly Rhys's books *Quartet* and *Wide Sargasso Sea* are rich in imagery. Rhys is fond of evocative adjectives and adverbs ('soft rain') and heavily connotated verbs, and an iconography of colour. Anna, Annette and Antoinette are all emotional romantics and Rhys chooses coded images to describe them. For example, Antoinette resembles Coco the green parrot. Turning herself into a commodified object, Annette sells her wedding ring to buy the white muslin for herself and Antoinette that will enable her to buy a second marriage to Mr Mason. Antoinette's most prophetic dream is of her future husband 'holding up the skirt of my dress. It is white and beautiful and I don't wish it to get soiled. I follow him sick with fear ... but it trails in the dirt, my beautiful dress.' [23] Yet it is not easy to use, as Rhys does here, the signifiers of romance, for example 'white' or 'birds'. Such writing allows its cognitive functions to be invaded by associations. The narrative of romance, its fantasies of sensuality and female thraldom is visible in a limited iconography of colour, of 'Black' and 'white' morality. Romance is both a potent *and* regressive account of femininity.[24] Romance is both part of a politics of consumerism aimed at women and also read by women as if it represents their social aspirations.[25]

Imperialism has always portrayed its own(ed) women as romantic emblems of white purity against the Black other, for example in Tissot's paintings of Edwardian women luxuriating in white dresses.[26] Rhys is, on the other hand, insistent on the relation of white women to Black. A significant example is the scene of Antoinette's nurture from nightmare by Sister Marie Augustine the coloured nun who 'had large brown eyes, very soft and dressed in white, not with a starched apron, like the others had'.[27]

The convent, like Coulibri, is a crucial environment in *Wide Sargasso Sea*. In both, the absence of racial and class antagonisms perform their enchantment in stark contrast to the masculine world outside. It might be more accurate to see the stasis of such places as idealised female worlds. Yet Rhys takes other paths of response away from atomised masculinity. We need to listen carefully for other frames of reference watching Antoinette entering *Wide Sargasso Sea* recording the daily lives of those around her. A neighbour, Mr Luttrell, kills himself because he cannot 'live at Nelson's Rest? Not for love or money.' [28] That casual saying is freighted with import. In the first page of the novel Mr Luttrell, another white Creole, has chosen suicide as *his* response to the economic exigencies of the Emancipation Act. Annette, on the other hand, chooses to connect 'love' and 'money' in a nexus of bourgeois patriarchy, sexual politics and racial exploitation in order to survive. She 'sells' herself to Mr Mason as his fantasy of a West Indies girl 'a pretty woman ... light as cotton blossom'.[29] Through the institution of marriage white patriarchy appropriates the full bounty of nature – her plantation estate together with its flower. The opening establishes the racial/ sexual constraints of Antoinette's life. Acting as a mirror of her mother, Antoinette will replicate not only her mother's name but also her mother's history by selling herself to the next patriarch, Mr Rochester. She and Annette are as similar in their appearance as they are in their histories, sharing a particular way of frowning and a 'sitting posture'. Christophine italicises the sexual politics of colonialisation: 'Money have pretty face for everybody, but for that man money pretty like pretty self.' [30] Antoinette's double/ triple consciousness placed between Black and white cultures heightens her awareness of difference and her ambivalence about fixed sexual values.

In literary criticism feminist critics *have* been working during the last decade to rescue Rhys from obscurity and restore her, not to a traditional canon, but to a parallel tradition of women's writing.[31] Judith Kegan Gardiner judges Rhys's honesty to lie in her unabashed attention to heroines alienated from others and themselves because they are female, poor and sexually active: 'They are also misdefined by a language and literary heritage that belong primarily to propertied men.' [32] Yet

Gardiner's detailing of sexual exploitation is a mere oxymoron of marginality. It accepts the binary oppositions: men/women, surface/absence. This stress on victimisation *per se* cannot adequately orchestrate that more complicated relation Rhys describes between the language of colonial culture and Black, white and coloured women's mimicry and desire.

It is a problem both of language and of politics. Writing about Derrida, Jonathan Dollimore reminds us that binary opposites are 'a violent hierarchy where one of the two terms forcefully governs the other. A crucial stage in their deconstruction involves an overturning.' [33] Rhys's overturning of opposite colours, her fictional figures, cannot be celebrated *tightly inside* the boundary of traditional literary criticism but require another story – the story of cultural theory. How is the other constructed in cultural theory? How does cultural theory tell its story? Cultural theory works through processes of signification which establish race in specific ways. Repression has a meaning in cultural theory which uses linguistic instruments of authority like 'primitivism'.

The Third World women in Rhys's writing are no primitives, no monolithic constructs. The mimicry of Annette/Antoinette, Antoinette/Amélie or Antoinette/Christophine refuses the codified categories where Black and white women are opposite portraits drawn by white culture. *They* are never *She*. Amélie's song of the 'white cockroach' metaphorically emphasises the shared outsider position experienced by both the Black servant and the Creole woman. Colour plays an important part in a character's self- identification of what I have called border crossing. Anna, in *Voyage in the Dark*, is a fifth generation Creole who figures Creolisation as part of her sexual and cultural response to Europe. If it is the active ideology of imperialism which provides that discursive field placing the Creole on the boundary of acceptable society, Anna collapses binary oppositions. In control of the text as its narrator, she is a free woman *and* a prostitute, having a personal morality which is both Black and white. Rhys's use of a Creole figure has two functions. It enables Rhys to explore the relation of gender and race while, at the same time, it *expresses* that relation, rather than the trap of what Homi Bhabha has called 'fetishistic identification' with Black culture.[34] Homi Bhabha, in his account of excess in 'The Other Question', has explained the way the coloniser encloses the colonised in legal, psychoanalytic or historical fiction. Bhabha criticises existing cultural theories of colonialism, the particular those of Franz Fanon and Edward Said. Fanon's *Black Skins White Masks* and Said's *Orientalism*, Bhabha finds are ultimately unsatisfactory because both writers believe that colonial discourse is only intent on creating a unified object – the racist stereotype of the 'lying Arab' or 'bestial African'. A colonial discourse which can only rule and conquer by such endless repetition is a discourse of *excess*. Bhabha argues, in turn, that excess reveals both a dualistic fear of, but *desire for*, the native. It is, paradoxically, the power of such stereotypes which allows disjunction (from the perspective of the colonised). Bhabha's statement of the problem is elegant.

From the direction of feminist psychoanalysis comes a similar argument. The same concern to deconstruct the stereotypes in patriarchal discourse occurs in *The Enigma of Woman*. Here the psychoanalyst Sarah Kofman works to establish the 'truth' of Freud's stereotypes of femininity. She asks: 'Why did he seem panic-stricken?' [35] It is the *excess* in Freud's exaggerated account of femininity, Kofman claims, which reveals his fear of women. 'Woman in general becomes unapproachable, a forbidden Mother.' [36] If the instability of women needs to be so frequently stereotyped it might also, Kofman makes clear, be a source of disruption. Both Bhabha and Kofman successfully link racist or sexist activity with racist or sexist language. I have put both accounts in tandem because, since Freud's account falls on nature – on women's irresponsible desires – his notion of excess, I would argue, matches the coloniser's appropriation of the native into childhood.

Rhys signals a rupture with conventional stereotypes because she demonstrates their excess. Only by expressing, and hence engaging with, the power of colonialist language can a writer begin to produce, as Rhys does, it seems to me, an adequate ideological critique. If we listen to Mr Mason and Mr Rochester, informed by both Bhabha and Kofman, we can hear how their language is both misogynist and racist. Bhabha and Kofman agree that colonial or patriarchal ideologies contain Blacks or women by codification. Rhys allows the excess of the coloniser to be heard. After Annette marries Mr Mason:

> we ate English food now, beef and mutton, pies and puddings. I was glad to be like an English girl but I missed the taste of Christophine's cooking. My stepfather talked about a plan to import labourers – coolies we called them – from the East Indies ... 'the people here won't work ... they are children – they wouldn't hurt a fly.'
> 'Unhappily children do hurt flies,' said Aunt Cora.[37]

To impose English customs and language is a normalising act whose work is to codify difference, to fix the other,

Christophine, outside the boundary of the civilised. Mr Mason's strategic aim is to create a subject space for natives through the production of knowledges about them.

The overriding romance of colonial fictions, cultural theory tells us, is one of geography. One of the great narratives of colonial literature concerns a male protagonist coming into rightful possession of his territory and 'seeding' it, twice over, marrying the white heroine and entering into a mutually redemptive relationship with indigenous natives.[38] Rhys's courageous stand against that narrative of imperialism is abundantly clear in her letters. Writing to Selma Vaz Dias she says that her writing will be 'more an escape from time and place as we know them – or think we do' and she quotes St Teresa of Aquila's moving address to the Conquistadores: 'I will find that country which is ever new and ever young. *Come with me and you will see.*' [39]

Rhys continually depicts a continuum between geography and sexuality. Paris is a vivid character in her European novels and short stories because the city evokes and reflects the sexual politics of the men and the women who live there. An insistent theme in colonial writing is its tendency to abstract relationships as mappable geographic space. The map is the colonial signifier of a dominated race, its economy, and topography. It is also a trope for that other colonial geography – the body of woman. Rochester identifies his estates with his wife. At Coulibri Antoinette and the house are intimate in their iconography of fertility. The family garden is a convincing image of the power and the danger of the semiotic balanced as it is between dead flowers and flourishing orchids.[40] It is the maternal space of Antoinette's childhood with its markers of nature – flowers, intense smells, and the rhythms of birds and animals. 'Wild untouched, above all untouched with. And it kept its secret.' Rochester knows that 'what I see is nothing – I want what it *hides* – that is not nothing.'[41]

Thrown out of the 'symbolic' civilised world of England, Rochester faces the wild zone of femininity. Rhys deliberately juxtaposes Rochester's fear of the environment with his fear of Antoinette's sexuality. After Antoinette is forced to bite him, Rochester finds 'everything around me was hostile. The telescope drew away and said don't touch me. The trees were threatening.' [42] Rhys's childhood and fiction are in dynamic interaction here. Her father placed a telescope on the verandah of their home above Massacre in order to overlook the geography. We shall come in a moment to Rhys's depiction of telescopes as signifiers of the paternal eye and its limited gaze. Without his telescope, Rochester fears entanglement in nature and makes his narrative construct an apartheid between his own socialised speech and Antoinette and Christophine's language of songs and body movement. Rochester finds safety in mappable boundaries. He possesses Antoinette's Granboise, like her body, by mentally mapping its rooms, steps and limits. Rochester refuses its romance through his knowledge of boundary: 'The barrier of the cliffs and the high mountains. And the barrier of the sea. I am safe.' [43] It is the possibility of blurred boundaries on the honeymoon island which causes Rochester's terror and demonstrates the limitations of a monocular patriarchal gaze. It is Rochester, not Antoinette, who is speechless, whose mind has blanks 'that cannot be filled up'.[44]

Questions about the representation of identity, difference and race are interestingly at issue. Collapsed into colonial writing are two myths about Black identity. The first is that all natives are childlike and the second myth is that all natives are lazy. An awareness of these forms of racism informed Rhys's story 'Overture and Beginners Please':

> Winks, smiles. Is it 'honey don't try so hard' or 'honey don't cry so hard?' 'How should I know?' 'Well, it's a coon song, you ought to know.' But when I discovered that although they never believed the truth, they swallowed the most fantastic lies, I amused myself a good deal.[45]

What Rhys reveals in her account of racism in an English public school is the boundary of its language. Such racism works, can have effectivity, only in constant excess, either through paternal metaphors of the child or the extremity of 'coon'. Yet, although the game of linguistic fantasy is a complex form of pleasure/unpleasure for a Creole girl, it does secure her a brief psychic space.

The fetishism of the other, cultural theory argues, is at its most transparent when the coloniser substitutes natural or generic categories (of emotion, or deviancy) for those that are socially determined. Mr Mason fears Annette is 'always at one extreme or the other. Didn't you fly at me like a little wild cat when I said nigger. Not nigger, not even negro, Black people I must say.' [46] Rochester's equation of Black/women's emotions with insanity is profoundly in debt to a nineteenth-century cultural framework in which notions of gender influence definitions of madness. As Elaine Showalter points out in *The Female Malady*, it was in the nineteenth century that 'the dialectic of reason and unreason took on specifically sexual meanings'.[47]

The Manichean bifurcation of Black = emotion, white = sanity are the extremes of the colonial script. Deconstructive cultural theory takes the biography and the book to be each other's 'scene of writing'. In her letters Jean Rhys experiences no bifurcation but rather interconnects her motive for writing – the figuration of 'the vanished West Indies of my childhood' – with her *own* body 'this is the first time I've felt half alive'.[48]

Interviewed for the *Paris Review* Rhys said:

> I was a bit wary of the Black people I've tried to write about I gradually became even a bit envious. They were so strong ... They had lovely dresses ... They had swarms of children and no marriages. I did envy them that.[49]

In the crude taxonomy of values that Rhys describes – strength, spectacle and sexual freedom – it is possible to hear the voice of a white woman's desire. Nor is *Wide Sargasso Sea* homogeneously subversive of colonial thought. It embodies some recognisable colonial tropes, namely that of the Caribbean as the infallibly good and free place. With the Black Tia, Antoinette is free to boil 'green bananas in an old iron pot and ate them with our fingers out of an old calabash'.[50] But rapidly Rhys historicises colonial experience and works to examine how that experience contains women in particular. Antoinette gradually loses her land, her dowry, her freedom and finally her sanity to Rochester. Rhys gives to the nurse Christophine, the most radical insight into this racial and sexual economy:

> These new ones have letter of the law. Same thing. They got magistrate. They got fine. They got jail house and chain gang. They got tread machine to mash up people's feet. New ones worse than old ones.[51]

Both Mason and Rochester fear the 'promiscuity' of the native body and take Annette and Antoinette away from their 'coloured' relatives. To Mason and to Rochester the sexuality of Annette and Antoinette is a sign of racial miscegenation. Both Mason and Rochester simultaneously fear, and ambivalently desire, the taint of race. In the colonial psyche the Black/white female catharsis is expressed in the sexual bifurcation white goddess/Black she-devil ('Magdalene'/'nigger'). Rochester's search for the 'true' history of Antoinette is an attempt to transfer white responsibility for miscegenation on to Black 'history'.

> One afternoon the sight of a dress which she'd left lying on the bedroom floor made me breathless and savage with desire. When I was exhausted I turned away from her and slept, still without a word or caress ... if she was a child she was not a stupid child but an obstinate one ... her mind was already made up. Some romantic novel, a stray remark never forgotten.[52]

The eliding of the otherness of a coloured woman with a feared lack of sexual control has a long-term history in Victorian literature written by men, for example in *Pierre* by Herman Melville and *Blithedale Romance* by Nathanial Hawthorne.

Rochester tries to contain female sexuality through denying Antoinette access to speech and hence to recognition in the symbolic. Since the other might transform the rational patriarch into a 'breathless savage' she must be entirely knowable as a child. Among Rochester's progeny in Rhys's exploration of atomised masculinity is Mr Mackenzie who inscribes women as sexual objects existing outside his self-protective moral code. His world of Blacks, Creole or coloured women is chaotic, uncontrollable and can only be fixed in the Manichean allegory of intelligence/random thoughts, father/child, subject/object. Similarly, in *Wide Sargasso Sea*, Rochester's gratification is impaired by alienation from his own unconscious desires. So that Rochester's narrative remains pertinently nameless. He is identified only as 'a younger son' while women's names are eternally in play. Women name each other easily and constantly without compromise. The historical crystallisation of Rochester's identity is in doubt. Daniel Cosway, the bastard son of Antoinette's father, is a hideous parody of Rochester's lack of a close father.

Rochester, in his section of narrative, constantly tries to 'name' his position, and the past. Rochester's imagined and actual letter to his father, and his reduction of Antoinette to a 'child's scribble', are then desperate attempts to reinscribe the father as telos. Yet the power of patriarchy is swamped by the categories it needs to tell its tale, so that Rochester desperately swarms in the subjectivity of his pronouns, first objectifying Antoinette as 'she' and then moving to an intersubjective 'you' in order to maintain his power of designation. Yet it is clear that simply to amass the many 'languages' of *Wide Sargasso Sea* cannot by itself answer the question of its effect, especially its effect on a woman reader. What we seem to need to understand Rhys's complex discursive subversions, it appears, is some way of talking about her fiction which is neither the 'imagistic' practice of literary criticism nor the continual 'performativity' of cultural theory.

Rhys said that she began and could finish *Wide Sargasso Sea* because of a dream of giving birth. Implicitly evoking the pre-Oedipal bond between mother and daughter in her autobiography, Rhys progressively develops the theme in her fiction that the nature of women is determined by the maternal. Rhys makes constant recourse to what we might conveniently call the psycho-analytic. A psychoanalytic examination of gender identity might be in order. My debt to psychoanalysis is clear in the structure and language of this chapter, for I use a vocabulary of repression,

Oedipal relations, and the scopic drawn from Freud's original conceptualisation of femininity and masculinity and pursued by feminist psychoanalysts ever since. Rhys, too, moves through tropes of displacement and a psychoanalytic symbolism that occupy strategic positions in her writing. Rhys's heroines display the Freudian characteristics of femininity – 'passivity', 'narcissism' and 'masochism' – combined with low self-esteem. Rhys's aim in deploying these models of femininity is to show how the social inscription of women are marked by these characteristics of alienation and inadequacy and, in turn, to inscribe women into a more positive language and gender identity gained from knowledge of the maternal.

Certainly Antoinette's character and situation reveal the imperative for the maternal bond, for example she tries to inscribe Rochester into a pre-Oedipal sensuality at Granbois. Antoinette is prepared to cross psychic boundaries. She finds pleasure in becoming an other in the mirroring and reflection of Tia. Similarly in *Voyage in the Dark*, it is the Black Francine who nurtures Anna through into femininity with her clear and honest description of Anna's first period. The representation of mirroring and mothering allows Rhys to rescue women from the allegorical closure of the colonial imaginary.

The iterative nature of mirroring structures the narrative of the *Wide Sargasso Sea* so that characters and scenes can only be apprehended through *other* characters and scenes just as the novel itself mirrors *Jane Eyre*. Rhys adapted the symbol of the mirror from her source text where mirrors are also crucial to meaning, for example in the scene where Jane perceives Bertha (reflected in a mirror) as her mother. Fleeing the burning Coulibri Antoinette is hit by Tia's stone: 'I looked at her and I saw her face crumple up as she began to cry. We stared at each other, blood on my face, tears on hers. It was as if I saw myself.' [53]

Yet transference is also the repetition of *paternal* prototype relations, of unconscious desires in the Oedipal relation. If Rhys, psychoanalytically, comes to grips with the ambiguities of white women's desire for, and dependence on, the Black other woman, desire itself has a contradictory nature. There is also the female desire for the father which is the theme of Antoinette's psychic and physical need for older men. Jane Gallop sums up the daughter's desire for her father as 'desperate'. [54] In *Speculum of the Other Woman* Irigaray argues that the only redemption of a woman's value as a girl would be to seduce the father. [55]

Rhys tells us in her autobiography that 'I probably romanticised my father, perhaps because I saw very little of him.' The signifier 'romance' is the sign of the intricate tangle of masochistic relations into which Rhys thrusts not only Antoinette and Rochester but also her other heroines and their patriarchal lovers. Rhys, like Charlotte Brontë, matches this desire to literary precedents. Both writers adapt *Paradise Lost* to establish Rochester as simultaneously threatening and desirable. Masochism informs their shared obsession with apocalyptic sexual encounters. For Rhys, the struggle reaches back into adolescence. As she tells us in her autobiography, 'Satan existed ... he could be a very handsome young man, or he could be so ugly that just to see him would drive you mad.' The Satanic paternal contributes to a masochistic regression in *Good Morning Midnight*, where Sasha ends the novel in a swoon of sadomasochistic desire for 'his mean eyes flickering'. But in *Wide Sargasso Sea*, Rhys brilliantly stays the 'omnipotent' power of the daughter's desire for seduction with the contradictory fantasy of maternal nurturance. For example, Antoinette takes no simple 'primitive' delight in Rochester's domestic violence, rather it is revealed only, and significantly, by Christophine: 'I know more than any doctor. Undress Antoinette so she can sleep cool and easy, it's then I see you very rough with her, Eh?' [56] Christophine, the Black nurse, recuperates Antoinette with the skills of transference from the anxiety of the daughter's desire. Freud's term for transference 'uberzetzung' is, in German, the word for translation, or the replacement of disturbance by the person of the therapist.

On the other hand, Rochester has a schizophrenic split between physical activity and mental detachment which occurs as part of his response both to geography and to sexuality. He rapes Amélie as a representative Black but distances her as excess since 'her skin was darker, her lips thicker than I had thought'.[57] Rochester has the same dichotomous relation to the 'body' of Grandbois which he encounters only when detached by alcohol. The sense that a better understanding of sexuality can occur in maternal surroundings inspires the scene where Antoinette crosses the boundary of menstruation into womanhood among the red flowers in the wilderness of Coulibri. The juxtaposition of the contradictory psychoanalytic paternal and maternal makes *Wide Sargasso Sea* into not an incoherent text but an extraordinarily accurate representation of the contradictions of femininity. *Wide Sargasso Sea* is able to express that yearning for a maternal bond which emerges in the Antoinette/ Christophine relationship by fashioning a story which displaces the paternal heterosexual romance plot in order to displace a 'colonised' femininity. Rhys's writing centres, emotionally and thematically, on the sensuality of women and on the bonds between them. In the fine story 'Let Them Call It Jazz', Selina is succoured in her imprisoned marginality by a deep identification with a same-sex role model. 'Liberated' from a white father and fair-coloured mother, Selina structures her desires and gratifications in her grandmother's image because 'she's quite dark and what we call "country-cookie" but she's the best I know'.[58] *After Leaving Mr Mackenzie* emphasises, and prescriptively stresses, the importance of women's bonds with women in Julie's gorged satisfaction with her female companions.

Racial/sexual difference is often described as if it is uniform. In Rhys's writing, difference is multiform. Through her Black mothers and white fathers Rhys sets up a psychoanalytic articulation of difference and contradiction which escapes the misrepresentations of colonialism. It may be colonial patriarchy which brings Antoinette to Thornfield and fixes her into the ideological order, or disorder, of madness. It is not Jean Rhys or her readers.

The most thorough example of the syncratic possibility of self/other identification informs Rhys's preference for the voice over the scopic gaze. The authority of colonial writing depends on its repeated recognition of the *visible* difference of the Black other, for example when Rochester displaces his guilt by signifying Amélie as more *visibly* (and bestially) Black. Jean Rhys herself experienced the specular seclusion of the colonial world during her girlhood in Dominica. In Bakhtian fashion the colonial gaze could be overturned at carnival when 'we could watch from the open window'.[59]

The antagonism of the look to the other is the position of domination. Rhys recasts the positions of dominant and muted in songs, folk singing and stories. The iteration of the feminine in *Wide Sargasso Sea* and in her other books is in its voice(s). Rhys's desire to speak difference erupts in the several Black, Creole and white voices which actively break the specularity of colonial knowledge. In her short story 'Temps Perdi' Rhys describes how Caribbean women 'carried on the old language and its traditions, handing them down from mother to daughter. This language was kept a secret from their conquerors.'[60] Anna Morgan in *Voyage in the Dark* strongly identifies with the Caribs, the indigenous people of the West Indies, and she makes equally careful distinctions between the languages of Black Creole and white.

Yet, as Hélène Cixous and Catherine Clément argue so acutely in *The Newly Born Woman*, each time there is a repetition of memory, a return of the repressed, it will be in a specific cultural and historical context. Fictional representations of difference must carry the impress of history. Women's identity may be malleable but malleability itself is differently established in different times. To unpick Rhys's representations, to understand her tactics better, we need finally to read the story of history.

Now the telling of history elevates politics and the social. What I should do is to write the history of post-emancipation politics and the social history of Jean Rhys. I should proceed by an exhaustive listing of events and their *conscious* literary representations. But Rhys is dead and, unlike David Plante in his book about Jean Rhys, *Difficult Women*, I do not want to make Rhys difficult; Rhys is an indirect historian but she is not a historical writer. Rhys gives conscious attention to public history. She carefully delineates with dates and exact cultural objects and vocabulary the historical moments in which her short stories are set. For example *Good Morning Midnight* contains little political detail about its period but does have a great sense of the economic fears that were a part of 1930s history, and Rhys's 'The Insect World' is a graphic account of blitz life during World War Two. Like a good post-modernist, Antoinette vents her hostility against (is 'mad about') the *teleological* unfolding of family history. She translates British history into childish songs: 'A Benky foot and a Benky, for Charlie over the water.' [61] Antoinette turns patriarchal history into the aberrant texts which it cannot repress.

Like Antoinette what I need to do, aberrantly then, is put an account, which is more or less a historical sociology of the 1840s (the moment of Antoinette) against an account of Black British women in the 1960s (the moment when Bertha became Antoinette). There is no question of direct influence at issue. We do not know exactly how much Caribbean history Rhys studied, but her letters reveal a great interest in, and knowledge about, the Caribbean. Nor, of course, can criticism any longer make simple one-for-one analogies between autobiography and fictional representations.

The customary elision of literature and history is effected when critics uncritically rewrite novels as historical narratives, as if literature could directly encode an external social world. Yet this elision does not satisfy the question of writing *movements*. Part one of *Wide Sargasso Sea* is set in 1834, the year after the Emancipation Act which replaced slavery with 'apprenticeships'. Yet in a strong sense *Wide Sargasso Sea* is intelligible only in relation both to its own contemporary history of the 1960s and from the point of view of Rhys's personal history. We need to speculate about *Wide Sargasso Sea* in the context of the dominant ideologies of race and sexuality of the 1830 and 1840s, *and* of the 1960s to understand how the text finally crosses and criss-crosses the boundary of historical representation.

Rhys felt herself to be in and out of history:

Eventually I got back to being a Creole lunatic in the 1840s. Quite an effort. Sometimes am almost there, sometimes I

think I'll stay there!! ... the Creole in Charlotte Brontë's novel
... attacks all and sundry – *off stage*. For me (and for you I
hope) she must be right *on stage*. She must be at least
plausible with a past.[62]

The word 'Creole' itself personifies imaginary history. It
originated from the Spanish *criar* (to imagine) and *colon* (a
colonist). In general terms, *Creole* can refer to European settlers
or to people of mixed race living in the colonies. Very briefly, the
Creole Caribbean of the 1830s and 1840s was a society of
bankrupt post-emancipation white plantationers who saw 'their'
Blacks in animal guise 'their noses flat like Dutch dogs' and
whose girls decline very fast from puberty 'until they grow
horribly ugly. They are lascivious.' [63]

The epistemic violence of the colonial world is savagely
misogynist: 'It is quite common for an attorney to keep ... thirty
or forty doxys.' Women most of all must not cross the boundary
of white and Black but accept linguistic and sexual apartheid.
Otherwise:

> we may see ... a very fine young woman awkwardly dangling
> her arms with the air of a negro servant ... the Creole
> language is not confined to the negroes. Many of the ladies ...
> speak a sort of broken English that is very tiresome if not
> disgusting.[64]

The description leads to Hester in *Voyage in the Dark* who
berates Anna for sounding exactly like a nigger while they are
living in Dominica, 'I tried to teach you to talk like a lady and
behave like a lady and not like a nigger and of course I couldn't
do it.' [65] In terms of the colonial/Creole order the action by
British law in emancipating the slaves from 1833 allowed Caribbean racial groups to enter society carrying with them their
cultural backgrounds. Creolisation in this sense was an aspect of
white control which was, necessarily, intensely specular.

> Sambo: child of mulatto and negro
> Mulatto: child of white man and negress
> Quadroon: child of mulatto woman and white man
> Mustee: child of quadroon and white man [66]

The hierarchy of colour continues through 120 possible gradua-
tions. The frontier quality of Caribbean culture has often been
noted. It was also, and mainly, a man's world because the
Deficiency Law was 'peculiarly oppressive to white females possessing small properties'.[67] Adding to the economic crisis, the
British government withdrew its protection of Jamaica's sugar
market in 1846.

A close reading of these observer accounts of the 1840s

Caribbean, when the system of apprenticeship was finally abolished, serves to remind us once again that writing is always a form of sexual politics and that sexual politics, no matter how specifically historical the context, is always constructed. Victorian travellers describe the Caribbean as if it were a displaced paradigm of the dangers in, and their fears of, gender and class in Victorian England; the Caribbean highlights the subterranean shifts and fissures in the British social terrain, as Britain was *settling* to support the material practices of imperialism.[68] Colour, or what G. Lewis calls a 'multilayered pigmentocracy' structured class position, and its genetic values, inevitably underlined the elision of women with blood and family history. The novel is set at that crisis point in Caribbean history when the white Creole in particular was most at risk of loss of place. Jean Rhys hoped to size the 1840s as an intact object of knowledge. Writing to Diana Athill in 1966 she promises that 'it [*Wide Sargasso Sea*] wouldn't take long ... I mean all the action to take place between 1834 and 1845 say. *Quick!*' [69]

Fortunately the novel is not that unitary historical text. The heterogeneity of its various narratives, its various locations, its complex mirroring of characters and its open ending provide Rhys with the space in which to express, and to negate, that complex interdependence of capitalist imperialism, sexual relations and race in relation to women. Daniel Cosway explains to Rochester the relation between mixed marriages, Annette's identity and emancipation economics:

> Then comes the glorious Emancipation Act and trouble for some of the high and mighties. Nobody would work for the young woman and her two children ... She have no money and she have no friends ... We all wait to hear the woman jump over a precipice ... But no. She marry again.[70]

Imperialism depends on a firm belief in evolutionary time. Traditionally anthropology cements imperialism to science by placing western linear time in opposition to primitive cyclical time. As Johannes Fabian argues, the subjectivity of the other's time is permissible only inside the duly qualified autobiography of the ethnographer consciously choosing to record a marginal culture.[71]

Just as anthropology focuses on the ethnographer's time and exiles the native to the continuous present tense so, too, David Plante battled with Jean Rhys's 'monumental' time:

> One grey day in late March we tried to organize the bits of her life chronologically ... 'Come on Jean, when did you and your husband stay at ... and for how long?' She raised herself from the pillow. 'All I can remember is the sea.' 'Try!' I said.[72]

Wide Sargasso Sea charts that masculine 'excess' in the winding course of Rochester's imperialism.

Rochester disparages Baptiste's refusal of economic history.

"Plenty of rum," he said. "Is it really a hundred years old?" He nodded, indifferently. A hundred years, a thousand years all the same to le bon Dieu and Baptiste.[73]

Rochester's commodity chronology is disrupted by the songs of Antoinette and Christophine which call on a potent alternative of dream and memory. Rochester fears the strength of 'women's time'. 'Someone was singing *"Ma belle ka di"*, or was it the song about one day and a thousand years. But whatever they were singing or saying was dangerous. I must protect myself.' [74] Similarly, in 'Let Them Call it Jazz', it is the songs of women prisoners in Holloway prison which enable Selma metaphorically to 'jump' the gates of the jail. Antoinette, frightened that Christophine is ageing, blots out demographic distance with anthropomorphic memories: 'All this was a long time ago, when I was ... sure that everything was alive, not only the river or the rain, but chairs, looking-glasses, cups, saucers, everything.' [75]

Antoinette's account of history is a phenomenology of physical characteristics. The world of everyday concrete objects has more explanatory value, for her, than the past which Rochester unravels. So, for example, Antoinette's Proustian memory of her mother's death is a more potent and vivid conception than the event in itself. By the end of the novel Antoinette rejects colonial time altogether by imposing a unitary world where word equals thing.

Nights and days and days and nights, hundreds of them slipping through my fingers. But that does not matter. Time has no meaning. But something you can touch and hold like my red dress, that has meaning.[76]

Antoinette thinks that time possesses the power of feminine sensuality – with looking-glass, rain and red dress. She asserts her own physical history – her memories of the island – against Rochester's historical prison. The red dress represents her real name. Red is the colour Antoinette chose when she embroidered her canvas at the Mount Calvary Convent and signed, along with her name, her place in time: 'Antoinette Mason, née Cosway, Mount Calvary Convent, Spanish Town, Jamaica, 1839.' [77] Rhys makes Antoinette speak out the animated subjectivity of physical reality over the colonial boundary of history.

Rhys's other texts also confidently dialogue with the past in the light of the present. In *After Leaving Mr Mackenzie* the detail of rooms reflects women's history. The descriptions of Julia's

room, her wallpaper and her bed, indicate her feelings and anxie-
ties. They are textualised images of the existence of her past –
made up of maternal imagery when her mother had been the
warm centre of the world. 'You loved to watch her brushing her
long hair; and when you missed the caresses and the warmth you
groped for them.' [78] This is a phenomenology of the maternal
espoused in a vocabulary of the body – of hair, gestures and
warmth. Julia's mother, a Brazilian by birth, 'sickens' in England
for the sun, and her invalid existence cannot finally offer Julia the
reciprocal support which Antoinette enjoys with Christophine.
Anna Morgan *is* the history of *Voyage in the Dark*. The potency
of her recollections is the only real event in the novel. As in *Wide
Sargasso Sea*, Rhys retreats from chronology to emphasise the
physical, intending to disrupt patriarchal history through the
figuration of a feminine and alternative story. We watch Anna's
history on a screen of double exposures. Anna continually super-
imposes the memory of her childhood on to her contemporary
history by describing the West Indies with the immediacy of the
present tense in contrast to the third-person account of English
experience. The introduction of Anna's memories is far more than
a narrative device to create plot contrasts. These textual tactics,
of a confused chronology and disembodied dreamlike state,
specifically occur with Anna's memories of her mother and of her
servants. So that, as Anna drifts into prostitution and loses
control over her body, so her memories of the Caribbean have to
darken. Past and present continually struggle against each other.
The tension in Anna's mind between them shows how Rhys's
women characters need to stand outside the boundary of the
contemporary and how a woman's maternal history draws a truer
picture of her sexuality than external chronology. Anna finds *the*
meaning of experience in her reflections, specifically in her
memories of Francine, the Black servant girl.

Significantly, throughout the novel Francine is portrayed as a
mother. She nurses Anna cooling Anna's head with a palm leaf in
an episode which foreshadows Christophine's nurturing care in
Wide Sargasso Sea: 'It was she who explained to me, so that it
seemed quite all right and I thought it was all in a day's work like
eating or drinking.' [79] And Francine's knowledge about women's
bodies (she explains here about menstruation to Anna) and about
women's language (her singsong rhythmic 'nigger-talk') represents
a now lost, sensuous, semiotic past. Memory and sexual desire
are often compared. *Voyage in the Dark* gives us women's history
as an epistemological alternative to linear chronology. Like
Monique Wittig, Anna chooses childhood as a form open to
history.[80] One understanding of dreams is to see them as active
dramas of events passively felt in childhood.[81] In the *Ritual*

Process the anthropologist Vincent Turner explains that movements in and out of time, through dawn and dusk, are characteristics too of liminality, of 'threshold people'.[82] Rhys rewrites 'time' to challenge the effacement of threshold women as historically muted subjects.

Wide Sargasso Sea is Rhys's own intertext of childhood and adulthood. For example, the landscape of Coulibri resembles Rhys's birthplace Dominica not the less equatorial Jamaica where the novel is ostensibly set. Rhys's family history is the plot of *Wide Sargasso Sea*. In October 1837 James Lockhart, Rhys's great-grandfather, died leaving his widow (significantly called Jane) to manage his plantation. In the Black riots which followed a colonial census the house was burnt down.[83]

Jean Rhys describes in her letters how she was also constantly pressured by contemporary history. Trying to explain that tension to Selma Vaz Dias, she says: 'If you do talk about my short story will you remember that they were all written during the war and in London. That explains a lot. One couldn't imagine any end to that time.' [84] *Wide Sargasso Sea* provides points of concentration, what we might call historical symptoms of resistance, to the different configurations of race and gender that Rhys experienced. These configurations are embedded both in her cognitive experience of the late 1840s, and in her *affective* experience of childhood and her likely encounters with Black women in the early 1960s. In the novel these configurations may, or may not, captivate a resistance ideology but, I would argue, it is the juxtaposition of these experiences which enabled Rhys actively to alter the traditional representations of race.

Rhys wrote *Wide Sargasso Sea* self-consciously from within the epistemological crisis specific to the early 1960s, a crisis occasioned by the break up of the British empire, and the need, in British culture, for fresh thinking about the Black subject, specifically the Black female subject. 'Race' is a concept used to classify and its reference point is always physical appearance. In the 1960s race was spoken in a new public voice, forced into speech by the Nottingham and Notting Hill riots against Black immigrants in 1958. The Conservative Party discussed the possibility of using 'Keep Britain White' as an electoral slogan as early as 1955.[85] The 1962 Commonwealth Immigration Act 'legalised' English racism and the 1964 Smethwick election returned a white racist MP, Peter Griffiths. A fresh vocabulary of the enemy within, of white men and of the sexual contagion and disease of Blacks was named as such by Enoch Powell in his famous 'Rivers of Blood' speech. In other words, the period during which Rhys was writing *Wide Sargasso Sea* was a period in which a truly popular language of race and nation flowered in Britain.[86]

Notions of Black subcitizenship and Black people as objects of social reform were already current in the post-war period, drawn from debates about Indian independence, but the path travelled by racism in the late 1950s and early 1960s was strewn with a taxonomy of the Black body and specifically of gender. The Eugenics Society, in 1959, argued that miscegenation was impossible to unmix, and much racist writing was striking for the way in which images of race were gendered.[87]

Equally the vibrancy of Christophine, Antoinette's nurse, and the strange excitement of their interdependence also have a relation to the elderly and alcoholic Rhys's dependence on, desire for, or distaste of, Black nurses in the many nursing homes and hospitals she attended while writing *Wide Sargasso Sea*. Jean Rhys was intensively rewriting the manuscript from the 1950s until its publication in 1966. During these years her husband, Max, was often in hospital and Jean herself was hospitalised in Exe Vale Hospital and Surrey Hills Clinic for several months, and continuously on medication for a heart condition. These were also the years when Britain's hospitals were radically transformed by the recruitment of West Indian nurses.

From 1944 the National Health Service and the Ministry of Labour, working in consultation with the Colonial Office, set up a recruiting system with offices in Jamaica and Trinidad. It is notable that subsequent restrictions in immigration were not applied to unskilled ancillary labour where West Indian women were concentrated.[88] Nursing was the specific occupation of Black women's employment, and in addition 78 per cent of ancillary workers and 84 per cent of domestic workers were from overseas. In 1964 Jean Rhys was 74 years old and Max was 80. In 1964 Jamaican women were seen as providing one *crucial* source of cheap labour to enable the National Health Service to meet the demands of Britain's changing demography. It was migrant, Caribbean women who catered for the ever-increasing numbers of geriatric men and women in nursing homes and hospitals throughout Britain.[89]

In the *Paris Review* Rhys dramatises her psychic separation from the first Black nurturer: 'At the start I hated my nurse. A horrid woman. It was she who told me awful stories about zombies and sucriants, the vampires.' [90] The early stereotype reveals something of Rhys's desire for, but initial defence against, her relations with older Black women. By *Voyage in the Dark* Rhys could use directly the names of the significant Black women of her childhood. In later encounters with Black nurses Rhys more adequately addresses the demands of her dependence and desire. At first, with Max in hospital, she felt 'Oh Lord: *If only they'd let us alone* ... the nurses aren't very nice ... the matron and most of the nurses are dreadful he says and they are *beastly. I saw how they treated him when I was there.'* [91] But, by the time of her own hospitalisation in St Mary Abbots, Rhys was too weak to 'separate' from care. Although the following two months in geriatric wards made her 'not mad about the welfare state' her letters also reveal her deep need more accurately to signify the Black woman in her fiction: 'I've made the Black woman, *the nurse* [my italics], too articulate. I thought of cutting it a bit ... [but] there's no reason why one particular negro shouldn't be articulate enough.' [92]

The hospital is the place of Rhys's desire for a Black mother/nurse. Homi Bhabha hints at the symmetry of darkness with a maternal imaginary. Darkness, he suggests, signifies a desire to return to the fullness of the mother.[93] In Rhys's text this is visible in the extent to which the Caribbean woman of the late 1840s is flooded with maternal images.

> When I was safely home I sat close to the old wall at the end of the garden ... Christophine found me there when it was nearly dusk, and I was so stiff she had to help me up. She said nothing, but next morning Tia was in the kitchen.[94]

Later Christophine takes care of every physical detail of Antoinette's existence.

> I wake her up to sit in the sun, bathe in the cool river. Even if she dropping with sleep. I make good strong soup. I give her milk if I have it, fruit I pick from my own tree. If she don't want to eat I say 'eat it up for my sake, *doudou*' ... I let her have rum.[95]

The scenes are nodes of allusions to the nursing required by a geriatric alcoholic. David Plante describes a similar moment with appalling clarity: 'She [Jean] fell in the bathroom last night, getting up to pee. It was a struggle, I had to roll her on to a blanket and drag her back to bed.' [96] *Wide Sargasso Sea*'s emotional strength derives in part from the impression it gives of the total loving care of a Black to a Creole woman and their reciprocal faith in the power of the maternal.

The equation patient = child, which recalls the fictive status of 'childlike' accorded to the attributes and identities of patients by most medical thought, provides another metaphorical space in which Rhys might see the Black nurse as 'mother'. In 'Sexual Division of Labour' Eva Gamarnikow describes how the ideological identification of good nurse with femininity is signified as motherhood.[97] Add the category Black to this equation and the representation becomes specific to post-war British healthcare. It is the imaginative engagement with Black women, through her childhood, her adult illness and in reading about the Caribbean, which enables Rhys to develop a complex expression of race and sex. Black 'other', in Rhys's writing, is not the colonial's other but characters like Tia who is Antoinette's alter ego and Christophine who evokes the maternal. Rhys places the pyschodynamics of mother/daughter relations in historicised narratives.

Rhys is disarmingly casual about her accomplishment:

> The big idea – well I'm blowed if I can be sure what it is. Something to do with time being an illusion I think. I mean that the plot exists – side by side with the present, not behind it, that was what it was – is. I've tried to do it by making the past (the West Indies) very vivid.[98]

Rhys continually writes the marginalised woman back into history not simply by celebrating marginality but by rewriting history itself. She 'remembered the last part of *Voyage in the Dark* written like that – time and place abolished, past and present the same – and I had been almost satisfied. Then everybody said it was 'confused and confusing'.'[99] Rhys actively replaces chronology – linear history – with maternal memory, dream, process.

The attraction of the mother is not reliably constant. Rhys never once portrays a scene of warmth and understanding in her autobiography between her own mother and herself. Nor is the mother always a Black mother. Grace Poole's narrative also hints at the reciprocal voice, in this case one speaking across class boundaries as well as across boundaries of race. Grace Poole's class language is specifically that of a servant but where, in Charlotte Brontë's *Jane Eyre*, Poole is an unsympathetic reactionary invocation of a working-class woman, Rhys's Poole has an authentic voice. She echoes and shares Antoinette's concerns. Grace Poole's introductory monologue to the final section set in Thornfield mirrors Antoinette's dreams both verbally and conceptually by sharing their vocabulary of 'darkness' and 'shelter'. Rhys openly revises a nineteenth-century literary text by adopting the point of view of its marginal character. Yet by choosing to represent psychic mothering in *Wide Sargasso Sea* through the 'mother' text *Jane Eyre*, Rhys gives powerful attention to the literary, as well as to the semiological, mother. Rhys's fiction, then, is the historical romance of the mother. Rhys wrote, as all writers write, to possess what is irretrievably lost. Surrogate mothers, usually Black servants, function in many women's texts and lives as alternative role modes to white patriarchs. The complementary that develops between white women and Black servants is heightened when the Black woman acts as receptacle for the white woman's fantasy of being mothered. Other writers have shared Rhys's negotiation of that desire. For example Lillian

Hellman explains that

> my own liking for Black people maybe came a few days after I
> was born when I was put into the arms of a wet-nurse
> Sophronia ... It was she who taught me to have feelings for
> the Black poor ... and she gave me anger, an uncomfortable,
> dangerous and often useful gift.[100]

Where Lillian Hellman conflates, somewhat unproblematically, the
representation of desire and the representation of progressive
philanthropy, Adrienne Rich is more honest and more radical:

> I had from birth not only a white but a Black mother. This
> relationship, so little explored, so unexpressed, still charges
> the relationship of Black and white women ... We have been
> mothers and daughters to each other.[101]

Rich understands that when a white woman identifies with a
Black other this risks dependence, even infantilisation. Black and
white women have to steer between the Scylla of the white
woman's 'infantilisation' and the Charybdis of the Black woman's
'childlike intellect'. Such is, I believe, the moment of Rhys's text.
Reciprocal dependence binds Antoinette with Tia and with
Christophine and informs the discursive and political effect of
Wide Sargasso Sea. A similar sentiment of interdependence structures *Voyage in the Dark*. Anna seeks to recapitulate the mother/
child dyad and, in her memories, bifurcates between the sensual
nurturing of Francine and the morality of a white stepmother
Hester. Rhys makes the important statement here that Anna's
pain is only relieved by her memories of women 'mothering' her
during a period of her history which predates her heterosexual
encounters.

In 'Three Women's Texts and a Critique of Imperialism',
Gayatri Spivak acknowledges that Rhys allows Christophine to
be 'first interpreter and named speaking subject'.[102] The essay
contains Spivak's usual subtle and sophisticated placing of texts
in economic as well as in critical theory. Yet even Spivak
judges the novel to *refract* the project of imperialism because
Antoinette, and the 'commodified' Christophine, are finally
caught in an imperialist hegemony. If Rhys does mediate
historical events through women who remain inevitably marginal
to dominant society, there are ways in which Rhys invites the
reader to circumvent that domination. What Spivak downplays
is the recognisable sociopsychological trope, namely that of
mother/nurse that enables Christophine to be that intelligent,
articulate spokeswoman for oppressed femininity.

Christophine is the visible role model of the other, self-made
into self, in the full density of otherness with her powerful

language and the medical power of obeah. Christophine links Antoinette to a more complex knowledge made up of magic, earth gods and Arawak history. There is a strong focus to Christophine throughout the novel, which begins with the opening description of her specialness and continues in Rhys's sympathetic portrayal of an alternative and purer Arawak mythology, for example in Christophine's song 'ma belle ka di maman li' which deliberately places the maternal in a Black and patois voice. It is Christophine who both makes and tells Antoinette's history. In *Wide Sargasso Sea* Rhys with vehement pleasure celebrates an articulate Black female woman, Christophine, who is authentically subversive of patriarchal history only *because* she is positioned on the boundary between races, between languages and between histories. Christophine, Antoinette, Tia and Amélie retrieve the maternal from its nexus of misogyny and racism. In *Gynesis*, Alice Jardine points out that it is in the nature of the 'European ensemble/confronted with systems of production and belief foreign to its own', to colonise or retreat into its own boundaries.[103] The space outside of the conscious colonial subject has always connoted the other, either/or feminine and Black. As Jardine observes, this space carries 'feminine connotations' which intersect the female body with maternity.[104]

Jean Rhys challenges the boundaries of such 'systems of production'. In *Wide Sargasso Sea* the reciprocity of Black women and white women, as mothers and daughters is a microcosmic reversal of the failure of culture and history to consolidate a progressive new identity of women. Jean Rhys fissures colonialism with discrete breaks: first she disrupts paternal history with the maternal semiotic by replacing chronology with a 'women's time' of maternal imagery and memories; second she plays out differing Creole and Black voices to refuse the specular aesthetic.

Of course, although her writing makes a monumental effort to subvert the colonial script it necessarily raises in its very strategies some problematics of boundary crossing. For example, the pre-Oedipal is inevitably implicated in a nostalgia for lost origins which cannot, by itself, provide the grounds for a counter-discourse. There is an inevitable tension, too, when constructing a new 'history' of women, between 'women' as a discursively constructed group and women as material subjects of their own history. Again, linguistically, discursive formations of marginal women might be misheard as articulating a limited scale. It is not possible for Rhys to replace *fully* the taxonomy of colonial racism with a white/Creole/Black discursive feminine.

What, then, are the maternal/sexual theories of boundary crossing? As we have seen, Nancy Chodorow, in *The Reproduction of Mothering*, argues that female children do not accept any boundary between themselves and their mothers because mothers cannot represent 'difference' for girls in the same way that mothers represent all that is not masculine for boys. The other significant theory of the maternal is the one proposed by Julia Kristeva, in *Desire in Language*, where she defines maternal imagery as the semiotic subtext of symbolic language. Plato 'intuitively' understood, Kristeva suggests, that there is 'a *chora*, receptacle, unnamable, improbable, hybrid, anterior to naming, to the one, to the father, and consequently maternally connoted'.[105] The chora is the place of orality, sensuality and 'laughter'. Rhys took that further journey across the frontier of the imperial dominative terrain. Rhys's project is to break not just the boundary between the maternal semiotic and paternal symbolic but to break the boundary of 'race', as constituted in paternal symbolic language, by working towards a warm and incestuous understanding between women of different races in mother/daughter dyads.

What is really meaningful in her writing is not just its radical *content* – an attack on the racist misogyny of colonial men – but its portraits of authentic Black and Creole women subjects addressing the instability of difference. Her work is charged with the conditions of its creation. It does not present a unified category 'woman' but represents the multivocal and personal narratives of different women of different colours:

> About my book. It is done in the way that patchwork would be done if you had all the colours and all the pieces but had not yet arranged to make a quilt.[106]

Notes and References

1. See V. Turner *The Ritual Process* London: Routledge and Kegan Paul 1969.
2. Hortense Spillers, although concerned primarily with the mulatto figure in Faulkner's *Absalom, Absalom!* and *Light in August*, similarly argues that the mulatto/mulatta is the metaphor of liminality and a paradigm of racial and gender discrimination. See Spillers 'Notes on an Alternative Model: Neither/Nor' in M. Davis et al ed *The Year Left 2* London: Verso 1987.
3. Jean Rhys *Wide Sargasso Sea* London: André Deutsch 1966.
4. Jean Rhys *Voyage in the Dark* Harmondsworth: Penguin 1969.
5. Jean Rhys *Good Morning Midnight* Harmondsworth: Penguin 1969.
6. Jean Rhys *Letters* Harmondsworth: Penguin 1985.

7. Jean Rhys *Smile Please* Harmondsworth: Penguin 1981.
8. To be fair, V.S. Naipaul and other Caribbean writers' adoption of a European perspective may be because, as Incke Plaf points out in 'Women and Literature in the Caribbean', there is as yet no broad view of Caribbean literature as a whole, in M. Schipper ed *Unheard Words* London: Allison & Busby: 1985.
9. Rhys *Letters* 1985 p. 172.
10. Rhys *Wide Sargasso Sea* 1966 p. 102.
11. E. Y. Nunez-Harrell 'The Paradoxes of Belonging: The White West Indian Woman in Fiction' *Modern Fiction Studies* 31 1985 pp. 281–93.
12. Rhys *Smile Please* 1981 p. 79.
13. Rhys *Wide Sargasso Sea* 1966 p. 111.
14. M. M. Bakhtin *Problems of Dostoevsky's Poetics* Manchester: Manchester University Press 1984 p. xxxvii.
15. Mikhail Bakhtin's concepts of dialogy and extopy are discussed in detail in the Introduction.
16. Rhys *Smile Please* 1981 p. 78.
17. Nancy Chodorow *The Reproduction of Mothering* Berkeley: University of California Press 1978.
18. This is, of course a sweepingly tendentious summary of the literary criticism about deconstruction. For an overview see C. Belsey *Critical Practice* London: Methuen 1980; H.J. Bloom ed *Deconstruction and Criticism* London: Routledge & Kegan Paul 1979, with essays by all the leading deconstructive critics – Harold Bloom, Paul de Man, Jacques Derrida, Geoffrey Hartman and J. Hillis Miller; and Vincent Leitch *Deconstructive Criticism: An Advanced Introduction* New York: Columbia 1983; and C. Norris *Deconstruction: Theory and Practice* New York: Methuen 1982. For feminist deconstruction see G. Spivak and B. Johnson *The Critical Difference: Essays in the Contemporary Rhetoric of Reading* Baltimore: Johns Hopkins 1980 and A. Jardine *Gynesis: Configurations of Woman and Modernity* Ithaca: Cornell 1985. J. Culler argues the case that deconstruction has a radical politics in *Deconstruction: Theory and Criticism after Structuralism* Ithaca: Cornell 1982. R. Rorty has drawn attention to deconstruction's need paradoxically to 'create' a historically determined practice against which it can react. See 'Deconstruction and Circumvention' *Critical Inquiry* 11, 1 pp. 1–23.
19. Jean Rhys *Quartet* Harmondsworth: Penguin 1973.
20. Jean Rhys *After Leaving Mr Mackenzie* Harmondsworth: Penguin 1971.
21. Rhys *Wide Sargasso Sea* 1966 p. 85.
22. Ibid. p. 17.

23. Ibid. p. 60.
24. See T. Modleski *Loving With a Vengeance* New York: Methuen 1984.
25. See J. Radway 'Women Read the Romance' *Feminist Studies* 9, 1, 1985. In Britain, it is traditionally the left which argues, by and large, that romances represent conservative ideologies. Feminist accounts of romance point out that romances are *read* by women for enjoyment because in them heroines are at the centre of expert care. Romances represent contradictory divisions of the psychic life. See J. Radford ed *The Progress of the Romance* London: Routledge & Kegan Paul 1986.
26. A marked example of the sequestration of the white woman in a colonial context is the generic cliché of Anglo-Indian romances such as *Ralph Darnell* (1879) or *Pretty Miss Neville* (1884). See B. Moore-Gilbert ed *Literature and Imperialism* London: Roehampton Institute of Higher Education 1983. In an alternative, and later, context Paul Gilroy describes the different responses of whites along gender lines to mixed-race couples in British ballrooms of the early 1950s, arguing that racist ideologies depend on fears of miscegenation. See *There Ain't No Black in the Union Jack* London: Hutchinson 1987.
27. Rhys *Wide Sargasso Sea* 1966 p. 52.
28. Ibid. p. 17.
29. Ibid. p. 29.
30. Ibid. p. 113.
31. The most direct and forceful feminist critics of Jean Rhys are: J. Miller *Women Writing About Men* London: Virago 1986; S. James *The Ladies and the Mammies: Jane Austin and Jean Rhys* Bristol: Falling Wall Press 1983; H. Nebeker *Jean Rhys: Woman in Passage* Montreal: Women's Publications 1981; D. Kelly Kloepfer *Jean Rhys: and the Novel as Women's Text* Chapel Hill: University of North Carolina 1988; J. Kegan Gardiner *Rhys, Stead, Lessing and the Politics of Empathy* Bloomington: Indiana University 1989.
32. Judith Kegan Gardiner 'Good Morning Midnight; Good Night Modernism' *Boundary* 2, 7, 1, 1982–3 p. 233.
33. J. Dollimore 'The Dominant and the Deviant: a Violent Dialectic' *Critical Quarterly* 28, 1/2, 1986 p. 190.
34. H. Bhaba 'The Other Question' *Screen* 26, 6, 1983 pp. 18–37.
35. S. Kofman *The Enigma of Woman* Ithaca: Cornell University Press 1985 p. 65.
36. Ibid. p. 83.
37. Rhys *Wide Sargasso Sea* 1966 p. 35.
38. B. Gale Chevigny and G. Laguardia continue on a more positive note (for decolonialisation) that this imperialist manoeuvre always ends in stasis because colonial romances

find solutions to problems either in the colonial past or in Europe itself. The contemporary *reality* of the geography does not provide these writers, as it did Rhys, with comfortable materials. See B.G. Chevigny and G. Laguardia *Reinventing the Americas* Cambridge: Cambridge University Press 1986.

39. Rhys *Letters* 1985 p. 144.
40. Rhys *Wide Sargasso Sea* 1966 p. 16.
41. Ibid. p. 87.
42. Ibid. p. 149.
43. Ibid. p. 27.
44. Ibid. p. 64.
45. Jean Rhys *Tales of the Wide Caribbean* London: Heinemann 1987 p. 69.
46. Rhys *Wide Sargasso Sea* 1966 p. 171.
47. Showalter's focus is on the treatment of female insanity by psychiatry and its misrepresentation in social as well as in cultural contexts. Her pertinent and forceful argument is that changes in cultural fashions, psychiatric theory and public policy all combine to keep madness a female malady. See *The Female Malady* London: Virago 1987. Since psychoanalysis depends conceptually on women's imaginary need for the phallus, Jane Gallop, in *Feminism and Psychoanalysis: The Daughter's Seduction* London: Macmillan: 1982, intercuts between Freud and Lacan to challenge the concept of specularity which this essentialism presupposes.
48. Rhys *Letters* 1985 p. 133.
49. E. Vreeland *Paris Review* 1979 pp. 219–37.
50. Rhys *Wide Sargasso Sea* 1966. p. 26.
51. Ibid.
52. Ibid. p. 93.
53. Ibid. p. 45.
54. J. Gallop *Feminism and Psychoanalysis* London: Macmillan 1982 p. 70.
55. Irigaray's insertion into psychoanalysis, and her departure from Lacan, is her creation of a female imaginary which represents woman's desire for the mother. See *Speculum of the Other Woman* Ithaca: Cornell 1985.
56. Rhys *Wide Sargasso Sea* 1966. p. 151.
57. Ibid. p. 115.
58. Rhys *Tales of the Wide Caribbean* 1987 p. 169.
59. Rhys *Smile Please* 1981 p. 52.
60. Rhys *Tales of the Wide Caribbean* 1987 p. 157.
61. Rhys *Wide Sargasso Sea* 1966 p. 148.
62. Rhys *Letters* 1985 p. 151.
63. See E. Brathwaite *The Development of Creole Society in Jamaica* Oxford: Oxford University Press 1971. The Emanci-

SEXUALITY AND REPRESENTATION 77

pation Act of 1833 followed the abolition of the slave trade in
1807. However, emancipation was to be gradual and, just as
former slaves remained the property of their owners after
abolition, so emancipation instituted a system of apprenticeship binding former slaves to their owners until 1840. This led
to much unrest. See D. McLoughlin 'Notes' to the *Wide
Sargasso Sea* London: Hodder and Stoughton 1989

64. Brathwaite *The Development of Creole Society in Jamaica* 1971
    p. 301.

65. Rhys *Voyage in the Dark* 1969 p. 65.

66. Brathwaite *The Development of Creole Society in Jamaica* 1971
    p. 295.

67. Ibid. p. 147.

68. See J. Davy *The West Indies, Before and Since the Slave
    Emancipation* London: Frank Cass 1971 (1854); G.K. Lewis
    *Main Currents in Caribbean Thought: The Historical Evolution
    of Caribbean Society in its Ideological Aspects 1492-1900*
    Baltimore: Johns Hopkins 1983; E. Williams *From Columbus to
    Castro: The History of the Caribbean 1492–1969* London:
    André Deutsch 1970.

69. Rhys *Letters* 1985 p. 297.

70. Rhys *Wide Sargasso Sea* 1966 p. 96.

71. Johannes Fabian points out that anthropology achieved its
    scientific respectability at a time when the natural histories of
    evolution reintroduced a history of retroactive salvation. The
    epistemology of anthropology therefore takes shape from an
    evolutionary sequential taxonomy based on the episteme of
    natural history which matches very well with an imperialist
    discourse employing such terms as 'primitive' and 'underdevel-
    oped'. See J. Fabian *Time and the Other: How Anthropology
    Makes Its Object* New York: Columbia University Press 1983.

72. D. Plante *Difficult Women* London: Victor Gollancz 1983 p.
    32.

73. Rhys *Wide Sargasso Sea* 1966 p. 16.

74. Ibid. p. 149.

75. Ibid. p. 37.

76. Ibid. p. 193.

77. Ibid. p. 44.

78. Rhys *After Leaving Mr MacKenzie* 1971 p. 106.

79. Rhys *Voyage in the Dark* 1969 p. 68.

80. Monique Wittig's central focus is on the construction of the
    feminine subject in psychoanalysis which she believes trivial-
    ises experiences of subjectivity in childhood and in lesbianism
    which are not defined in existing discourses. See M. Wittig
    'The Straight Mind' *Feminist Issues*, 1, 1, 1980 pp. 103–110,
    and *Les Guérilliéres* New York: Viking 1971.

81. A. Miller *Thou Shalt Not be Aware* London: Pluto Press 1990 and New York: Farrar, Strauss and Giroux 1984.

82. Turner argues that attributes of liminality are necessarily ambiguous because liminal people elude static cultural classifications. However their ambiguous attributes are expressed in a rich variety of symbols in many societies, for example in the instillation rites of the *Kumukindyila* or *Bwiti* baptismal ceremonies. See V.W. Turner *The Ritual Process: Structure and Anti-Structure* London: Routledge & Kegan Paul 1969.

83. See L. James *Jean Rhys* London: Longman 1978. Jean Rhys writes about her family history in *Smile Please:* '[my mother] was born in Dominica on what was the Geneva Estate, and Geneva Estate was part of my life.' The estate was founded by James Gibson Lockhart who left Scotland for Dominica in the eighteenth-century and it was the freed slaves who burned down the first estate house in the 1830s.

84. Rhys *Letters* 1985 p. 66.

85. See P. Gilroy *There Ain't No Black in the Union Jack* London: Hutchinson 1987.

86. Gilroy *There Ain't No Black in the Union Jack* London: Hutchinson 1987 p. 47.

87. Ellis Cashmore traces the interconnections between class, race and gender since World War Two in terms of structured inequalities in *United Kingdom?* London: Unwin Hyman 1989. Paul Gilroy examines categories of 'race' and anti-racist mobilisation, specifically focusing on the complex and dynamic patterns of Black definitions in postwar Britain in *There Ain't No Black in the Union Jack* 1987.

88. See A. Mama "Black Women, the Economic Crisis and the British State' *Feminist Review,* 17, 1984 pp. 21–36.

89. Mama 'Black Women' 1984 pp. 21–37 describes the connections between women's immigration and the social services. There is some information about Black women's employment in V. Beechey and E. Whitelegg eds *Women in Britain Today* Milton Keynes: Open University Press 1986. But a more thoroughgoing account is in S. Westwood and P. Bhachu *Enterprising Women* London: Routledge 1988. Issues of Black women and education are described in eds G. Weiner and M. Arnot *Gender Under Scrutiny,* Milton Keynes: Open University Press 1987. Women's autobiographical accounts are in S. Grewal et al eds *Charting the Journey* London: Sheba Press 1988 and in E. Dodgson *Motherland: West Indian Women in Britain in the 1950s* London: Heinemann Educational Books 1984.

90. E. Vreeland *Paris Review* 1979 p. 230.

91. Rhys *Letters* 1985 p. 222.

92. Ibid. p. 297.

93. H. Bhabha *The Other Question* Screen 26, 6 1983.

94. Rhys *Wide Sargasso Sea* 1966 p. 23

95. Ibid. p. 154

96. D. Plante *Difficult Women* London: Gollancz 1983 p. 52.

97. E. Gamarnikow 'Sexual Division of Labour' in A. Kuhn and A. M. Wolpe (eds) *Feminism and Materialism* London: Routledge & Kegan Paul 1978.

98. Rhys *Letters* 1985 p. 24

99. Ibid. p. 253.

100. L. Hellman *Scoundrel Time* Harmondsworth: Penguin 1978 p. 33.

101. A. Rich *Of Woman Born* New York: W.W. Norton 1976.

102. Spivak 'Three Women's Texts and a Critique of Imperialism' in H.L. Gates *'Race', Writing and Difference* Chicago: University of Chicago Press 1986.

103. A.A. Jardine *Gynesis: Configurations of Woman and Modernity* Ithaca: Cornell University Press 1985.

104. Alice Jardine examines the breakdown in the master narratives of religion, philosophy, history and cultural criticism which, she argues, ritualise the principle of uncertainty, of loss as feminine. See *Gynesis* 1985.

105. J. Kristeva *Desire in Language* Columbia: Columbia University Press 1980 p. 133.

106. Rhys *Letters* 1985 p. 162.

CHAPTER 4

Acts of Defiance: Celebrating Lesbians

Gabriele Griffin

> Let's stop this shit. I love women. I'll never marry a man and I'll never marry a woman either. That's not my way. I'm a devil-may-care lesbian.[1]

Thus speaks Molly Bolt, the protagonist of Rita Mae Brown's *Rubyfruit Jungle*, at once *defying* heteropatriarchal conventions that demand that women marry and that they marry men, *subverting* that demand by suggesting and rejecting an alternative formation of marrying a woman, and *asserting* her stance as oppositional to both positions of submission to and subversion of heterosexist conventions by identifying herself as a *lesbian*.

Molly Bolt is not alone in her defiance of these conventions; she belongs to a generation of defiant lesbian heroes[2] who started to surface in women's writing during the 1970s and 80s. The defiant lesbian hero was and still is hugely popular with diverse audiences as indexed by the fact that two novels featuring such a character, Jeanette Winterson's *Oranges Are Not the Only Fruit* and Alice Walker's *The Color Purple*, both won literary prizes and were turned into commercially successful mainstream films, the former for TV, the latter for cinema. With reference to these two novels and to *Rubyfruit Jungle*, the question I want to raise in this chapter is why is the defiant lesbian hero so popular with diverse audiences?[3]

From the point of view of a lesbian audience there are a number of very good reasons why such a figure might be popular. For one thing, she breaks with the tradition that dominated representations of lesbians through the first 60 years of the twentieth century, a tradition which cast the lesbian as 'deviant' and as the victim of her psychosexual identity as well as her heterosexist environment.[4] The prototype for that figure is Stephen Gordon, protagonist of Radclyffe Hall's *The Well of Loneliness* and variously replicated in Hall's other lesbian characters such as Joan Ogden in *The Unlit Lamp* and Miss Ogilvy of 'Miss Ogilvy finds herself'.[5]

Hall's lesbian characters share a number of characteristics: they are single (= the only one) and singular individuals, extraordinary beings existing without any sense of a lesbian community.[6] They are born into and live in a middle-class environment whose ideology dominates British culture and with which they grapple while sub-scribing to it. They are *afflicted* by a sense of difference which translates itself into a feeling of perpetual conflict as they strive for the 'normalcy' denied them by an identity they cannot fully come to terms with. While Hall's protagonists themselves are unquestion-ably lesbian, meaning that they are sexually as well as emotionally attracted to women, the women they desire frequently are not. For this reason the lesbian relationships of Hall's central characters tend to be temporary, unsatisfactory, unconsummated or repressed. Hall's lesbians are certainly not 'proud to be gay'. They are loners, unfulfilled, unable to establish or sustain relationships with other women, leading lives of perpetual alienation in an environment hostile to their needs.

The effect of this image of 'the lesbian' on *The Well*'s lesbian readership cannot be underestimated. One lesbian writes:

> I read *The Well of Loneliness*, and this confirmed me in my belief that I was a lesbian ... I identified with Stephen Gordon, and I thought it was tragic and I wept buckets and went around in a daze, for days.[7]

Not all lesbian readers, however, identify with Stephen Gordon:

> The only thing I'd ever read was *The Well of Loneliness*. My lover was no Stephen Gordon, and neither was I. And there was nowhere, nowhere at all we could go. It was the loneliness and the wondering where we fitted. Of course, we always dressed in dresses and matching accessories.[8]

While testimonies by older lesbians suggest the extent to which the image of Stephen Gordon dominated notions of the cultural representation of lesbians,[9] they also indicate that that single image could not account for all lesbians. In the wake of the women's and gay liberation movements of the late 1960s and early 70s, lesbians – as part of a wider move by women towards revisioning themselves – began to react against the image of the lesbian established through *The Well of Loneliness*. Thus Elana Nachman/Dykewomon maintains that she wrote *Riverfinger Women*, another lesbian novel featuring a defiant lesbian hero, because of her 'stubborn wilfulness not to be a tragic queer'.[10]

Rubyfruit Jungle, *The Color Purple* and *Oranges Are Not the Only Fruit* share this stance. As texts they belong to the category of what Rita Felski in *Beyond Feminist Aesthetics* calls 'the narrative of female self-discovery' which she regards as 'the genre which is most clearly identified with contemporary feminist writing'.[11] Like the Bildungsroman or novel of development/

education[12] they chart their protagonist's development from child-hood/adolescence to adulthood, recording this development in roughly chronological thought not metronomic form. As in the Bildungsroman the central character assumes her subjecthood in the course of the novel but it is, in these instances, critically determined by the intersection of her relation to the community of which she is a part and her lesbianism.

The positioning of the protagonists of *Rubyfruit Jungle*, *Oranges*, *The Color Purple* vis-à-vis their communities at the opening of each text continues the tradition popularised by Radclyffe Hall of constructing the lesbian as 'different' from those around her.[13] All three figures occupy extreme though not necessarily ex-centric spaces in relation to their respective community, determined by the details of their specific origins. *Rubyfruit Jungle* opens with Molly learning that she is a bastard, with its two attendant meanings of illegitimacy and of being 'bad'. Jeanette of *Oranges* in detailing her genesis – and the biblical allusion is important here – offers as one of her opening statements the comment 'I cannot recall a time when I did not know that I was special.' [14]

Despite coming from opposite ends of the value spectrum, being marked as 'a bastard' and as 'special' share the underlying function of separating the lesbian hero out from others, of constructing the 'unbelonging'. This is reinforced by the fact that Molly and Jeanette are adopted which generates uncertainty concerning their biological origins. Celie in *The Color Purple* begins her life in a state of utter subjugation which denies her any subjecthood. As the husband she is forced to take asserts at one point: 'You Black, you pore, you ugly, you a woman ... you nothing at all.' [15] In her case, too, the blood ties she assumes are hers turn out not to be so – she like Molly and Jeanette is cut loose from her biological origins.

This absence of biological roots and relative separation from the communities in which they live mark an important pre-condition of the lesbian hero's development. As Felski states:

> ... the last twenty years have seen the emergence of a distinc-tive new narrative for women, tracing the process of *separation* as the essential precondition for any path to self-knowledge ... the novel of self-discovery proceeds from the recognition of women's estrangement within a male-defined environment ...[16]

In *Rubyfruit Jungle* and in *Oranges* this recognition of female estrangement from a male-defined environment does not go hand in hand, as it did in eighteenth- and nineteenth-century novels such as Mary Wollstonecraft's *Mary* or Charlotte Brontë's *Jane Eyre*, for example, with a sense of men's ultimate power and authority and the female's gradual move towards social integration through hetero-romance, but rather translates itself into a counter-narrative of men as insignificant and/or grotesque.[17] Jeanette's adoptive father in Oranges is described as 'never quite good enough' [18] and she is haunted by the story of the woman who 'told us all she had married a pig'.[19] The notion of men as animals and as physically grotesque recurs later when Jeanette, defending herself against her mother's charge that lesbians are 'aping men', maintains that 'a homosexual is further away from a woman than a rhinoceros' and that 'a man is a man, wherever you find it [sic]'.[20] Not dissimilarly, Molly Bolt's entrepreneurial spirit first manifests itself when she enters into an arrangement with Broccoli Detwiler to show off his penis 'billed as the "strangest dick in the world".' [21] The male body here becomes a site of disgust in contradistinction to conventional romance plots in which the male body, framed as 'tall, dark and handsome', is presented as desirable. Female self-discovery thus proceeds in part through differentiation from the male (body) which is not, as the Freudian Oedipal narrative would have it, constructed as the positive pole to female absence.[22] Felski suggests: 'The defining feature of the feminist text is a recognition and rejection of the ideological basis of the traditional script of heterosexual romance ...' [23]

This includes the notion of the male (body) as desirable. In the case of The Color Purple the rejection of the traditional hetero-romance script takes the form of replacing one type of heterosexual encounter – the physical embrace of heterosexual lovers living out their sexual 'destiny' which functions as the climax and affirmation of the heteropatriarchal romance plot and which projects a vision of female fulfilment determined by being (physically) possessed by a male – with another, the rape of the female by the male. This latter plot, while still highlighting male ownership of the female body, explodes the notion of female consent and complicity. The resultant disgust of Celie with the male body expresses itself in yet another subversion of a heterosexual romance narrative, that of the fairytale in which by kissing the physically undesirable male (whether this be a frog or a beast) the princess turns him into a desirable prince. Refuting this narrative, Celie maintains: 'Take off they pants, I say, and men look like frogs to me. No matter how you kiss 'em, as far as I'm concern, frogs is what they stay.' [24]

In Oranges the same type of fairytale is referred to when Jeanette, confused by the woman's story about marrying a pig, wonders if that woman had read the story of 'Beauty and the Beast', another transformatory tale in which woman's love for man turns him into a desirable commodity:

> I wondered if the woman married to a pig had read this story. She must have been awfully disappointed if she had ... It was clear that I had stumbled on a terrible conspiracy. There are women in the world. There are men in the world. And there are beasts. What do you do if you marry a beast? Kissing them didn't always help.[25]

With men no longer transformable through the love of a woman, in the feminist novels of self-discovery their inadequacy to women's sexual needs is exposed. In the three texts under consideration this inadequacy is presented as one major determinant of the protagonist's lesbianism. Celie tells Mr-unambiguously that her early experiences of being raped by the man she thought was her father have turned her against men as sexual partners.[26] The views of men which dominate Jeanette's childhood in *Oranges* have already been referred to. In the light of these perceptions it is not surprising that Jeanette is completely uninterested in men:

> As far as I was concerned men were something you had around the place, not particularly interesting, but quite harmless. I had never shown the slightest feeling for them, and apart from my never wearing a skirt, saw nothing else in common between us.[27]

Jeanette, unlike Celie and Molly, never has either an enforced or a voluntary sexual relationship with a man.

Molly Bolt's starting point is different from Celie's and Jeanette's. She is neither abused by nor uninterested in men. She embodies the demands of early 1970s feminism which focused on women's ability to choose, including being able to choose in the sexual realm.[28] The exposure of hetero-romance as a patriarchal plot designed to subordinate women[29] had led to feminists re-visioning sexuality as socioculturally constructed, therefore potentially open to choice. The political lesbian was born.[30] In line with this choice-based vision of sexuality,[31] Molly Bolt in her adolescence, with both a lesbian and a heterosexual encounter behind her, decides to take control over that aspect of her self – her sexuality – and to experiment:

> Well Leroy, I thought ... you can't hold a candle to Leota ... But I'm not gonna base my judgment on one little fuck with ole Leroy. We got to do it a lot more and maybe I'll do around twenty or thirty men and twenty or thirty women and then I'll decide.[32]

Instead of being the object and, as Celie is, the victim of male sexuality, Molly assumes agency in relation to her sexual self, eventually coming to the conclusion which is the death knell to hetero-romance that:

Once you know what women are like, men get kind of boring. I'm not trying to put them down, I mean I like them some-times as people, but sexually they're dull. I suppose if a woman doesn't know any better, she thinks it's good stuff.[33]

Molly is constructed as affirming a sexual preference for women from a position of *informed choice*; her preference is positive rather than, as Celie's might be interpreted, negative. For a lesbian audience, the debunking of male sexuality as appropriate to women's sexual needs within a frame of deliberate and positive choice can be highly gratifying, particularly in a hostile hetero-sexist context in which lesbians are still told that what they need is 'a good fuck' by a male to 'put them right'.

Simultaneously, and this too makes them interesting to a contemporary lesbian audience, *Rubyfruit Jungle*, *Oranges* and *The Color Purple* all celebrate lesbianism specifically in terms of its expression of female sexuality. Celie is sexually awakened by another woman who considers her a virgin[34] because she has never experienced an orgasm. This woman, Shug, initiates Celie into her body and she does so in the 'classic' fashion of the consciousness-raising women's groups of the 1970s: she tells her to look at her vagina with the help of a hand-held mirror.[35] Shug tells Celie how her body might function sexually. When Shug later asks whether Celie's sexual relationship with her husband has improved as a result of Celie now knowing about the clitoris, here termed 'button',[36] Celie responds negatively. It is then that Shug begins her sexual relationship with Celie in which the latter's sexual desire is for the first time awakened and satisfied. The fact that Celie's lesbian relationship with Shug does not improve her relationship with her husband undercuts the conven-tional notion that lesbian relationships function as a transitory phase prior to woman realising her 'true' sexual destiny in the arms of a man.[38] Celie's commitment to Shug never wavers, even when Shug falls in love with yet another man.

Like Celie, Molly and Jeanette have predominantly positive sexual experiences with women which reinforces their sexual pref-erences. Lesbianism in all these texts is unquestionably marked as a commitment to women which *prominently* includes sexuality rather than being detailed in terms of some form of emotional bonding. Given the debates about the definition of lesbians in the wake of the women's liberation movement and Adrienne Rich's proclamation of a 'lesbian continuum' which included non-sexual relationships between women,[39] the affirmation of the specifically *sexual* nature of lesbian relations is likely to be welcomed by contemporary lesbian audiences.

Additionally, the protagonists' attitude towards their lesbian-ism is crucial in the re-visioning of the image of the lesbian as projected by Hall's work. This becomes evident when one considers the 'before' and 'after' (women's liberation) images of the lesbian provided in *Sappho was a Right-on Woman* in which the pre-women's liberation lesbian is described as suffering from terrible guilt feelings: 'Guilt is at the core of the Lesbian's life experience. It is her heritage from the past; it controls her present and robs her of her future.' [40] None of the protagonists of the texts discussed here feel guilty about their lesbianism. This is not the same as saying that attempts are not made to make them feel guilty. On the contrary. But all three refuse that guilt. To Molly and Jeanette their sexual experiences with other women, because they are so satisfying, seem 'natural'. Celie never questions her sexual preferences. Molly, Jeanette and Celie project an almost 'instinctive' affirmation of lesbianism; not they, but those around them, agonise about their lesbian experiences. Unlike Hall's lesbian characters, these protagonists are no longer presented as suffering from guilt or conceiving of their lesbianism as either a problem, a disease, or a sin. These views are held by their communities but not by them and in rejecting their communities' positions they reject negative stereotypes of lesbians. The difference between Hall's and the post-1971 writers' depiction of lesbians is perhaps most joyously incapsulated in the scene in *The Color Purple* in which Shug tells the assembled extended family that she is taking Celie with her to Memphis:

> You bitch, [Celie's husband] say. What will people say, you running off to Memphis like you don't have a house to look after? Shug say, Albert. Try to think like you got some sense. Why any woman give a shit what people think is a mystery to me. Well, say Grady, trying to bring light. A woman can't git a man if peoples talk. Shug look at me and us giggle. Then we laugh sure nuff. Then Squeak start to laugh. Then Sofia. All us laugh and laugh. Shug say, Ain't they something? Us say um *hum*, and slap the table, wipe the water from our eyes. Harpo look at Squeak. Shut up Squeak, he say It bad luck for women to laugh at men.[41]

Here a reverse narrative of the conventional heteropatriarchal one in which men do not take women seriously is offered in the form of a group of women bonding to laugh at men who cannot protect themselves against this force of female laughter,[42] grounded in the women's recognition that only they can help each other, sexually and otherwise.

This celebration of female bonding, expressed in Shug helping Celie towards her sexual self, goes hand in hand with the lesbian characters' openness about their sexual relationships. It is indeed this openness, the refusal of the traditional closet, which is also the 'undoing' of both Molly and Jeanette who find themselves excluded from their communities as these 'discover' their lesbian relations. When Jeanette begins her first lesbian relationship she soon reaches a point when she decides to tell her mother what is going on.[43] This ushers in her mother's 'betrayal' of her to the congregation whose help the mother seeks in trying to rid Jeanette of her 'sinful ways'. As Jeanette is told later by another lesbian character: 'No one need ever have found out if you hadn't tried to explain to that mother of yours.' [44] Analogously, Molly finds that her scholarship at college is not renewed when her relationship with another woman becomes known.[45] In each instance, the community seeks to extrude its lesbian member which leads Molly to conclude: 'Looks like nobody wants their queers, not the whites, not the blacks. I bet even the Chinese don't want their queers.' [46] However, in both Jeanette's and Molly's case, finding themselves castigated by their communities does not lead them to repress or sublimate their sexual desire. Both articulate their refusal to be subordinated to others' views as a necessary aspect of their sense of themselves. Thus Jeanette's sense of (sexual) self is shaped through a dialogue with an imaginary other, the orange demon, who appears to help her decide in how to handle the community's accusation of sinning and their demand for repentance. The demon identifies itself as 'different and difficult' rather than 'evil'[47] and maintains of demons:

> We're her to keep you in one piece, if you ignore us, you're quite likely to end up in two pieces, or lots of pieces, it's all part of the paradox.[48]

The demon suggests to Jeanette that the way to keep her integrity is by keeping the demon. Jeanette is thus split into an inner and an outer self; to the congregation she lies about repenting her lesbian experiences in order to be able to remain part of her community; inwardly, however, she does not repent. In a similar fashion, Molly Bolt tries to keep up appearances at various stages in her adolescence while secretly engaging in lesbian relationships. She, like Jeanette, learns to 'play the system', following her adoptive father's injunction to 'go on and do whatever you want to do and the hell with the rest of the world ... listen to nobody but your own self' [49] and her own sense that she '[wants] to go [her] own way'.[50] One of the best examples of Molly 'playing the system' occurs when she successfully fools a psychiatrist to whom she is sent about her 'condition'.[51] As Jeanette offers her congregation an outward image of being 'Calm, cheerful, and ready to accept' [52] when she 'repents', so Molly is 'calm and cheerful' [53] as she acts up to the expectations of the psychiatrist trying to cure her of her lesbianism:

I invented horrendous stories to ground my fury in the past.
It's also very important to make up dreams. They love dreams.
I used to lie awake at night thinking up dreams. It was
exhausting. Within a week, I was released ...[54]

Both Molly and Jeanette manage to 'play the system' but eventually are forced into a situation where they have to choose between belonging to the community and exercising self-denial, or
remaining 'true' to their lesbian selves and leaving. Both choose
the latter. Indeed, *Rubyfruit Jungle*, *Oranges* and *The Color Purple*
all construct lesbianism as a one-way choice the protagonist in
the course of her development decides in favour of. It is not,
these texts argue, possible to be a lesbian *and* to remain in the
community in which you grew up. You have to put a space –
literally – between you and it. Separation is thus acted out
geographically; the defiant lesbian hero is an itinerant figure,
catapulted into movement through her affirmative choice of living
a lesbian lifestyle.

So far the term 'community' has been used to suggest a
unitary body of people. However, in considering what precisely
the lesbian hero needs to separate from in order to assume
agency in her life, that concept of the community needs to be
more closely interrogated. Considered in terms of their economic
and geographical bases, the lesbian heroes' originary communities
in all three texts occupy a particular end of the scale. *Oranges*
portrays a lower middle-class/working-class small-town community; *Rubyfruit Jungle* is situated in the poor, rural south of the
United States. Molly is, as another lesbian in the novel describes
her, a 'member of the proletariat' [55] Celie, too, begins life in the
poor, rural south. But her community is a pre-industrial rural one
in which people produce what they consume and live at subsist-
ence level. In terms of their economic and geographical 'locations', then, the three texts differ significantly from Hall's *The
Well* and, as I shall suggest later, this is a significant contributory
factor in making these texts popular during the late 1970s and
1980s with diverse audiences, for one of the things the lesbian
hero needs to separate from in order to achieve subjecthood is
the poverty of her environment, in every sense of that phrase.

Ideologically, the communities in all three texts project con-
servatism, a subscription to notions of hierarchy and authority.
Thus Molly's adoptive mother, for instance, is described as someone 'whose politics are to the right of Genghis Khan'.[56] Jeanette
writes of her adoptive mother that 'At election times in a Labour
mill town she put a picture of the Conservative candidate in the
window.' [57] The emphasis on the respective mothers' rather similar ideological positions is significant here as opposition to the
mother becomes a vital element in the lesbian hero's separation

process. In *The Color Purple* Celie's adoptive mother is framed in rather different terms, physically weakened through the poverty-stricken, pregnancy-dominated life she is forced to lead, both in need of protection from her husband and unable to protect Celie from his sexual assaults on her. Her early death leaves Celie to assume the role of mother without having had an intervening adolescence.

The depiction of the community in all three texts shares, as part of its conservative ideology, the representation of gender difference as absolute. This difference can be expressed in capitalist terms as: men own, women are owned. The nature of men's ownership differs across the novels. In *The Color Purple* Celie is literally treated as chattel, as a possession to be passed from man (adoptive father) to man (husband) once her sexual utility for the former has waned.[58] She is owned body, but not, as the text indicates, soul. In Molly's case, the attempt is made to own her both body and soul through attempts to contain her by confining her (this is done, predominantly, by her mother), through trying to reorient her sexually (by exposing her to a male psychiatrist) and by attempts at excluding her from resources which will enable her to become independent (at the film school Molly attends, for example, men are given privileged access to cameras, etc.). In Jeanette's case the initial attempt is to own her spirit through mapping out her future as a celibate missionary in Africa; when she begins to have sexual relationships with women, this is widened to the attempt to own her body by determining what she can do with it. In all three texts men are constructed as owning the power of ultimate authority, whether they use this power in the lesbian protagonist's interest (as does Molly's adoptive father Carl in defending her against her adoptive mother) or against her (as does Mr – in withholding Celie's sister's letters from Celie). All three characters resist being thus owned. In consequence, one of the issues explored in all three novels is the effect that the impossibility of sustaining such a gender differentiation has on individuals or, put another way, what happens when women refuse to be owned.

In this refusal, the lesbian protagonists' relationships with other women is crucial. Broadly, a distinction can be made between women who support the lesbian protagonist in her resistance and those who act as gatekeepers to patriarchal regulatory prohibitions. In this respect *Rubyfruit Jungle* offers the bleakest picture, projecting the majority of its female characters as unsupportive towards each other and submissive to a system which disempowers them and keeps them in positions of self-denying dependence. Molly's adoptive mother, who herself never had what she wanted, offers Molly no support; on the contrary, when Molly

is thrown out of college for her lesbianism and attempts to rejoin
her mother, the latter throws her out,[59] thus forcing her into a
brief period of homelessness and hussling in order to survive.
Similarly, at college, the dean of the school, herself a lesbian,
does not support Molly but forces her into leaving the institution.[60] Another lesbian woman, Holly, tries to deflect Molly from
her decision to become a film maker by suggesting to her that
she, like Holly, become the mistress of a well-to-do lesbian willing
to keep her economically. These three instances index the extent
to which both economic dependence and having a stake in heteropatriarchy by being given power in its structures divides
women from each other.[61] Molly finds no refuge, even in the
women's movement. As she says at the end of *Rubyfruit Jungle*:

> My bitterness was reflected in the news, full of stories about
> people my own age raging down the streets in protest. But
> somehow I knew my rage wasn't their rage and they'd have
> run me out of their movement for being a lesbian anyway. I
> read somewhere too that women's groups were starting but
> they'd trash me just the same.[62]

I would argue that this portrayal of women as divided among
themselves reflects Rita Mae Brown's rather negative experiences with the women's movement in the late 1960s and early
1970s, particularly in relation to NOW (the National Organisation of Women) which in the period between 1969 and 1971
was anti-lesbian because a pro-lesbian stance, so it was argued,
would 'hurt the organisation politically'.[63] Due to this anti-
lesbianism:

> In January 1970, Rita resigned from NOW ... accusing NOW
> members of being middle-class club women not ready to think
> about issues of race, sexual preference, or their own class
> privileges.[64]

In *The Color Purple* women's relations with each other are depicted very differently from the way they are presented in *Rubyfruit Jungle*. In the former subjugated women bond together and
support each other through their various life crises. Celie, for
instance, suffers persistent rape by her adoptive father to protect
first her mother, 'My mama she fuss at me an look at me. She
happy, cause he good to her now.' [65] and then her sister Nellie 'I
see him looking at my little sister. She scared. But I say I'll take
care of you.' [66] From the beginning of the novel, Celie's relationship with women is different from that with men: 'I don't even
look at mens. That's the truth. I look at women, tho, cause I'm
not scared of them.' [67] Her positive response to women, conditioned by her not being oppressed and exploited by them,[68] never

wavers and predisposes her towards having a lesbian relationship. Only on one occasion does Celie betray a woman, Sofia, the first woman able to resist men's oppression whom she encounters. When she betrays Sofia by encouraging her husband to beat her in order to subjugate her, Celie suffers terrible pangs of remorse,[69] alleviated only by her reconciliation with Sofia.[70]

Sofia, Celie's sister Nettie, as well as several other women, encourage Celie to resist her oppression[71] at the hands of her husband but she is in a state of such disempowerment that she is incapable of generating the fighting spirit necessary for that purpose: 'I don't know how to fight. All I know how to do is stay alive.' [72] Where Molly Bolt is constructed as a fighter, only waiting to 'bolt' from any confinement of either body or spirit, Celie is reduced to a such a state of abjection that she cannot change her situation by herself. And whereas Molly manages to defy conventions *despite* the absence of support from women, Celie is enabled to defy her oppression by men *because* a woman comes to her aid and that in very concrete terms. What is interesting about that woman is that she is cast as 'strong', as someone who herself defies convention both sexually and otherwise. Shug in that sense acts as a foremother and role model for Celie. Having come from the same background as Celie and being labelled a 'bastard' just like Molly is, Shug has transcended her background and, significantly, is in a position of moving freely in and out of that background by the time Celie encounters her. Shug is thus also an itinerant, independent of her originary community. This independence is fuelled by her economic self-sufficiency. She makes a living as a singer. She chooses her sexual partners. And she chooses how to live her life. As Celie is unable to take control of her life when they first meet, Shug sets in motion the moves which will liberate Celie from her oppression. She awakens her sexual self. She removes Celie from her home environment, taking her to Memphis. She encourages Celie to consider how she might make a living and when the pants Celie makes turn out to be a success, she helps Celie set up in business as a clothes designer. Celie becomes a small-business woman, eventually able to generate her own income. Her subsequent inheritance of her adoptive father's house enables her and her sister Nettie as well as their children to be reunited under one roof. In contradistinction to Molly Bolt, Celie does not 'make it' by herself but is enabled to become defiant through the help of another woman. Celie has to move out of her original state of poverty and objectification by men but she does not, like Molly, and indeed like Jeanette, have to leave behind the female members of her community.

In ways not unlike those of *The Color Purple, Oranges*

presents a female community who offer each other support
through crises. However, this text divides women more
pronouncedly along lines of heterosexuality and homosexuality
than does *The Color Purple*. In that text Celie is helped by
another woman who also has a sexual interest in her and who,
at the same time, due to her economic situation is independent
of but not uninterested in men; however, women are represented as generally supportive of each other, irrespective of
their sexual orientation. In *Oranges* the situation concerning
women is somewhat different and operates along divisions
dictated by sexual orientation. One typical expression of this
division is offered in a conversation between two married
women about two girls spending time together which Jeanette
overhears:

> 'If they're not careful folk will think they're like them two at
> the paper shop.'

> 'I like them two,' said Nellie firmly, 'and who's to say they do
> anything?'

> 'Mrs. Ferguson across saw them getting a new bed, a double
> bed.'

> 'Well what does that prove? Me and Bert had one bed but we
> did nothing in it.'

> Doreen said that was all very well, but two women were
> different. Different from what? I wondered ...[73]

As she is castigated by her congregation for being a lesbian,
Jeanette discovers that she is not the only one.[74] There are a
number of lesbians in the community, not all visible to the
community's eye, but it is these women, like Elsie and Miss
Jewsbury, rather than the heterosexual females of the community,
who rally around to support Jeanette, offering her advice, shelter,
and protection.

In terms of help from other women, *Rubyfruit Jungle* places
women as least supportive of lesbians and *The Color Purple* as
most supportive, with *Oranges* hovering somewhere in the middle. In the instances of *Rubyfruit* and *Oranges*, the lesbian
hero's defiance is therefore directed in the main towards resist-
ing the women who act as gatekeepers to patriarchal rule. In
these two texts the female communities are presented as having
internalised that rule and utilising women to enforce it. This
gendered division into an androcentric legislative and a gynocen-
tric executive obscures somewhat the ways in which the gate-
keeping women themselves are expressive of their victimisation
within a system which allows them no independence.

In considering how the lesbian hero is oppressed in each of these three texts, I return to the question of why these texts are popular with diverse audiences and I want to link that issue with a brief comment on representations of defiant figures, for which there exists a long-standing narrative tradition in western culture. The most important of these is, perhaps, provided by Christian mythology, offering images for encoding rebellion that have taken a sustained hold in our culture. These images are 'usually' and significantly couched in specifically masculine and hierarchised terms as the insurrection of son against father and of man against God. It is the revolt of the younger against the older, the powerless against the powerful. In each instance rebellion is quoshed and the rebel falls, is driven from heaven, out of paradise. The territorial fights between – usually two individual – males encoded here are relevant to subsequent representations of female revolt as they offer the precedents upon which female insurgence bases itself and from which, in the unfolding of its narrative, it departs. *Rubyfruit Jungle*, *Oranges* and *The Color Purple* all make reference to this mythology. Thus one of her lesbian lovers says to Molly: 'Remember we're the hottest couple since Adam and Eve. Wrong metaphor – since Sappho and whoever.' [75] Celie in *The Color Purple*, driven to confiding in God, turns away from him when she realises that 'the God I been praying and writing to is a man. And act just like all the other mens I know. Trifling, forgitful and lowdown.' [76] And Jeanette who views her whole life in terms of its relationship to the brand of Christianity her community embraces comes to agree with the statement that 'Once created, the creature was separate from the creator, and needed no seconding to fully exist.' [77]

The Bible, however, presents not only the story of paradise lost but also of paradise regained, of defiance of authority leading to greater glory. This counter-narrative to the story of the fall of man, in the Bible usually associated with resistance to worldly authorities, can be found, for instance, in the ending of Christ's story, in his resurrection and ascendence to heaven. As riches-to-rags and rags-to-riches tales these two types of plot have permeated western culture, surfacing in Faust legends, in nineteenth-century novels such as *Great Expectations*, and, more recently, in the construction of the anti-hero of the 1950s and 60s. However, as suggested above, these narratives tend to focus on males and, typically, both narratives, whether they detail the fall or the rise of man, serve to affirm *his* identity, define his sense of self.

Both types of tale, paradise lost and paradise regained, raise the issue of 'rightful' authority, of who can and who cannot be defied with impunity. What do the specific lesbian heroes of

Rubyfruit Jungle, Oranges and *The Color Purple* defy? Molly defies
the poverty and constraints of her originary community, embodied
in her adoptive mother Carrie's attempts to prevent her from
'bettering' herself. From the early stages of Molly's childhood
Carrie, jealous of the former's independence, treats Molly's drive
towards self-improvement with contempt:

> I've got a good mind to throw you outa this house. You and
> your high and mighty ways, sailing in the house and out the
> house as you damn well please. You reading them books and
> puttin' on airs.[78]

Molly combines her desire for self-improvement with laying herself open to a variety of (sexual) experiences. The latter create
impediments in her advance and might be a source for condemnation from a heterosexist or bigoted audience, especially in this age
of AIDS (which, it has to be remembered, had not been heard of
in the early 1970s). However, the former, Molly's drive to self-
improvement, towards an education that will enable her to earn
an independent income, and her guts in standing up for her
values are all part of an ideological frame that constructs her as
an all-American ideal which, as the blurb on the back of my text
suggests, implies that 'Being different isn't really so different.'
Molly's desire is to be in control, to give orders, and to make an
impact on society. Following an argument with another child
about who will be doctor or nurse in a game they are playing,
Molly asserts:

> Course I didn't want to be a doctor. I was going to be
> president only I kept it a secret. But if I wanted to be a
> doctor I'd go be one and ain't nobody gonna tell me other-
> wise.[79]

Wanting to be the president of the United States, again an
all-American dream of the rags-to-riches variety, gives way to
wanting to be a woman film director. Her competitiveness in the
all-male context of the film school is conjoined with the desire to
be unique in her work:

> My movies ... [will not be] soppy romances about hapless
> heterosexuals, not family dramas about sparkling white
> America, not Westerns that run red from first reel to last or
> science fiction thrillers where renegade white corpuscles fill
> the screen – my movies [will be] real movies about real people
> and about the way the shit comes down.[80]

Molly's all-American ambition to make it against the odds – the
odds being a poverty-stricken rural background unsupportive of
women wanting to break out of that environment – is what would
endear her to an audience who consider this fighting spirit and

desire to succeed as inherently positive traits. Her simultaneous commitment to the disadvantaged in her society, expressive of the civil rights movements of the era in which the novel is set, and ultimately encapsulated in her fly-on-the-wall style movie featuring her mother,[81] reconciles her to those audiences who might regard the representation of her as an epitome of the all-American self-made woman as conservatively inflected, offering a false vision of the possibilities of self-help. *Rubyfruit Jungle* thus appropriates the narrative of the self-made person (usually a man) – and Holly, one of Molly's lesbian friends, significantly compares Molly to her father[82] – but with the difference that Molly tries to integrate past and present, rather than leave behind one for the other, and in so doing incorporates those marginalised in society into the story of her own advancement.

As in *Rubyfruit Jungle*, Celie at the beginning of *The Color Purple* is placed in an environment which *anyone*, whether lesbian or heterosexual, would want to transcend. Defying the poverty and sexual oppression of which she is the object can only be endorsed, especially as her oppression includes what at the beginning looks like incest. The taboo which this type of sexual abuse constitutes in all societies not only validates Celie's defiance once she gains support from Shug but, in a sense, also offers the validation of her lesbian identity. For a heterosexual audience this text makes it easy to argue that it is not surprising that Celie's sexual identity comes to rest in a lesbian self. The condemnation implicit in the novel is clearly of men who force women sexually, especially incestuously and paedophilically. The fact that Shug enjoys sex with men counteracts the stance taken by Celie of rejecting men as possible sexual partners and, unlike *Rubyfruit Jungle*, removes the insistence of male insufficiency to female sexual need which threatens heteropatriarchy so much more overtly in the latter text. Celie's defiance of Mr – with the help of Shug is thus cast in terms understandable by *any* audience. At the same time, like *Rubyfruit Jungle*, it offers a narrative of a victim transcending her victimisation and emerging as an independent and reconciliatory figure. Having laid down her sexual life for her mother and sister she is resurrected by another woman and through this love for her is enabled to forgive those who sinned against her. The biblical analogies are obvious though, as I shall argue below, the ending of *The Color Purple* strikes me as very problematic precisely because it models itself too closely on the Christian myth of the New Testament.

Where *Rubyfruit Jungle* combines the plot of the self-made man story with the American dream of being able to fashion oneself in one's own image, *The Color Purple* rewrites the Christian myth of the son being saved by the father as that of the dependent female being remade by the independent one. In this difference of constructing self-madeness and other-madeness both texts are expressive of the time in which they were written. They share the optimism of the possibility of change. But *Rubyfruit Jungle* picks up on a sense projected in much lesbian writing during the early 1970s that, as Julia Penelope put it in 1974:

> Because our culture has ignored us, we have the unique opportunity few people have: we can set about constructing our lives and deciding who we are.[83]

The notion of voluntaristic self-generation expressed here, indicative of the optimism that the individual lesbian can, through an act of will, assert and fashion herself as she desires to be, was one of the dominant traits of lesbian self-representation in the 1970s. By the time *The Color Purple* emerged, that notion had been revised since the quest for autonomy, so central to the demands of the women's movement, had been re-visioned as problematic for women as it simultaneously underwrites a masculine stance of independence not achievable and possibly not even desirable in any social formation and devalues women's socialisation into bonding, cooperation and attachment.[84] Without wishing to argue the relative merits or otherwise of these positions, in the context of reading *Rubyfruit Jungle* and *The Color Purple* it is important to note that an ideological shift had taken place in feminist views of 'what women want' between the points of production of the two texts, replacing autonomy with adequate social and sexual bonding.

In the case of *Oranges*, the audience is confronted with an environment marked not so much by material deprivation as by spiritual narrowness. Again, the particular environment depicted makes it very easy for *any* but the most zealously religious to appreciate why Jeanette might want to leave this community behind. Winterson in this text, as Brown in *Rubyfruit Jungle*, uses humour to create a distance between the persons represented and the audience; to the extent that as we, as readers, laugh about the foibles of that community we can dissociate ourselves from it which, in turn, helps us to accept Jeanette's need to dissociate herself from it. Further, the text also indirectly and directly offers sociocultural explanations for Jeanette's lesbianism, thus, rather like Hall's *The Well*, creating an ambiguity concerning its origin. Both essentialist views (you are born one) and social constructionist views (you are made one) on lesbianism are offered.[85] On the latter front, one of the more obvious potential contributing factors in Jeanette's lesbianism might be that her community is composed of strong women who offer models of independence and nurturance while men either do not feature or are cast in a negative light.

Marriages are not represented as fulfilling for women. As in *The
Color Purple*, bonding, where it occurs, happens among women. On
the essentialist front, not only does Jeanette never show any interest
in men; it is also suggested – possibly following arguments of
congenital influence – that her mother had lesbian inclinations (see
the interesting incident around the photo of Eddy's sister) [86] which
she sublimates through her activities in the church at the same time
as avoiding heterosex by going to bed at different times from her
husband. Jeanette herself argues:

> At first, for me, it had been an accident. That accident
> had forced me to think more carefully about my own
> instincts and others' attitudes. After the exorcism I had
> tried to replace my world with another just like it, but I
> couldn't.[87]

Like Molly, Jeanette moves to get herself an education, passport
to a different life from the one her mother leads. Like Molly and
indeed Celie, she also moves to the city, continuing the tradition
of urban migration as the salvation for the beset lesbian character. But this migration does not constitute a break with the past.
Significantly, all three texts end on a note of reconciliation. Part
of this move reflects an appropriation of the narrative structures
of the Bildungsroman which proclaim the eventual 'arrival' of the
protagonist in terms of a maturation which allows that individual
to review his experiences (and I use the masculine term advisedly
here) in a sufficiently dispassionate light to be able to 'forgive'
those who sinned against him and to see their own dependence
on the deforming structures whence he has emerged. Jeanette
sees her life in terms of choices between conformity which holds
you in known structures and defiance which propels you into the
unknown:

> I could have been a priest instead of a prophet. The priest has
> a book with the words set out. Old words, words of power ...
> The words work. They do what they are supposed to do;
> comfort and discipline. The prophet has no book. The prophet
> is a voice that cries in the wilderness, full of sounds that do
> not always set into meaning. The prophets cry out because
> they are troubled by demons.[88]

What is missing from this representation of choice between conformity and divergence is that priest and prophet – at least
traditionally – are held in place by a yet higher authority, God or
the gods. Implicit here is therefore an assertion of the inescap-
ability of the structures which hold one, a fact reinforced by
Jeanette's sense, as she returns to visit her mother, that 'I seemed
to have run in a great circle, and met myself again on the
starting-line.' [89] Returning to the mother, in both *Oranges* and in

Rubyfruit Jungle, becomes an imperative for the lesbian hero whose defiance leads to an acknowledgement of difference, embodied in the title line *Oranges Are Not the Only Fruit*.

In the case of *The Color Purple*, the final reconciliatory set-up of Celie inheriting the house of her stepfather who raped her repeatedly and took away her children, followed by a friendship and working relationship with Mr –, the husband to whom she was handed as chattel and who sustainedly mistreated her, is rather different from that of the other two texts.[90] In *Rubyfruit Jungle* and *Oranges* the mothers are willing to be on speaking terms with their daughters but there is no suggestion of the daughters returning home to live. The mothers represent a past to which the daughters are bound but by which they are not tied down. Celie, on the other hand, seems to move into an upmarket version of her former home with more control over what happens to her and surrounded once more by those with whom she started. In the case of her sister, her children and Shug this may be understandable, but concerning the men from her past this seems much more problematic, at least from my viewpoint. For, what *The Color Purple* seems to be saying is that the maltreatment and sexual abuse Celie has suffered can be overcome,[91] that in Christ-like fashion, she can move beyond the scars of these experiences to a position of forgiveness in which the fact that she does not want to have sex with men anymore does not matter that much – after all, not only has she had children and thus fulfilled her 'destiny' in heteropatriarchal terms, but by the end of novel she is also well into her middle age and therefore, again in heteropatriarchal terms, moving outside the range of supposedly (hetero)sexually desirable females. I would argue that this ending of *The Color Purple*, in contradistinction to the endings of the other two texts, catapults *The Color Purple* firmly back into the frame of the heteropatriarchal narrative of the traditional Bildungsroman in which the protagonist arrives at a point of integration with a more desirable version of the heteropatriarchal community in which s/he started and lives happily ever after. Such a closure, it is worth noting, is not granted the protagonists of the other two texts which, for this very reason, operate a more sustained version of lesbian defiance.

Some concluding remarks: the defiant female figure is, of course, not an invention of the late twentieth century. However, whereas in pre-twentieth-century versions of this protagonist, defiance of heteropatriarchal norms is either temporary (the eponymous heroine of Eliza Haywood's *The History of Miss Betsy Thoughtless*, for instance, marries Mr Trueworth in the end), or leads to (self)destruction of the heroine (consider Anna Karenina) or to permanent exile (the fate of Maria in Jane Austen's

Mansfield Park), here defiance is sustained, finally acknowledged as an assertation of difference which, however, does not inevitably make the lesbian hero 'happy ever after'. At the same time this defiance is not as uncompromisingly presented as it is in Joanna Russ's *On Strike Against God*,[92] for instance, which may be *one* reason why these three texts are more successful with diverse audiences than is Russ's. This striving towards the recognition of the self and its distinctness, the desire for self-improvement as well as the entrepreneurial spirit shown by at least two of the protagonists, Molly and Celie, fit in well with the prevailing conservative ideologies which took hold in western culture from the second half of the 1970s onwards. This, I would suggest, is in part the price paid for popular success. It constitutes one of the marked differences to Hall's *The Well* in which the heroine comes from a supposedly unimpeachable background rather than from a materially deprived one where she is the object of physical and/or sexual abuse. Brown, Walker and Winterson all provide multiple reasons for their lesbian heroes' defiance which offer different audiences diverse vantage points from which to identify with the protagonists' defiance.

Notes and References

1. Rita Mae Brown *Rubyfruit Jungle* London: Bantam Books 1983 p. 220.
2. In 'Lesbian BiblioMythography', Nickie Hastie writes: 'I prefer to use the word "hero" to refer to female protagonists instead of the more conventional "heroine". The word "heroine" implies to me a diminutive sort of "hero", and I think oppressively gendered language needs to be challenged.' For a more sustained lesbian feminist analysis of oppressive genderisation in language see Julia Penelope *Speaking Freely: Unlearning the Lies of the Fathers' Tongues* Oxford: Pergamon Press 1990.
3. For another discussion of this phenomenon with specific reference to *Oranges Are Not the Only Fruit* see Hilary Hinds's 'Oranges Are Not The Only Fruit: Reaching Audiences Other Lesbian Texts Cannot Reach' in Sally Munt ed *New Lesbian Criticism* London: Harvester Wheatsheaf 1992 pp. 153–72.
4. Two articles which offer extended comment on this problematic are Sonja Ruehl's 'Inverts and Experts: Radclyffe Hall and the Lesbian Identity' in Judith Newton and Deborah Rosenfeldt eds *Feminist Criticism and Social Change* London: Methuen 1985 pp. 165–80, and Judith Newton's 'The Mythic Mannish Lesbian: Radclyffe Hall and the New Woman' in Martin B. Duberman et al eds *Hidden from History: Reclaim-*

ing *the Gay and Lesbian Past* London: Penguin 1991 pp. 281–93.

5. Radclyffe Hall *The Unlit Lamp* London: Jonathan Cape 1934; *Miss Ogilvy Finds Herself* London: Hammond 1959; *The Well of Loneliness* London: Virago 1982.

6. The fact that Hall presents her lesbian characters as living with a sense of a lesbian community does not mean that these did not exist. Renee Vivien's *A Woman Appeared to Me* (rpt. Tallahassee: Naiad Press 1982) portrays such a community and so does Shari Benstock's *Women of the Left Bank* London: Virago 1987.

7. Suzanne Neild and Rosalind Pearson *Women Like Us* London: The Women's Press 1992 p. 97.

8. Neild and Pearson *Women Like Us* 1992 p. 92.

9. See, for example, Marcy Adelman *Long Time Passing: Loves of Older Lesbians* Boston: Alyson Publications 1986 pp. 67, 133, 164 or Neild and Pearson *Women Like Us*, 1992 pp. 23, 34, 97, 119, 127.

10. Elana Nachman/Dykewomon *Riverfinger Women* Tallahassee: Naiad Press 1992 p. 185.

11. Rita Felski *Beyond Feminist Aesthetics* London: Hutchinson Radius 1989 p. 122.

12. In *Beyond Feminist Aesthetics* Rita Felski discusses feminist appropriations of the Bildungsroman extensively.

13. The suggestion that lesbians (indeed, homosexuals in general) are not only different from but possibly superior to heterosexuals (because representing a more advanced position on the evolutionary scale) was promoted by, among others, Edward Carpenter in *The Intermediate Sex* London: Allen & Unwin 1921, especially in the 'Introductory' and concluding chapter.

14. Jeanette Winterson *Oranges Are Not the Only Fruit* London: Pandora 1985 p.3.

15. Alice Walker *The Color Purple* London: The Women's Press 1983 p. 176.

16. Felski *Beyond Feminist Aesthetics* 1989 p. 124.

17. The convention of regarding the female body as grotesque is explored in Mary Russo's essay 'Female Grotesques: Carnival and Theory' in Teresa de Lauretis ed *Feminist Studies/Critical Studies* London: Macmillan 1988 pp. 213–29.

18. Winterson *Oranges* 1985 p. 11.

19. Ibid. p. 71.

20. Ibid. p. 128.

21. Brown *Rubyfruit* 1983 p. 5.

22. The showing off of Detwiler's penis replays the 'making use of scopophilia' described by Freud as a necessary ingredient of children's psychosexual development, not resulting, however, in the girls' being 'overcome by envy for the penis' (Sigmund Freud *On Sexuality* Pelican Freud Library vol 7 Harmondsworth: Penguin 1983 pp. 112, 114) but in the

commodification and exploitation of the grotesque penis for financial gain, thus granting Molly who organises the spectacle mastery over the organ which is not hers but which she comes to 'own' temporarily by way of controlling its display.

23. Felski *Beyond* 1989 p. 129

24. Walker *Color* 1983 p. 215.

25. Winterson *Oranges* 1985 p. 72.

26. Walker *Color* 1983 p. 221.

27. Winterson *Oranges* 1985 p. 127.

28. The importance of the possibility of choosing whom one relates to sexually has recently been re-emphasised through Rosemary Auchmuty et al's paper 'Lesbian History and Gay Studies' (Rosemary Auchmuty, Sheila Jeffreys and Elaine Miller 'Lesbian History and Gay Studies: Keeping a Feminist Perspective' *Women's History* 1/1 1992 pp. 89–108) in which they point out that many lesbians do not begin life as lesbians but have heterosexual relationships at some point in their lives.

29. In her famous essay 'Compulsory Heterosexuality and Lesbian Existence' Adrienne Rich explores the utility for hetero-patriarchy of conflating procreative/reproductive sexual function with romantic love.

30. Ti-Grace Atkinson discusses the significance of this concept in *Amazon Odyssey* New York: Link Books 1974 pp. 135–89.

31. For a recent representation of lesbianism as social constructed see Celia Kitzinger *The Social Construction of Lesbianism* London: Sage 1987.

32. Brown *Rubyfruit* 1983 pp. 69–70.

33. Ibid. p. 159.

34. Walker *Color* 1983 p. 69.

35. Ibid. p. 69–70.

36. The use of the word 'button' for clitoris has been made famous by Gertrude Stein's poetry in which the term acquires the same meaning.

37. Walker *Color* 1983 p. 95.

38. Depicting lesbian relationships as interludes prior to assuming one's 'proper' place in society was quite common in the early part of this century. Two examples are Lillian Hellman's play *The Children's Hour* and Clemence Dane's novel *Regiment of Women*.

39. While underlining the erotic attraction of women for women seems to me to be an important part of the representation of lesbians, the danger of demarcating lesbians solely in those terms is frequently that it privileges sexually active lesbians over ones who are either celibate or do not have a sexual relationship.

40. Sidney Abbott and Barbara Love *Sappho was a Right-on Woman* New York: Stein and Day 1985.

41. Walker *Color* 1983 p. 171.

42. A similar scene of female bonding expressed through laughter and in the light of male incomprehension concerning women's needs can be found in Marleen Gorris's brilliant 1982 film *A Question of Silence*.

43. Winterson *Oranges* 1985 p. 102.

44. Ibid. p. 106.

45. Brown *Rubyfruit* 1983 p. 131.

46. Ibid. p. 151.

47. Winterson *Oranges* 1985 p. 108.

48. Ibid. p. 109.

49. Brown *Rubyfruit* 1983 p. 92.

50. Ibid. p. 88.

51. A comic exploding of the usefulness of such 'treatment' is offered in Judy Grahn's 'The Psychoanalysis of Edward the Dyke' *The Work of a Common Woman* London: Onlywomen Press 1985 pp. 26–30.

52. Winterson *Oranges* 1985 p. 109.

53. Ibid. p. 129.

54. Brown *Rubyfruit* 1983 p. 129–30.

55. Ibid. p. 161.

56. Ibid. p. 242.

57. Winterson *Oranges* 1985 p. 3.

58. The tradition of such an objectification of women as objects of (discursive) exchange between men in nineteenth-century texts is explored in Eve Kosofsky Sedgwick's *Between Men* New York: Columbia University Press 1985.

59. Brown *Rubyfruit* 1983 p. 135.

60. The literary history of the representation of lesbians working in educational establishments and feeling unable to support their lesbian students has been discussed in Martha Vicinus's 'Distance and Desire: English Boarding-School Friendships' in Estelle B. Freedman, Barbara C. Gelpi, Susan L. Johnson and Kathleen M. Weston eds *The Lesbian Issue: Essays from Signs* Chicago: University of Chicago Press 1982.

61. Another version of the same phenomenon is portrayed in Emily Prager's short story 'A Visit from the Footbinder' in the book by the same title, London: Hogarth Press 1993 pp. 11–39.

62. Brown *Rubyfruit* 1983 p. 246.

63. Sidney and Love *Sappho* 1985 p. 111.

64. Ibid. p. 111–12.

65. Walker *Color* 1983 p. 3.

66. Ibid. p. 5.

67. Walker *Color* 1983 p. 7.

68. One could argue that Celie is exploited by her mother as the mother allows her to be sexually abused by the father. However, Celie forgives her, writing: 'Maybe cause my mama cuss me you think I kept mad at her. But I ain't. I felt sorry for mama. Trying to believe his story kilt her.' (Walker *Color* 1983 p. 7.)

69. Walker *Color* 1983 p. 37.
70. Ibid. pp. 38–9.
71. For example Walker *Color* 1983 p. 17, 21.
72. Walker *Color* 1983 p. 17.
73. Winterson *Oranges* 1985 p. 76.
74. Ibid. p. 106.
75. Brown *Rubyfruit* 1983 p. 118.
76. Walker *Color* 1983 p. 164.
77. Winterson *Oranges* 1985 p. 46.
78. Brown *Rubyfruit* 1983 p. 7.
79. Ibid. p. 81.
80. Ibid. p. 174.
81. From the 1970s onwards a fascination with 'ordinary' lives began to be influential in western culture, resulting in fly-on-the-wall programmes for radio and TV, oral history projects, volumes of interviews with diverse people, etc. This constitutes part of the decanonisation of culture.
82. Brown *Rubyfruit* 1983 p. 173–4.
83. Julia Penelope 'Lesbian Separatism: The Linguistic and Social Sources of Separatist Politics' in Sarah Lucia Hoagland and Julia Penelope eds *For Lesbians Only* London: Onlywomen Press 1988 p. 46.
84. Two of the perhaps better-known explorations of a revaluing a supposedly feminine socialisation traits are Nancy Chodorow's *The Reproduction of Mothering* Berkeley: University of California Press, and Carol Gilligan's *In a Different Voice* Cambridge, Mass.: Harvard University Press 1982.
85. Winterson *Oranges* 1985 p. 128.
86. Ibid. p. 36.
87. Ibid. p. 128.
88. Ibid. p. 88.
89. Ibid. p. 173.
90. It may be that this difference is a function of *The Color Purple* being constructed by a heterosexual woman while the other two texts were written by lesbians.
91. This representation contradicts the reports of incest survivors. For one example, see Anji Watson's 'No Longer a Victim' in Pearlie McNeill, Bea Freeman and Jenny Newman eds *Women Talk Sex* London: Scarlet Press 1992 pp. 47–63.
92. Joanna Russ *On Strike Against God* Trumansburg, NY: Crossing Press 1980.

CHAPTER 5

Weaving Our Own Web: Demythologising/Remythologising and Magic in the Work of Contemporary Women Writers

Gina Wisker

> Resurrect the ashes of the women burnt as witches
> resurrect the ashes/mould the cinders
> stir the cauldron/resurrect those witches ...
> Resurrect
> Resurrect
> Resurrect
> And as for the boys playing with their power toys
> Entoad them all[1]

> You have only to look at the Medusa straight on to see her.
> And she's not deadly. She's beautiful and she's laughing.[2]

Recuperation, revaluation and celebration are the modes and tones with which many contemporary women writers revive and rewrite the myths that denigrate women, upholding an outdated male power. Prophetesses and witches were feared as subversives but their alternative insights stitched them into a female-based culture, one whose myths seemed to have been entirely written and culturally evaluated by the men whose very power they subverted. So too this is true of the Medusa, a fearsome figure throughout mythology, powerful in an evil sense. Heroes destroy such power and are rewarded for it, as social conventions lead to the drowning and burning of witches, the hounding of other women with magical powers. Obviously the myths are not taken literally today, if they ever were, and it seems a little silly, even perverse, to bother to engage with what appears straightforwardly in books and films for children, parodied and reimagined in mouthwash adverts, pantomimes and musicals, power dressed in American soap operas. But even that list suggests the very broad, insidious, scope of the continuation of meanings and relationships underlying these myths. They are as much a popular cultural shorthand as they ever were.

> Myth deals in false universals, to dull the pain of particular circumstances. In no area is this more true than in that of relations between the sexes ... All the mythic versions of women, from the myth of the redeeming purity of the virgin to that of the healing, reconciling mother, are consolatory nonsenses; and consolatory nonsense seems a fair definition of myth anyway.[3]

For contemporary women writers intent on subverting the oppressive status quo there are several choices in relation to these myths, these shorthand symbols representing gender and power relations. Myths can be deconstructed and denounced, or rewritten and reclaimed. Mythical and historical women whose powers suggested irrationality and disorder are reinscribed into a different version of culture, one which invests them, or reinvests them with alternative powers. Reappropriation of myths, and revaluation of the powers of magic, the supernatural, and the spiritual: these characteristics are embraced by contemporary women writers.

Demythologising I

As Barthes says:

> One can conceive of very ancient myths, but there are no eternal ones; for it is human history which converts reality into speech, and it alone rules the life and death of mythical language.[4]

Dominant cultural myths do not necessarily reflect our authentic experiences, but somehow we internalise their versions of our lives, ourselves. Myths can be rewritten to suggest the changing shape of our lives. Judith Pintar comments:

> There have been many religious, philosophical and psychological systems which are meant to apply to everyone, regardless of cultural background or personal history. Not only do these systems require that we find within ourselves the qualities or motivations that the authorities describe, but once found, they cannot be altered or declined. Throughout history, myths have been used by the powerful to influence social custom: mythmaking is a political process which disguises itself in the sacred. When we set ourselves free from the tyranny of these myths, there is nothing to stop us from retelling our lives.[5]

Alice Walker's *Possessing the Secret of Joy* [6] focuses in on the tyranny of male myths which seek to oppress women. Taking the character of Tashi, who haunted her imagination since *The Color*

Purple, she traces the painful and politically raw subject of female circumcision, showing it to be founded upon a myth of a dangerously (for men) powerful sexuality in woman which challenged that of man, and which needed therefore to be excised, removed, cut out and down in order to ensure that the kind of lively female power which could accompany some control over one's own destiny, sexual and otherwise, could be prevented, under patriarchy. The myth of uncleanliness, and that of upholding the political, religious and historical beliefs and culture of the tribe persuade Tashi to embrace this disfiguration and pain. Ironically, instead of making of herself a defiant tribal woman in the face of white encroachment, she succumbs to the other power, that of sexism, in this maiming:

> I recognized the connection between mutilation and enslavement that is at the root of the domination of women in the world.[7]

She learns that the downcast eyes and submissive sliding walk, thought so attractive among Olinka women, comes from pain, and that all collude in a humiliating, potentially fatal ritual (her sister was one of those thousands who died yearly from the operation). The myth is explicit:

> In a culture in which it is mandatory that every single female be systematically desexed, there would have to be some coded, mythological reason given for it, used secretly among the village elders. Otherwise they'd soon not know what they were talking about. Even today there are villages where an uncircumcised woman is not permitted to live. The chiefs enforce this.[8]

Tashi recalls hearing the elders laugh and talk about an image and myth of woman as Queen bee, whose sweetness made them mere workers but who needed to be rendered inert, unable to fly:

> Number three: If left to herself the Queen would fly
> ... Number four: But God is merciful.
> Number one: He clips her wings.
> Number two: She is inert.[9]

Men tell women they look beautiful weeping; their sexual pleasure and sense of ownership depend on the operation. The cultural pressures to conform, to be accepted, complete the picture. Power rests with the men, and ancient myth combines with taboos about health, purity, correct behaviour as useful controlling mechanisms.

Pierre, Tashi's husband Adam's illegitimate son, aids Tashi's discoveries of original myths in which woman's sexual powers were felt to be threatening by a ravishing God. She also is made aware of the continued existence of small dolls representing a self-aware, happy female sexuality, a kind of cultural response denied in the Olinka and frowned on by white America. Even in the land Tashi initially idealised, female circumcision developed in some cases as a control for hysteria!

She cannot live with the recognition of the reality this myth forces upon women under patriarchy of whatever form. As Evelyn, renamed in America, to her Adam she is the first woman to reject the repressions of the myth, and her murder of the national hero, M'Lissa, who carried out the operations, is an act of psychological freedom even though it leads to her own death. The novel is tragic, poignant, gripping, and the examination of the destructive power of the gender myth which lies behind mutilation is horrific. Alice Walker explored these enslaving, physically realised myths of male dominance and female submission and offers as (largely imaginative) alternatives not a rewriting of the myths but a reinvestigation of their sources and an explanation of their necessity to the continuation of male power. She also offers the reclamation of female sexuality and self-awareness as a first step towards identity, independence, full being. The polemical cry which remains with us from the novel is one which overturns the initial description of black women's possession of the secret of joy being dependent on their submissive role. 'Resistance is the secret of joy.' [10]

Demythologising/Remythologising II

> For fantasy is true, of course. It isn't factual, but it is true. Children know that. Adults know it too, and that is precisely why many of them are afraid of fantasy. They know that its truth challenges, even threatens, all that is false, all that is phony, unnecessary, and trivial in the life they have let themselves be forced into living. They are afraid of dragons, because they are afraid of freedom.[11]

> Fantasy violates the real, contravenes it, denies it, and insists on this denial throughout.[12]

It can represent alternatives as equally valid, show that what is taken for real is but the product of arbitrary arguments.

> Breaking single reductive 'truths', the fantastic traces a space within a society's cognitive frame. It introduces multiple, contrary truths: it becomes polysemic.[13]

It points to the 'edges of the "real" '.[14]

But writers such as Angela Carter, Toni Morrison, Fay Weldon, Emma Tennant, Sara Maitland and Alice Walker are actually more likely to represent the fantastic, the supernatural and the magical with the same factual details as they would the historically 'real' or credible in a recognisable sense. Using the figure of the oxymoron they suggest both the everyday acceptable 'real' which details a world dominated by one set of values, including that of law-abiding status quo, and the 'unreal' or otherly real, the magical, at the same time. The very form disposes of the rigid philosophical beliefs that shore up logic and social norms.

> Feminist fantasy explores the contradictions elided by the (patriarchal) real; for example, that women are both inside patriarchal ideology, as the essential Woman, and outside it, as the (repressed and denied) experiential subjects.[15]

Winged women, flying, dragons, conjuration, mysticism and mediumship, folklore and midwifery, tangible ghosts, the devil in suburban clothing, the witch who is your aunt, metamorphosis and telepathy: these are some of the everyday occurrences in fiction which celebrate the power of a magical, a fantastic, reality and a vibrant female other.

The reclamation and redefinition of myths, symbols, legends, fairytales, the culturally produced forms which underly our visions of ourselves as women, is one major way in which contemporary women writers subvert culturally conditioned gender inequalities. Similarly the abyss between the recognised 'real' and the world of dreams, alternatives, magic, prophesy, and a philosophy of multiplicity and possibility is challenged by the text which gives equal value and credibility to the supernatural, the magical. A feminist reading position is constructed which renegotiates relationships of power, suggesting differences between the real and unreal, the valued and the valueless. It enables us to read and construct a different subject position. It is liberating and exciting and usually also amusing, for the renegotiations and the rereadings, the assertions of alternative realities and different values frequently render ironic the established conventional versions and evaluations.

For me, Medusa remains the much maligned central figure of this collusive myth making. When we visited Istanbul not long ago we were fascinated to see there the magnificent underground cistern which once fed the whole water supply of the city in Justinian's time. Recently discovered was another part of it, we were told. There were two huge pillars helping to hold up the roof. At their base, upside down in the water, were two enormous stone heads of Medusa. Supporting patriarchy, neutralised because reversed and only her reflected image staring up at us, she was nevertheless nurturing the city. Medusa remains for many women writers, as she does for me, the paradigm for woman's misrepresentation in myth, classical and contemporary. For celebrating life and jouissance – making love in a temple – she was turned into a snakey-headed monster only conquerable by the archetypal hero Perseus, by force and trickery. She is the subject of dozens of poems which rewrite her, reclaim her, and so reinvest her with female power and value. May Sarton's 'The Muse as Medusa' sums up much of this. Looking Medusa in the eye, the poet is not turned to stone but freed into a watery, creative and procreative fluidity:

> I saw you once, Medusa, we were alone
> I looked you straight in the cold eye, cold
> I was not punished, was not turned to stone –
> How to believe the legends I am told?[16]

Rediscovering and reinterpreting the myths is a powerful way to discover why and how women have been misrepresented and constrained, and goes some way towards the development of new representations, dispensing with all the virgin/whore, Eve/Lilith nonsense perpetuated in tale, legend, media, and common parlance.

Language is power and representation is power. In the history of phallogocentrism woman has been inscribed as other, as secondary, as mythically deadly, devouring, destructive, and any magical or mystical powers she has had have been distrusted as undermining the fabric of society, undermining the system of values and meanings embedded in language and in social formations. Much contemporary women's writing aims at the deconstruction of those old established myths. They explode the tight cobweb of language and belief and image which constricts the way we see and represent ourselves as women. What is so exciting, so liberating, about this writing is the energy and the laughter which sweeps away all the old formations, takes them apart and rewrites them in language which seizes different values, which enables a reclamation of the body. Both the polemical piece by Cixous and the poem by Grace Nichols, above, express this sweeping away the old representations. Cixous urges a specifically female libidinal energy and voice and constantly writes against forms of knowledge which constrict vision within the language of the dominant culture. She reinvests the world of fairytale, myths, religion, the spiritual by her poetic, anarchic, fluid writing which encourages ever-changing shifts in meaning according to the reader and the context. Carving out new, writing Cixous aims to 'liberate the New Woman from the Old' [17] and as Morag Shiach argues:

> The gesture that characterises the relation of women to the cultural is one of flying and stealing (voler). Women, Cixous

argues, must steal what they need from the dominant culture, but then fly away with their cultural booty to the 'in between', where new images, new narratives and new subjectivities can be created.[18]

Flying, stealing, deconstruction and reconstruction, fluidity, reclamation and new naming of the body and the relationship with the mother, laughter, the reinvesting of the power of magic and imagination, celebration and carnival; these are the tones of much contemporary women's writing as it seeks to re-vision the world and women's space(s) within it. 'To think I really fooled you' [19] cries the flying winged woman, Fevvers, the revitalised, wings unclipped Queen Bee (see *Possessing the Secret of Joy*) in Angela Carter's powerful, energetic tale which troubles the distinctions between fact and fantasy in its formal use of magic realism, even as it takes literally the old myth of woman as bird/icon/angel (or whore) by having as its protagonist a 'genuine winged wonder'.

In *The Magic Toyshop*[20] Angela Carter investigates and makes ironic the way in which adolescent girls develop a sense of their gendered identity culturally based in male imaged popular and high art. From the Pre-Raphaelite and Impressionist posings in front of the mirror, Melanie moves on to imagining herself as a version of Lady Chatterley, after reading Lawrence, yet her version of sexuality is actually constrained by girls' magazine and Hollywood film images of squeaky clean hunky bridegrooms, and her vision of any actual sex act is hazy and deferred; the bridegroom cleans his teeth and husks 'darling' at her but there the mental cinematic reel ceases and any necessary connection between sex appeal, male and female roles, and the actual side of sexual relations shifts on to the figures of Edward Bear with his tummy swollen – pregnancy in a child's pyjama case – and Lorna Doone 'splayed out face down in the dust under the bed' [21] Wrestling with a wedding dress too loose for her body, Melanie climbs the apple tree of knowledge out of her own first Eden garden, and rips the dress, subsequently blaming herself for the deaths of her parents in an air crash. Woman, Eve like, takes on guilt. Carter's pastiche, her intertextual and palimpsestic use of myth, image, symbol, literary, artistic and popular cultural representation in this realistic/Gothic tale confronts the reader with a tightly woven web of links and relations. We perceive at every turn how high and popular culture continually invest certain myths of subordination and oppression, both gender and race/ religion related. The imperial/colonial tones of Queen Victoria as a broken statue and the oppression of the Irish Jowle family suggest the colonial. The myths are inscribed in an everyday reality.

The most powerful moment in the novel is the enactment of

the Leda and the Swan rape scene with Melanie forced to be a human puppet to Uncle Phillip's fantasy of power. In high art there are several representations of the story of Leda and the Swan, always with an adoring Leda cuddling a beautiful, powerful yet kindly swan. But the actual myth is sick. Jove descends to a variety of lucky women, each time in the shape of a beast, as a bull to Europa, a swan to Leda, and a shower of gold(!) to Danae. The resultant rape is always depicted in positive tones in art, and the myth suggests that woman is lucky to carry the seed of the gods, even if the power of an animal is mixed into the act. Yeats's poem 'Leda and the Swan' [22] hauntingly and languorously portrays the strangeness and the frightening (because of the non-human bird) yet rapturous (because of the god, and the sexual power) lack of resistance by Leda to the rape: 'those terrified vague fingers' are Leda's 'so caught up'. The poem emphasises the strangeness and the power but wallows in the sexual frissons at the same time. Carter uses 'loins' and some other of the same words as Yeats to indicate the poem as source, but she simultaneously actualises the horror and brutality of the act, and the ridiculousness of western male-dominated civilisation's imagining and repeatedly redescribing this myth of power and subordination. Melanie 'felt herself not herself' [23] she has her destiny wrested from her with the descent of the puppet swan; feathers fill her mouth; she screams: 'the obscene swan had mounted her' [24] and the near rape of girl by man-controlled, man-constructed beast of power is plain, violent, real, monstrous. But while the full reality of the horror of this enacted power relationship is emphasised, it is also debunked, satirised, laughed at. 'Like fate or the clock' [25] the plywood puppet is operated by a bully who pictures himself as godlike, caught up in his own myth of power, on his own petty stage in the toyshop which is his world. Phillip thinks of himself as having a sonorous voice, wreaking the will of 'Almighty Jove' but he is simultaneously a figure of fun, and a microcosmic figure of patriarchal power. The swan is a slapstick production: 'On came the swan, its feet going splat, splat, splat' [26] Carter enables us to laugh, to see the whole pretence as ridiculous, but also to feel that its reality is tangibly oppressive; real and fantastic at once. Laughter and deconstruction give the readers more power than Finn, who smashes the swan but can be smashed himself.

A carnivalesque, celebratory remythologising takes place in both *Nights at the Circus* and *Wise Children*,[27] Angela Carter's last two novels. While *Wise Children* deals directly with the central issues of the relationship between reason and imagination, logic and magic, in a reinterpretation of *A Midsummer Night's Dream*, *Nights at the Circus* flies in the face of patriarchy, em-

bodying Cixous's assertion of the importance of 'voler', to fly, and
to steal – or reappropriate and liberate.

As a Cockney Venus, Fevvers is the embodiment of several
realised myths, not least that of the East End whore with a heart
of gold, as well as that of the delicate, caged bird/woman and
ship's figurehead. She is a fusion of man's uneasy, contradictory
versions of woman. Yeats's idealisation and idolising of women
(Maude Gonne in particular) emerges here intertextually as a
paradigm for the masculine response of romanticising and ravish-
ment which links myth and contemporary twentieth-century
cultural representation. The Leda and the Swan myth, used in *The
Magic Toyshop*, here re-emerges alongside other myths. Capitalist
power structures entice as well as entrap Fevvers. Painted white,
she poses as icon of chastity and femininity in Ma Nelson's
whorehouse, moving on to help re-enact different, more perverse
male sexual fantasies fuelled by de Sade, in the Gothic dungeons
of Madam Schreck's house where Fevvers is one of the 'tableaux
vivants' of women in the 'profane altars' at which punters come to
worship. Myth, symbol, power and cash are recalled in the reference to Yeats's 'The Circus Animals Desertion' this 'lumber room
of femininity, this rag and bone shop of the heart'.[28]

It is specifically the mythologising leanings of Christian Rosencreutz, who wishes to ensure masculine ascendancy by sacrificing
Fevvers, which endanger her. His is a Gothic palace, his world
one of masculine power, 'the Times', leather seats, and a 'phallus
rampant' as emblem. Significantly Rosencreutz spouts his own
heresies about gender differences, but their resemblance to real
literary, medical, philosophical and political arguments against
women's emancipation in the nineteenth century render him
culturally representative of oppression and destruction, not merely
dramatically so within the context of this story. He argues that:

> women are of a different soul-substance from men, cut from a
> different bolt of spirit cloth, and altogether too pure and
> rarefied to be bothering their pretty little heads with things of
> this world, such as the Irish question, and the Boer war.[29]

Rosencreutz casts Fevvers as a sacrificial, rejuvenating figure, one
almost lethal for her.[30]

The contemporary version of response to woman in mythic
form emerges with that of the Duke, who wants to turn
Fevvers into the golden bird in a golden cage, like Yeats's
golden bird on a golden bough, the restrained artist offered
permanence in exchange for passive stasis, in 'Sailing to Byzan-
tium'. Woman is artifice for the Duke, and his collection includes woman as Aeolian harp, but will be crowned by the
ultimate exchange for jewels, Fevvers reduced to a tiny priceless

golden bird to fill the empty perch in the empty cage among the Fabergé egg constructions. The ice swan downstairs, reminiscent of Leda and the Swan, twin to the swan on top of the cage, melts as Fevvers's time drips out but she manipulates the Duke's own sexual needs to engineer her escape. While she 'contemplated life as a toy' [31] she ensures the Duke's climax coincides with the wet crash of the ice sculpture, and her own exit, leaping on to a model train which, fantasy intermingled with realism, turns into the full size 'real' trans-Siberian railway. Fevvers's jouissance triumphs. She defines and retains her own identity, revealing it to none, fooling Walser the journalist whose quest for the 'real' matches our own, and taking control of her own myth. She celebrates her life and her own sexuality, as the novel forces readers to redefine the boundaries of the real and the fantastic. Artifice, literary and artistic representations and mythic constructions are all deconstructed and reconstructed, their power base shifted, while western logic takes a similar tumble.

Nights at the Circus is a mixture of the fantastic and the realistic. It derives from the Gothic not merely in the settings of Madame Schrecks's living museum of sexual oppression and the grand turreted mansions of Christian Rosencreutz and the Duke, but most specifically in its shattering of the boundaries between what is acceptable in a novel as symbolic, relating through the imagination to cultural representations of the 'real' and what is imaginary. Fevvers's own potentially magical or freak status radically challenges cultural norms. Rosemary Jackson usefully defines the use of the fantastic:

> fantasies image the possibility of radical cultural transformation through attempting to dissolve or shatter the boundary lines between the imaginary and the symbolic. They refuse the latter's categories of the 'real' and its unities.[32]

Nights at the Circus examines myths and constructions of femininity through the arch construction herself, Fevvers. Angela Carter's Gothic, highly intertextual brand of magic realism ideally provides both an ironic critique of the power underlying and upheld through myths and symbols, and creates and recreates powerful new myths and symbols to enable a theft of power, a flight from patriarchy.

Woman as bird does not have to be caged, and flight can suggest power and freedom not a desperate escape. Elaine Feinstein in her poem 'Anniversary' uses bird imagery to epitomise this reclamation of the magical as an expression of woman's varied nature as she pictures herself putting a multicoloured birdlike flamingo leg over the sill of her scientist husband's lab, as he picks and sorts facts and details, only to be largely ignored as usual, but to move on and hint at power beyond the ordinary:

> Listen, I shall have to whisper it
> into your heart directly: we are all
> supernatural/everyday
> we rise new creatures/cannot be predicted.[33]

While Grace Nichols returns magic to the ordinary, reinvests the powers of women in the everyday world:

> My mother had more magic
> in her thumb
> than the length and breadth
> of any magician[34]

In fiction, magic realism is best suited to express that mixture of the factual, social, historical world and its cultural constructions, and the imaginative, fantastic, spiritual even magical other world, largely denied in our prosaic scientific restricted 'rational' times. With the reinvestment of the magical and the imaginative comes an investigation into those limiting social practices which have led to the repression of the different, of woman, of black and minority cultures. Some writers like Angela Carter and Fay Weldon start with traditional and contemporary mythic representations and take them to logical extremes, enabling the powers of the magical and the spiritual to have equal value with the everyday.

Author of 'The Laugh of the Medusa' and radical philosopher and critic, Cixous, like Angela Carter, comments on the power of myths and the need for their reinterpretation. She uses them and turns them around, as does Carter, yoking the real and the imaginary, denying binary oppositions:

> I owe almost everything to dreams ... I work a lot on the level of myths, as much as on that of dreams. In reality, myth was that which took the place of analysis in former times ... one never questions enough the traditions of interpretation of myth, and all myths have been referred to a masculine interpretation. If we women read them we read them otherwise. That is why I often nourish my texts, in my own way, at those mythic sources.[35]

Her work integrates the theory and poetry, and she denounces binary oppositions, producing a creative flexibility, exposing the restrictions of phallocentric valuations and definitions as they appear in myth, the representation of the sexes, worldviews and the everyday reading and understanding of experience.

Of *La Jeune Née*,[36] Conley says:

> Continuing her search for passages (sorties out of a Hegelian
> system and phallogocentric entrapment) she denounces well-
> known hierarchical couples of opposites man/woman, activity/
> passivity, sun/moon, culture/nature, day/night, father/mother,
> head/feeling, intelligence/sensibility, logos/pathos and the
> primacy of form over matter .... These oppositions extend to
> the positioning of bodies in society and to the codification of
> sexual difference found in all symbolic practices: myths,
> legends, books, and major discourses governing society. The
> ordering of values (with their connotation of presence and
> substance) are accompanied by moral values, good or bad.[37]

This deconstruction does not stop there. Cixous explores the
powers of woman as difference, celebratory in tone and dramatic,
poetic, expressive. Conley argues that Cixous notes:

> In man's fiction and poetic myths, woman is always absent,
> hence desirable according to a logic of desire based on lack.
> To this (phallocentric) notion making of woman the domestic
> other, Cixous opposes woman as the 'real' other, unknowable,
> non theorisable, distant in her proximity.[38]

In the face of 'two irrepresentables, death and the female sex' Cixous urges that we look at the defiance/vitality of the Medusa: 'She
is beautiful and she laughs.' [39] She rewrites, reinvests Eve, Demeter
and Koré, a female Prometheus and, more recently, Freud's Dora.
This echoes that seminal comment of Angela Carter's:

> I believe that all myths are products of the human mind and
> reflect only aspects of material human practice. I'm in the
> demythologising business ... How that social fiction of my
> 'femininity' was created by means outside my control, and
> palmed off on me as the real thing ... This investigation of the
> social fictions that regulate our lives – what Blake called the
> 'mind forg'd manacles' – is what I've concerned myself with
> consciously since that time.[40]

Not only does she identify the mythos of history and cultural
production as a constraint upon perceptions of identity and of
social role but she also equates this rigidity of thought and
practice with the rigid logic and reason Blake inveighed against,
so relating her feminist response to that of an attack upon
reductive western logic-dominated philosophies, later (i.e. post-
Blake) named Hegelian.

Like Angela Carter, Suniti Namjoshi reworks old myths and
tales in her *Feminist Fables*[41] which provides short, sharp, witty
reversals of several tales. She too has a Medusa poem, envisaging
Perseus as a pompous self-opinionated hero proving his manhood
by lopping off the head of the Medusa.[42] This severs the power

relations behind the myth, while contributing to the re-empower-
ing of woman with its tone of irony and mockery.

Demythologising often takes the form of asking fundamental
questions about the mythic woman, as Judith Kazantsis does in her
poem 'Clytemnestra' [43] which imagines the pain of the mother,
known only for the murder of her husband Agamamemnon. She
watched her daughter Iphigenia burn as sacrifice for the Trojan war,
a girl's sacrifice for a man's war to bring back an idolised woman,
Helen. A wicked gender-based irony.

Many women poets have written about other betrayed women,
among them Eurydice. Elaine Feinstein[44] sees the mythic tale not
from the point of view of the foolish Orpheus who turns round
and so loses his wife back to Hades, but from the point of view
of the newly awoken Eurydice who is then betrayed by the man's
selfish, stupid move.

These reworkings of myth go only skin deep but help women
reclaim the stories, rewrite them, refuse the construction of deadening, humiliating stereotypes of the passive earth woman, or
active devouring woman/whore/harridan, prime cause of sin and
sickness, and they have their parallels in the world of feminist art,
with images of Pandora rising like a cheeky butterfly from her
box, herself the richness of what she unleashes rather than all the
plagues upon the world.[45] Remaking the figures of mythology is
an artistic aim also of Nancy Spiro[46] who creates friezes of
leaping, powerful, goddess figures like the male athletes and gods
in historical friezes.

It is not always a rewriting and re-visioning of ancient mythic
figures that is the central concern of women writers, however. For
some writers, if these figures appear it is because they represent the
social and cultural oppressions women suffer now as they did in the
past, and the mythic women and mystic situations embody and
dramatise these situations. Other women choose to write about
contemporary mythology, the housewife enamoured of her washing
machine and dedicated to finding the powder to make all her whites
whiter; the eternal superwoman mixture of mistress/mother/even
professional worker. They also choose to expose oppressive myths
which contain black women in domestic service and figure lesbians
as deviant. Re-representing these stereotypes and culturally conditioned myths is an ideologically charged activity, and one that
requires a revision of the language and the established form that
perpetuate the myths and constraints. Poetry can take this
linguistic task on board more easily than prose fiction. However,
the stylistic yoking of the symbolic/imaginative/fantastic with the
historically/socially realistic is the main mode used formally by
fiction writers such as Angela Carter and Toni Morrison, to suggest
these radical re-visionings and rewritings.

It can be argued that the forms and the expressions *are* radically different because they are reinterpretations, re-expressions, new expressions by women. If we return to some of the arguments of Cixous we find a claim that women must write differently; that by setting words together in different patterns, changing the gender of words, even refusing the constraints of punctuation, a more fluid, changing, non-oppressive expression is possible. Rachel Blau de Plessis,[47] looking at the work of Denise Levertov, Adrienne Rich and Muriel Rukseyer, highlights the fundamental cultural and ideological critique which their work embodies with its radical use of myths, form, language:

> their poems analyse women's assumptions and patterns of action, revealing the cultural norms that uphold traditional consciousness of women. The poets discuss the role of the individual in history, especially in the creation of social change. Their myths have an unusual dimension, for critique becomes the heart of the myth. Their myths are critical of prior mythic thought; they are historically specific rather than eternal; they replace archetypes by prototypes.

In her book *Impertinent Voices*[48] Liz Yorke looks at the revisionary myth making of marginalised and oppressed groups of women, particularly black and lesbian woman, and sees their specifically marginalised position as actually enabling. From a position of the oppressed outsider it is possible to rewrite and re-envision. She argues that:

> Black and lesbian poets have played an important role in producing poetic revisionary mythologies. Their work has shown that dispossessed groups, however they are marginalised may devise specific strategies of writing to break against, through, out of those essentialist definitions and mythic models which still oppress, still and subdue them.[49]

Adrienne Rich often speaks directly for the silenced, unpicking the myths of motherhood and wifehood as eternally nurturing and rewarding, giving voice to their contradictions. So too, for example, does Susan Griffin unpick these myths in 'Three Poems for Women' [50] which has the silent and absent woman doing domestic chores and bringing up her children figured and given a voice. Elsewhere Liz Lochhead revisits other cultural myths such as the capitalist and materialist success of 'Page Three Dollies' [51] where the girls' manipulative 'and we're laughing all the way to the bank' slips into a more realistically manipulated 'and they're laughing all the way to the bank', highlighting the irony that the pin-up girls who make money out of their bodies feel in control, but are as exploited as any other commodity.

Demythologising is rampant, aware, bitter, ironic, but is

remythologising really possible? Angela Carter's *The Passion of New Eve*[52] gestures towards an idealised future of gender equality, leaving readers frustrated because it cannot be fully envisioned, while in Doris Lessing's sci-fi version *The Marriages Between Zones 3, 4 and 5*[53] the ideal balance between the sexes in the beginning of the novel appears utopian and static. In *The Passion of New Eve* the truism that man creates woman in his own dream image, preferring her suffering and subordinated, is enacted in the figure of Tristessa, the transvestite who acts out screen goddess roles in Hollywood films, watched by Evelyn/Eve in his/her youth and maturity. Man's ideal woman is shaped like man, with a few removals and enlargements. For the sexist Evelyn, in his/her castration and remodelling as a woman in the warrior community of women in the desert, the model of woman he becomes is that of his own fantasy, eminently vulnerable and artificial. Being made into this kind of sexy victim female is a punishment for his previous sexual domination and cruelties, specifically to Leila, who is made physically ill in her liaison with him. As part of the supersexist Zeno's harem, Eve/Evelyn gets a dose of his/her own exploitative and bullying medicine. Contemporary myths of gender roles are exposed as artifices, prisons of the body and the mind, licensing patterns of oppression and debasement. The destruction of Tristessa's glass palace shatters the myths philosophically and literally.

No real substitution emerges from this novel, nor does it emerge from the poems by Griffin, Lochhead, Feinstein, Kazantsis. Writing in new forms is an enormous task, positing new worlds a job for feminist utopians perhaps. The major role played by Angela Carter, Suniti Namjoshi, Liz Lochhead, Emma Tennant, Fay Weldon, etc. is to use the forms and images of myth and magic in order to both expose their hitherto *constrictive* nature, and, to revitalise positive myths and images for women, reinterpret and reclaim the male-defined negative images, enable us all to laugh, see through, see clearly, and move on. Use of the fantastic and of the magical (or in some cases spiritual) aids this exhilarating move.

Magic

Contemporary Gothic utilises the fantastic to critique and dissolve a repressive cultural order whose symbolism is a straitjacket, and whose modes of behaviour and relations devalue and denigrate whatever is perceived as other. Much contemporary Gothic writing by women also investigates the traditionally described dangers of reaching for new powers and new delights beyond the bounds of the western male-defined and restricted status quo. Transgression and subversion are threatening to cultural norms and their upholders, and a traditional form of punishment is the sudden recognition that one's challenges and transgressions are not merely radical, equally valid interpretations and assertions, but pacts with the devil. The Faust myth, playful or serious, lurks in the lives of transgressive, radical women reminding them sometimes that their challenges to the established order have a traditional punishment. Suburban normality rather than death and damnation is, often ironically, offered as this punishment. Emma Tennant's *Faustine*[54] pays her debt, while Fay Weldon's Carmen[55] gets it both ways, some rewards, and a final cheating of the devil, but a resolution in suburban bliss which leaves one wondering.

Magic, partly social, partly legendary, enables Ruth in the *Life and Loves of a She-Devil*[56] to wreak revenge on the philandering Bobbo, though her final transformation into a packaged artificial version of the romantic novelist Mary Fisher is an indictment of her fundamental collusion with the very consumer-oriented world which initially devalued and rejected her. While we enjoy and revel in the magic in operation in the novel we are reminded that Fay Weldon is being more than merely playful in giving women back their magical powers: she is pointing out that even when women are in the ascendant the models they have of success can be male dominated, male derived. Each of her novels returns her triumphantly imaginative and magical women to the kind of domestic situation which should surely be unpacked and unpicked as a result of the insights that liberation through magic could produce. The carnivalesque quality of the novels' centres is, then, undercut by their final reversions and reversals.

Fay Weldon's *Growing Rich* started life as a TV serial, then Weldon wrote the book out of the image, so confounding those readers who credit the novel as first and final version. *Growing Rich* brings temptation and the devil into the dully familiar, everyday Fenedge, the place we all want to escape from and where three Fenland girls, Carmen, Annie and Laura, grow up. Despite showing some promise at school, all three look set to deteriorate into female stereotypes: Laura gets pregnant and marries the dependable Woodie who makes sheds and shelves and presents her with four permanently small children; Annie meets a Mr Right from New Zealand, a bungie-jumping sheep farmer who flies her off to a similarly small-minded community the other side of the world; Carmen ends up chicken packing, her hideously dull parents regularly packed off to sun, sea and sand in sangria-swilling Spain. Carmen, however, is central.

Hers are the choices which control everything. Her temptations and decisions control the fates of the other girls as well as her own with rapid, various, and extreme results, depending upon whether or not she succumbs to the mythic promises with which she is continually propositioned by the kerb-crawling Driver, Mephistophelean chauffeur to the twentieth-century Magnate Sir Bernard's Faust.

Criticism of the dullness of everyday life brings Driver gliding ominously into view:

> Now it is dangerous to speak these thoughts aloud in case the devil, in one of the many forms he takes, is flying by: and he often is, especially in such places, for it is here that he locates his safe houses.[57]

Cultural cliché is realised:

> You can work your way out, you can sleep your way out, or you can sell your soul to the Devil.[58]

Carmen resists the temptations of wealth because Sir Bernard is not her type. She is herself, like Angela Carter's Melanie in *The Magic Toyshop*, a victim of teenage romance mythology, however, falling for her 'one true love', supermarket manager Ronnie Cartwright, whom she loses to the schoolgirl Poison Poppy.

Contemporary cultural mythology is scrutinised and satirised here, alongside the welter of local, literary and national myths and legends, fairytales and superstition – about grave mounds, about Faustus, about the devilish sources of sexual attractiveness. Driver (mistakenly) believes he taps the everyday woman's materially greedy, media-influenced soul when he deals with Carmen. If she looks momentarily like going along with his plans, she starts to metamorphose into every man's packaged dream woman, like Evelyn turning into Eve in *The Passion of New Eve*; uncomfortable and awkward for her as a woman, of course. The details are realistic, the actions magical, satirical, funny both on screen and in the novel:

> Something's wrong with me. It must be hormonal. I reckon I've gone from an A cup to a C overnight. It's disgusting. I flop when I walk. And my waist's got small, so my hips poke out in a ridiculous way. And I swear my legs are longer, or somehow my skirt's got shorter.[59]

Carmen feels she is a freak, and both detests and uses the absurd responses her new figure attracts from potential employers. Male myths show a preference for the silently perfect woman, however; Carmen finds her Cindy Doll mouth cannot utter criticism.

Magic is fun to show on the TV screen with conflagrations on the dunes and revelations of tortured souls, cathedrals struck by lightning, candlelit dinners under the trees, timely appearances from a BMW which can metamorphose into a Mercedes, all suddenly summoned up. In the novel these can be suggested, and literary references more widely used to provide hints and parallels, a different kind of reality and depth. The magical is used both as a potential threat, controlled by the devil, and as an amusing everyday actuality. As I have argued elsewhere,[60] feminist readers are left with contradictions and questions deliberately proffered by Fay Weldon when we seek a feminist utopia, a mythic or magical resolution to the story:

> The equations between conformity, conventional rewards (for Carmen, her family and her friends Laura and Annie and their families) and selling out to the devil are clearly stated; however, Carmen's assertion of independence, and her rejection of seduction for material worldly gain uncomfortably unite feminist principles with some old-fashioned, rather mythic ones about safety (of the soul!), value and the preservation of virginity.[61]

Carmen marries Sir Bernard, rendered rather ordinary and very mortal. Her version of bliss is stereotypical, thus reinforcing all the cultural myths both Laura and Annie have acted out. The use of the devil and of magic are great fun, however, and though occasionally ostensibly rather cosmic, ultimately they are more like the activities of Puck: domestic, everyday, fairly controllable with some commonsense. Fay Weldon exposes the myths, gives her women a little controversial power, but does not try totally, magically, to change the world.

Emma Tennant's *Faustine* is a similarly amusing, socially critical but not world shattering treatment of magic. In order to attain eternal youth and sexual potency, to escape from the constricting routines of childcare for her grandchild, grandmother Muriel, lured by a TV salesman, sells out to the media, to the 60s youth culture, and to the devil. She effectively colludes with the cosmetic images of the beautiful people, and like Ruth in Weldon's *She-Devil*, becomes an artifice, media-constructed herself. Initially a drudge and nurturer, when her granddaughter seeks out the maternal image she recalls, Muriel/Lisa Crane ensures that the dual myth of beautiful media success and nurturing grandmother can be maintained until the last minute, but no one can really be such a superwoman, and the losses and compromises are immense in the end. The man she nurtures along with her over the successful media-filled glitzy years as Lisa Crane eventually shows his cloven hoofs and either they walk off into the night together, each fond of their bargain, or the grand-daughter metamorphoses into the grandmother and she has to pay the price.

Generations of women are also the locus of Sara Maitland's *Three Times Table*.[62] Realism, logic, science initially oppose, then finally relate with imagination and magic. In this stratified house live Rachel the scientist grandmother, Phoebe her daughter, and Maggie, her granddaughter, an adolescent to whom the magical is an everyday reality in the shape of her dragon, Fenna. Rachel seeks final logical answers and finds the dinosaur link for which she searches, her 'dragon'. Her daughter Phoebe turns away from the certainties of pure maths, the hippy trail and finally to gardening. Preferring to nurture council estate flowers grown with scientific precision, her role is celebratory of life in the face of the disillusionment of her father's death, but she nurses the dark secret of her own cancer and cannot come to terms with it. Finally the granddaughter Maggie, on the point of a puberty she wishes to keep at bay, is sensitive and vulnerable to the lived experience of magic. The dragon is real for Maggie, as it is eventually recognisable to her grandmother.

While trapped into a merely reductive, logical version of scientific thought and discovery, Rachel sees Fenna as her enemy:

> Fenna was an assault, an attack, on all that she had stood for. Fenna was the wilful instrument of her own professional disintegration.

> Fenna was flame and fire, and moved on the wings of the night that were dragon wings to dance with taloned claws and mock scientific theory.

> Fenna was the dark force of the imagination as well as its golden dancing; Fenna was chaos as well as order, and brought, on fiery dragon breath, the full danger of the chasm.[63]

Like the goblins controlled by Beethoven in E.M. Forster's *Howards End* Fenna represents the existence of another non-logical, imaginative, chaotic world which is feared by rational man or woman who feel that with constant striving they can understand and label existence. Reason and imagination need equal balance: Fenna has to exist too, and Rachel's dinosaur, scientific proof of a theory, was a fake. So Rachel moves from the belief that 'mechanistic science could explain all phenomena even those of the heart and soul'.[64]

Through the figure of the two dragons Sara Maitland engages with the central dispute between the mechanistic and the magical other which lies philosophically behind so much of contemporary women writers' engagements with myth and magic. Cixous through polemic and poetry, Carter through magic realism and the oxymoron, others through myth reversals and magic agents, all undermine that reductive single vision which imprisons a woman in stultifying representations, as other in a binary mathematics which always leaves her registering less than one at the end of the equation.

Of course, merely alternative myths and merely imagination and magic are not put forward as woman's solution, however. Magic in itself can be real, but it is not all that is reality. It can be dangerous for Maggie, for example, in *Three Times Table*. With Fenna, Maggie explores the night world and he grows in size and power as her belief in him grows. His physical presence is real enough to cause the roof of the house to cave in when, concentrating on the decisions related to reaching maturity, Maggie realises she must destroy the hold he has over her. She travels with him one last time then rejects his existence. Realism and magic combine. The London fire brigade enter, seeking cups of tea and, although rational explanations for imploding glass roofs are run out to satisfy them, Fenna's anger has caused the damage. Leaving Maggie to grow up, he gives her both appetite and menstruation, but in passing on her knowledge of Fenna, Maggie also realises that magic will return and refill her life, in a new balance.

Rachel, initially denying dragons as undermining her own scientific rationalism, gradually moves to a realisation of the probability not of rational and logical development but of catastrophe theory. This makes space for and allows the existence of dragons and chaotic changes unplanned, unforeseen, uncontrolled and inexplicable to logic and to versions of science and maths as they have been enshrined in the male-dominated establishment represented in the museum in which she works and in the mathematically brilliant, excessively sexist husband she once had.

For Maggie and Phoebe, as for Rachel, dark powers and the powers of magic must be balanced – neither rejected nor fully embraced, but incorporated into a scheme which allows both the scientific rational and seemingly conformist everyday, and the supernatural, the magical, the imaginary, the magical. Grandmother's powers enable her to recognise this and the gradual flow of the storyline, paralleling the three women's lives through a day, a night and the following revelatory day, enables these different worlds to find their own related compartments as the women exist on different floors in the house yet merge together and depend on each other, naturally, like strata.

The novel celebrates the power and relationships of women together. In its dealings with science, rationalism, and the work-

ings of myth and the imagination as they daily coincide, it
reinvests the world with the alternative readings and powers of
the supernatural, as well as the rational, the male and the female.

Layers of women of different ages in a terraced house are the
subject also of Michèle Roberts's *In the Red Kitchen*[65] where
psychic powers are described as real and genuine. Flora Milk, a
young Victorian medium, makes contact ahead of time with the
late twentieth-century protagonist, settled into her decrepit new
house with her lover. For Hattie of the twentieth century the
death of her child is a traumatic experience, and with trauma
comes the contacts with Flora Milk. Hattie is confused and
conflated in Flora's contacts, though, with the pharaoh's daughter, Het, her father's bride and companion through death to a
promised eternal life. All three women are manipulated by men,
suffer through their lies and powers, though the loving relationship of the twentieth-century Hattie is the most positive of the
three. As links between the women are established, some due to
the place, others to the similarity of position or to the medium
powers of Flora, the magical and the afterlife and predictions
merge together; there is a continuity of experience through time.

Flora is both blessed and cursed with her gift of mediumship,
doubted and manipulated by her male protectors who are yet very
willing to promote and market it:

> I didn't ask to be a medium. It is not pleasant; I carry other
> people's suffering in my heart, I am a magnet for souls rushing
> irresistibly towards me and depositing in me their anguished
> histories.[66]

Flora herself is like the house. 'Vacant possession I am; they
move in on me.' [67] The Victorian cemetery that houses Flora and
her relations, visited by Hattie, resembles the Egyptian tombs,
linking the three worlds: 'the Victorian necropolis: Ancient
Egyptian city half buried in creepers and nettles'.[68] Hattie's own
convent escape into thoughts of God as female parallel Het's
sense of power as king/pharaoh following her father's death. But
both women find their alternative versions of power described as
perverse, and they are silenced, rendered nothing, an O. The lives
of Flora and her sister Rosina are confirmed by the family albums
and mementoes dug out by the old man who visits his old family
home, Hattie's house. A positive version of relationships, Hattie
moves on towards childbirth in her home, while the interwoven
stories of the other women testify in the house to suppression,
brave hopes, denials, oppression, and yet a continuity of contact,
a networking through space and time, via the female power of
mediumship. This too is a positive breaking of the silence in a
magical, real way.

While Fay Weldon introduces a little licensed wickedness with her she-devils and pacts (or avoidance of pacts) with the devil, while Emma Tennant's Faustine sells out, and dragons fly the London night sky with adolescent girls on their backs in *Three Times Table*, magic and the spiritual become palpable actants in the dramas of much of the writing of Toni Morrison and Ntozake Shange.

> This yoking and interweaving of the historical and the imaginative, the magical and the real breaks down the binary oppositions which Westernised, Hegelian philosophy asserts. We can no longer bear the situation of repression, of desocialisation, of desymbolisation, of inferiority.[69]

As in Michèle Roberts's *In the Red Kitchen*, mediumship, contact through history and time with lived memories, functions to link up through time and place the different characters in Alice Walker's *The Temple of My Familiar*[70] which traces cultural and race history through the women characters, through a central male character and, more appropriately, through Lizzie. She represents a lived racial and cultural memory, appearing in photographs which testify to her authenticity as many different women through time. Lizzie hears the voices of her ancestors and enables modern Americans to sense and trace roots with an Afro-American past, and with Indian and South American pasts also. There is a link to a central myth, a magical South American time when the powerful priestess was persuaded wrongly to give away her bird, her powers, and male power predominated thereafter, stolen, women's weaving of magical feathers devalued to sewing for men or producing trendy get-ups for pop stars.

The everyday appearance of magic, of the supernatural and of the spiritual is a feature also of much of Toni Morrison's writing. This is a different kind of magic realism but the intent and effects are similar to those of Angela Carter, Emma Tennant and Fay Weldon, though less straightforwardly funny. In *Beloved*[71] Toni Morrison renders tangible, domestic, personal and visible the unspoken historical pain of slavery in the form of the returned baby ghost, Beloved, whose succubus presence drains her mother as her previous presence as poltergeist scared her brothers away. Coming to terms with her death, the guilt, pain, and the need to move forward into a sense of self-worth and self-identity, without denying these sufferings, is the powerful message of the novel provided by the presence of the embodied ghost. Elsewhere, in *Song of Solomon*[72] flight is a metaphor chosen to suggest a new realisation of identity in relation to roots.

For Alice Walker and Toni Morrison, two Black Afro-

American women writers, the supernatural and spiritual provide the genuinely alternative vision of the world which sits alongside that logical, male-dominated world of 'reason' and historical fact. Like Angela Carter they both interweave the historical and the magical, showing that both are necessary and vital in their union. They each construct mythic configurations out of the specific conditions of poor black, oppressed people, particularly women marginalised under white patriarchal controls.

The last laugh is not on Medusa but on anyone male or female who accepts as fixed and given those cultural myths which shape and constrict our versions of ourselves. By rewriting the old myths and reclaiming the women of power, devalued and demoted in a patriarchal world, and by asserting as real, valid and celebratory the powers of alternative visions, those of magic, liberating, wild, subversive, joyous, women writers are reinvesting the world with the powers of the denied and denounced, the powers of women. The result is funny, ironic, powerful, and very positive. And, as Ursula Le Guin points out, it is important and necessary:

> Those who refuse to listen to dragons are probably doomed to spend their lives acting out the nightmares of politicians.[73]

Notes and References

1. Grace Nichols 'Twentieth Century Witch Chant' *Purple and Green: Poems by 33 Women Poets* London: Rivelin Grapheme Press 1985.
2. Hélène Cixous 'The Laugh of the Medusa' ('La Rire de la Meduse' in *l'Arc* 61 1975) transl. E. Marks and E. de Courtivron *New French Feminisms* Brighton: Harvester 1980 pp. 245–60.
3. Angela Carter *The Sadeian Woman* London: Virago 1979 p. 7.
4. Roland Barthes *Image/Music/Text* transl. Stephen Heath London: Fontana 1977.
5. Judith Pintar *The Halved Soul: Re-telling the Myths of Romantic Love* London: Pandora 1992.
6. Alice Walker *Possessing the Secret of Joy* London: Jonathan Cape 1992.
7. Ibid. p. 131.
8. Ibid. p. 217.
9. Ibid. p. 221.
10. Ibid. p. 264.
11. Ursula le Guin *The Language of the Night: Essays on Fantasy and Science Fiction* in Susan Wood ed New York: Petigree 1979 p. 44.
12. Joanna Russ 'The Subjectivity of Science Fiction' *Extrapolation* 15 Part 1 p. 52.

13. Rosemary Jackson *Fantasy: The Literature of Subversion* London: Methuen New Accents 1981 p. 23.

14. Irene Bessière *Le Récit Fantastique: La Poetique de l'Incertain* Paris 1974 p. 62.

15. Anne Cranny-Francis *Feminist Fiction* Cambridge: Polity Press 1990 p. 77.

16. May Sarton 'The Muse as Medusa' *Selected Poems* New York: W. W. Norton 1978.

17. Cixous 'The Laugh' 1980 p. 248.

18. Morag Shiach *Hélène Cixous* London: Routledge 1991 p. 23.

19. Angela Carter *Nights at the Circus* London: Chatto and Windus 1984 p. 295.

20. Angela Carter *The Magic Toyshop* London: Virago 1967.

21. Ibid. p. 166.

22. W. B. Yeats 'Leda and the Swan' *Collected Poems* London: Faber.

23. Carter *Magic* 1967 p. 167.

24. Ibid. p. 166.

25. Ibid.

26. Ibid.

27. Angela Carter *Wise Children* London: Chatto and Windus 1991.

28. Carter *Nights* 1984 p. 69.

29. Ibid. p. 79.

30. Gina Wisker 'Winged Women and Werewolves: How Do We Read Angela Carter?' *Ideas and Production* vol IV 1985 p. 92.

31. Carter *Nights* 1984.

32. Jackson *Fantasy* 1981 p. 178.

33. Elaine Feinstein 'Anniversary' in Couzyn ed *The Bloodaxe Book of Contemporary Feminist Poets* London: Bloodaxe 1985.

34. Grace Nichols 'Abracadabra' in *The Purple and the Green* 1985.

35. Cixous 'The Laugh' 1980

36. Hélène Cixous *The Newly Born Woman* transl. Betty Wing Manchester: Manchester University Press 1986.

37. V.A. Conley *Hélène Cixous: Writing the Feminine* Nebraska: University of Nebraska Press 1991 p. 56.

38. Ibid.

39. Cixous *The Newly Born* 1986.

40. Angela Carter 'Notes from the Front Line' *On Gender and Writing* London: Pandora Press 1983.

41. Suniti Namjoshi *Feminist Fables* London: Sheba 1981.

42. Suniti Namjoshi 'Look Medusa' in *The Purple and the Green*, 1985.

43. Judith Kazantsis 'Clytemnestra' in *The Wicked Queen* London.

44. Elaine Feinstein 'The Feast of Eurydice' in *The Bloodaxe Book* 1985.

45. Mouse Katz 'Pandora's Box' Painting Multi Media 1984.

46. Nancy Spiro *Let the Priests Tremble* Prints 1984.

47. Rachel Blau du Plessis 'The Critique of Consciousness and Myth in Levertov, Rich and Rukseyer' in S. Gilbert and S.

Gubar eds *Shakespeare's Sisters: Feminist Essays on Women Poets* Bloomington and London: Indiana University Press 1979 pp. 280–1.

48. Liz Yorke *Impertinent Voices* London: Routledge 1991.
49. Ibid. p. 16.
50. Susan Griffin 'Three Poems for Women' in The Raving Beauties ed *In the Pink* London: The Women's Press 1983.
51. Liz Lochhead 'Page Three Dollies' *True Confessions* Edinburgh: Polygon Press 1985.
52. Angela Carter *The Passion of New Eve* London: Virago 1978.
53. Doris Lessing *The Marriages Between Zones 3, 4 and 5* London: Jonathan Cape 1980.
54. Emma Tennant *Faustine* London: Faber 1992.
55. Fay Weldon *Growing Rich* London: Harper Collins 1992.
56. Fay Weldon *The Life and Loves of a She-Devil* London: Hodder and Stoughton 1983.
57. Weldon *Growing* 1992 p. 1.
58. Ibid. p. 8.
59. Ibid. p. 46.
60. Gina Wisker 'Feminism and a Fenland Faustus' in *Million: The Magazine About Popular Fiction* no 12 Nov/Dec 1992 pp. 37–9.
61. Weldon *Growing* 1992.
62. Sara Maitland *Three Times Table* London: Virago 1991.
63. Maitland *Three* 1991 p. 109.
64. Ibid. p. 178.
65. Michèle Roberts *In The Red Kitchen* London: Methuen 1990.
66. Ibid. p. 92.
67. Maitland *Three* 1991 p. 93.
68. Ibid. p. 116.
69. Conley *Hélène Cixous* 1991.
70. Alice Walker *The Temple of My Familiar* New York and London: Harcourt Brace Jovanovitch and The Women's Press 1990.
71. Toni Morrison *Beloved* London: Chatto and Windus 1988.
72. Toni Morrison *Song of Solomon* London: Triad Grafton 1980.
73. Le Guin *The Language* 1979.

CHAPTER 6

From Vases to Tea-sets: Screening Women's Writing

Marilyn Brooks

Speaking of her adaptation of her first novel for TV serialisation, Jeanette Winterson tells the following anecdote:

> A woman goes into an art gallery. She sees a vase and falls in love with it. She goes over to the sculptor and tells her how much she loves her work; the colour, the shape, the glaze, the particular wholeness of the piece. Naturally the sculptor is flattered. 'Yes,' says the woman, getting out her cheque book, 'your work is unique. Now, could you just smash it up and make me six cups and saucers out of it?' [1]

Adapting fiction for television or film is problematic. The text is appropriated by another form which has its own language, its own meanings, its own 'integrity'. These may collude or collide with each other. Technically what you see on the screen cannot be the same as what is written, but while some alterations are inevitable, the change of audience makes others desirable. Although discussion of adaptations tends to accommodate the idea that something has to be 'left out', in the case of minority writings, what is left out is exactly relevant within the context of deliberate evasion or silencing.[2] It suggests subverting the subversive in order to turn it into the televisual experience called popular entertainment.

Television and film are consumed by a varied mass audience whereas women's writing is not, being more often seen as subversive, unsettling and intellectual. This has implications for its screening as 'the values and attitudes of the small middle-class reading public might be incomprehensible to the mass film public'.[3] Much of women's writing invites enquiry and direct engagement from the reader, positions more conducive to the privacy of the text than to the screen, which assumes:

> the unit of consumption [...] as the family or household rather than the individual viewer. This is to situate individual viewing within the household relations in which it operates, and to insist that individual viewing activity only makes sense inside of this frame.[4]

Similarly, the comic or dramatic 'abnormality' of television drama acts to confirm:

> the normality of both the viewer and the viewer's presumed setting. The TV viewer is thus a viewer who is confirmed as isolated, even insulated, from the events of an outside world which is defined in opposition to the domestic and familial setting in which TV viewing is assumed to take place.

Thus, television is 'in a position to be disturbing for its viewers when it represents something that is repressed in most domestic situations'.[5]

Because much women's writing is deliberately provocative and challenging to preconceived ideas, the screening of this material might be seen as offensive within this affirmative situation of television viewing. Prime-time viewers are not expected to welcome confrontation and challenge. Visual discussion of issues such as family rejection or lesbianism can be seen to be antagonistic to this value system.

Technically, the visual image seems to say it all, presenting more of a *fait accomplait*, which is less conducive to 'open' discussion, nagging questions remaining just out of frame. Deliberate ambiguity is a hallmark of the openness of women's writing, with its invitation to discussion and ambivalence rather than to acceptance of the closure of conclusion. The visual image seems to militate against this openness, as it frames and emphasises decisive actions for the viewer, who is encouraged to adopt a passive role as collaborator. The viewer sees the action from the camera's 'truthful' point of view.

Similarly, the framing of TV images tends to promote characters and actions rather than ideas, yet ideas are often the foundation of much women's writing and, at the same time, produce its provocative stance. Tactics need to be adopted in order to circumnavigate this visual inadequacy because 'we cannot see what we cannot see; in fiction we can'.[6]

Strategies exist to minimise the effects of television and film's deficiencies, but there is a clear danger that the alternative strategies involved in the act of making marginal texts 'popular' for screening will *necessarily* defuse the meaning which makes them perceived as marginal to begin with. Offering these texts prime-time viewing is insisting on compromise. Popular TV tends to be just that, and consequently, challenging and radical positions have to be accommodated within the parameters existing. There is a potential danger that raising these issues and then containing them visually, simultaneously contains the issues themselves.

On the other hand, screening presents an opportunity for greater accessibility of marginal material which may be presented without the confrontational regalia of privileged reading matter. Hence, provocative material might be digested before this is realised, and in the very setting where it would normally be denied, as alternative comedians have been quick to exploit. Statistics show that 'the majority of viewers of a typical film adaptation will not be familiar with the original novel'.[7] Similarly 'television reaches three times as many people as those who claim to have encountered the literature directly'.[8]

Publishers like Pandora, The Women's Press and Virago have a 'knowing' market and this has tended to isolate texts as radical in the public's consciousness. However, the serials considered here were shown during peak viewing periods and were promoted by the broadcasting companies as being of popular interest. I am suggesting that the negotiation which makes this possible *necessarily* reduces what made the texts 'popular' for women readers.

This chapter will look at three adapted novels: Jeanette Winterson's *Oranges Are Not the Only Fruit*,[9] and Fay Weldon's *The Cloning of Joanna May*,[10] both of which have been highly successful television serials, and the film of Weldon's *The Life and Loves of a She-Devil*,[11] which has been promoted as a 'Hollywood blockbuster comedy'.[12]

Oranges Are Not the Only Fruit was screened in three parts during 1989. Viewing figures record an audience of 2.9, 4.4, 3.9 million which, for a mid-week screening is considered a success. The author of the novel, Jeanette Winterson, was scriptwriter.

It is a brilliant, kaleidoscopic exposure of religious intolerance. It marvellously depicts religion gone wrong and the bigotry of those who can't see this. It is vibrant with oranges, from Jess's hair to the ubiquitous bowls of fruit. Jeanette Winterson's involvement as scriptwriter ensures that much of the radical thrust of her narrative remains, although she acknowledged she had to 'smash up the original and do it justice in a different way'.[13]

The story of Jess's[14] upbringing by her bigoted, godly mother, and her experiences within an evangelical church, culminate in her open lesbianism, a controversial topic which, given the context of domestic viewing, might be expected to be the most resistible of the issues raised. Most of the 'negligible' criticism received by the BBC was directed at the portrayal of lesbian activities. But what the serial very successfully does, as early as the titles, is immediately to establish Jess's world as so bizarre as to normalise her own position as rebel and lesbian, conflating the two issues. Within her own domestic and social setting, which is depicted surrealistically, through images of a merry-go-round, beast-like congregations, etc., Jess's 'unnatural passions' are seen as understandable and acceptably reactionary. The viewer is invited to reposition herself towards it as counter to dominant values.

Lesbianism might well be accepted as a 'natural' outcome of an upbringing which sees 'unnatural passions' as consisting in passion itself.

It would be very difficult for anyone to view the graphic scene of the casting out of demons by Pastor Finch as anything but repulsive and sadistic. As such the serial clearly promotes this world as oppressive, resistible and antagonistic. (In the novel it is humorously summed up in a couple of sentences.) Close-ups of Pastor Finch suggest the pleasure he feels in this 'pastoral' work. Close-ups of Jess solicit sympathy for her plight as demon-harbourer. But there is a danger here. While visual emphasis on the sadistic violence of Jess's world encourages a greater transference of rejection away from 'unnatural' Jess, it simultaneously invites the viewer to disengage with it as a specific issue itself. The stress on religious oppression has reduced the amount of rebellious choice available to Jess, and one can only applaud her rejection of her distorting world. Becoming a rebel/lesbian is a reflection of Jess's upbringing, and the viewer is more likely to find this both acceptable and containable. Lesbianism is also elevated into a pre-lapsarian state of innocence as Jess and Melanie romp on Elsie's carpet. At the same time, the viewer might easily choose to be persuaded that the parameters which are defining Jess's experience may be repulsive, but not undeservedly restrictive, given the 'deviancy' of her behaviour. The novel minimises this risk by opening up Jeanette's behaviour as a concrete example of a more pervasive, and less tolerable, general oppression, its heroine being 'someone on the outside of life'.[15] Paradoxically, *Oranges* may become 'comforting' in the case of its viewers, through exclusion of the 'difficult questions' which produce this comfort for its readers.[16]

Winterson had had to confront the dilemma of what to leave out, and she was successful in negotiating with a new form, recognising it as 'the story I had decided to tell on television', which made it easier for her 'to identify the difference between real losses and fond farewells'.[17]

The novel resonates with inset narratives, fables and fairytales which 'worked as a kind of Greek Chorus commenting on the main events'. These were deemed expendable in the serial 'because their function could be taken over by the camera itself'.[18] The camera succeeds in this way, focusing the viewer's attention on what is objectionable, rejectable. However, their exclusion does enforce a very different point of view which the novel resists: that the oppression experienced by Jess is particular, rather than general. The danger is that a narrowing, rather than a widening, of prospects is being offered by the screen. The serial focuses on one issue by eliminating a more provocative one.

In the novel Jeanette's difficulty in finding an identity is a general problem. The quest for identity concerns all. The inclusion and recurrence of stories of Sir Percival's flight from the Round Table, Winnet's negotiation with the sorcerer's chalk circle, and the secret garden where 'all true quests end' bring questing to the fore and, importantly, stresses the central concern with possibilities, choices, decisions.

The serial viewer is protected from this self-examination, largely by the concentration on the abnormality of what is on offer for rejection. Jess takes on the opprobrium of the world for her deviant and defiant behaviour. In the novel this behaviour is used to represent more widespread dissatisfaction at the confinement meted out by 'normal' societal demands. The consistent imagery of closed circles, webs, circumferences, and their symbolic negotiation, ensures that this is at the forefront of Jeanette's representative experience. The reader is invited to see *her own* quest for individuality within the narrative supplied by Jeanette. Jeanette is everywoman, rather than lesbian woman. Breaking out of chalk circles and away from Round Tables means a negotiation with more than sexuality, central though this is to both forms.

Winterson acknowledged this reduction of the commentary provided by the recurrent tales, deciding that 'the power of the image means that you don't always have to spell it out'.[19] But the camera's very closeness often acts to isolate the individuality of Jess's plight which the narratives not only resist, but expand, and this can only reduce the more general application of the whole narrative.

Hence, the demon of the serial is the dismissible one of biblical evil, more containable by far than the demon of self-assertion and identity. The novel's demon has a far more general significance. The novel makes clear that Jeanette is 'demon-possessed' in a far broader sense than religious intolerance recognises. The orange novel-demon explains that 'we're here to keep you in one piece, if you ignore us, you're quite likely to end up in two pieces, or lots of pieces, it's all part of the paradox'.[20] Driving out of demons has more than a religious association, although this works (as in the novel) if it is seen as symbolic of other controlling restraints on the individual's development.

However much we are encouraged to reject Pastor Finch we are rejecting a distortion of a truth rather than rejecting the foundation of that truth. The biblical chapter headings of the novel keep re-emphasising the intrusive nature of historical 'truth'. As the chapter Deuteronomy points out, 'of course that is not the whole story, but that is the way with stories; we make of them what we will. It's a way of explaining the universe while leaving the universe unexplained, it's a way of keeping it all alive, not boxing it into time' whereas history, as in the Bible which contains Deuteronomy, is 'a means of denying the past' and hence refusing 'to recognise its integrity. To fit it, force it, function it, to suck out the spirit until it looks the way you think it should.' [21] The serial ensures that we reject Pastor Finch but perhaps not the distortion that is religion itself.

The difficulties of breaking with one's past no matter how confining that past are explored mainly through the inset narratives, as we see Sir Percival symbolically represented as a spider caught in a web. In the novel and in the serial Jeanette/Jess articulate the difficulty of escaping from a past dominated by cultural, familial and historical ties:

> I have a theory that every time you make an important choice, the part of you left behind continues the other life you could have had ... I seemed to have run in a great circle, and met myself again on the starting line.[22]

But circumferences are consistently shown as self-limiting. Jess's ambiguous relationship with her adopted mother and her consequent difficulty in breaking away from her, convincing though it is in the serial, is given a different emphasis in the novel as the insets insist that questing is seen as part of *normal* behaviour, and is not the prerogative of the young or the oppressed. The serial is in danger of particularising Winterson's concern with 'comforting' the individual who is not Jess but the more representative Jeanette:

> Everyone, at some time in their life, must choose whether to stay with a ready-made world that may be safe but which is also limiting, or to push forward, often past the frontiers of commonsense, into a personal place, unknown and untried.[23]

The consistent use of images of confinement in the novel extend the struggle beyond Jess's particular experience of religion and sexuality. Symbolic circles cry out to all to be breached, threads to be broken.

The serial undoubtedly opened up discussion in homes where, as the viewing figures show, the novel was not likely to be read, and happily it 'generated a great deal of debate and it seems that people found in it another way of looking at the world'.[24]

The serial confirms it as 'a threatening novel' which:

> exposes the sanctity of family life as something of a sham; it

illustrates by example that what the church calls love is actually psychosis and it dares to suggest that what makes life difficult for homosexuals is not their perversity but other people's.[25]

It very successfully utilises

[the] humour and lightness [so] that those disposed not to agree find that they do ... there is no doubt that in its double incarnation of page and screen, *Oranges* has broken down many more barriers than it has reinforced.[26]

But at the same time its generically subversive stance has been made legitimate for acceptance by an audience presupposed to find religious bigotry and intolerance unacceptable. Unfortunately, the surreal world offered by the serial reinforces the strangeness, rather than the normality, of Jeanette/Jess's existence and, as such, can only diminish their subversive significance. The popular medium of televised oppression upholds that oppression within controllable, rejectable parameters which are desensitised for popular consumption.

The paperback edition of *The Cloning of Joanna May* has sold over 150,000 copies, 100,000 before its screening in two parts in January 1992. Each televised episode attracted an audience of 10.5 million viewers (compared with, for instance, 18 million per episode for *Coronation Street*, 15–16 million for *Eastenders*) of whom 5.6 million were women, 4.2 million men, the rest children. The figure of 53 per cent represents a slightly higher female audience than is usual for a weekend showing. The serialisation and the novel are regarded as popular successes.

The screenplay of *Cloning* sets Joanna's predicament as cloned woman very firmly within the context of patriarchal control, even over nature through genetic engineering and the more general issue of nuclear waste treatment. The video blurb promises a story of:

sex, intrigue and high drama [which] dominate the lives of Joanna May and her former husband, a self-made multimillionaire. Carl's unreal adoration of Joanna can accept no human frailty, while her devotion to him easily transcends her own, largely meaningless, affairs with the younger gardener and the curator of Carl's museum of mankind.

Carl's obsessive love for Joanna dictates that he has her lovers brutally murdered and that he produces, by cloning her cells, a younger generation of three Joanna look-alikes. His notion is that he can choose one of these girls for his own. 'Not as you are now, but younger and free from the stain of betrayal.'

The girls reject with scorn this mad idea together with Carl's values and judgements. [27]

In the serial Weldon's narrative is firmly placed within the context
of male dominance and control over the lives of desired women.
The two-generation coverage immediately sets up Carl's ancillary
obsession with this control through the preservation of youthful
potency. According to this blurb the action is to be seen from the
point of view of Carl May and his position of power.

The paperback blurb, however, clearly situates Joanna and her
preoccupations at the forefront of the narrative:

> Joanna May thought herself unique, indivisible – until one day,
> to her hideous shock, she discovered herself to be five: though
> childless she was a mother: though an only child she was
> surrounded by sisters young enough to be her daughters –
> Jane, Julie, Gina and Alice, the clones of Joanna May ... In
> this astonishing new novel, Fay Weldon weaves a web of
> paradox quite awesome in its cunning. Probing into genetic
> engineering, *The Cloning of Joanna May* raises frightening
> questions about our identity as individuals – and provides
> some startling answers.[28]

Joanna May has allowed herself to be subsumed by Carl May
to the extent that her personal identity has been completely
eroded. By the end of the novel Joanna finds this identity:

> When I acknowledged my sisters, my twins, my clones, my
> children, when I stood out against Carl May, I found myself:
> pop! I was out ... I was no longer just a wife; I was a human
> being: I could see clearly now ... I, Joanna May. Or perhaps
> now, just Joanna.[29]

The televised form has repositioned the role of the heroine, making
her an example of her husband's power (as also in the novel) but by
so doing it deflects the novel's concern with the situation of all
women within the dominant power system of the male. Images of
Carl looming over Joanna, whether supernaturally, when she is
making love with the gardener, or in reality, against his office
monitors, underline his centrality. He is seen to have control over
the women in his life by his ability to frame, freeze frame, package
and clone them. The technology surrounding him is a visual symbol
of his masculine potency. The popular elements of sex and violence
are exaggerated to enhance this position. But, at the same time, the
serial has similarly refocused and blurred the central position of
Joanna and her representational role for all women. The serial
defuses the feminist aspect of its 'revolutionary' nature by zooming
in on the more overtly menacing and less gender-specific threat of
nuclear waste. Carl May's power over Joanna is another sign of his
power over millions. He is very visibly the chairman of British
Nuclear Agents, making on-site visits and television appearances.

By enclosing the implications of the cloning issue within the more general threat of the nuclear one, the serial invites the viewer to see the problem as external, rather than internal. Carl's megalomanic control over the life of Joanna blurs the novel's insistence that the individual has to take responsibility for her own identity, which she eventually does with the aid of the clones.

The novel is more concerned to utilise the threat of radioactivity as a sign of breakdown in human terms, 'a hideous black cloud of the spirit'.[30] Radioactivity, which is already falling, is an embodiment of general malaise between the sexes. As its controller, Carl May represents this breakdown in sexual relations.

The novel stresses genetic engineering more than the more topical radioactive waste because, although it is a similarly disturbing demonstration of control, it is one which has a more direct bearing on the lives of women. This is made clear by the emphasis placed on nature's equivalent control of women via the womb. Almost all the female characters are obsessed by reproduction; how to procure it or how to avoid it. At the same time, genetic engineering is also placed within the context of male power as Carl consistently contemplates utilising this to produce desired women. Carl acts as a modern God and, as such, can produce women if not in man's likeness at least to his liking: 'why then Carl May might create a perfect woman, one who looked, listened, understood and was faithful' [31] such as Joanna until her Eve-like betrayal through infidelity to Carl but not to herself.

Both 'texts' demonstrate fear of ageing but again the serial decentralises the novel's location of this as a specifically female concern. The novel-Joanna is 60 and well aware that 'time is against all women' [32] whereas Patricia Hodge plays an impossibly youthful 'older woman' to her attractive young lover, Oliver. Women's powerlessness against the biological clock is articulated by Joanna: 'Is this the sum of woman then – to be the instrument of reproduction, a walking womb?' [33] More importantly, the novel-heroine joins her 'lot with other women, universalizing an experience', and, simultaneously she attempts to find an identity by sharing herself with others, turning 'from "I" to "she" '.[34]

By focusing on Carl's ageing, which he thinks he can control through the second generation clones, the serial removes the stress on women's biological control. Sexual potency as symbol of power is demonstrated by his prowess with the compliant bimbo Bethany (who is under constant threat of replacement in the novel) but is undermined when the clones reject him as an anachronistic old man, an acceptable version of the January/May convention. But Carl can still pack them off, dispose of them by sending them to Joanna. In the novel Carl never meets the clones, initially wanting to avoid them *because*

of their likeness to the betrayer Joanna. After all, they are still
women.

The serial misses the complexity of human involvement that
the pasts of the clones foreground. The serial reduces them to
three, omits their pasts and only hints at their present lives. This
removal enables concentration on Carl's power position as creator
of them for his future sexual and self-fulfilling use. In the novel
Gina's, Julie's, Jane's, Alice's family backgrounds are carefully
documented as are those of Joanna and Bethany. These backgrounds enable Weldon to encourage awareness of the wider
'identity' issues of the novel as all four are unable to make the
changes necessary to gain control over their lives, a control which
tends to centre on their reproductive systems. For example, Gina
is Cliff's battered wife, and mother of three unplanned children.
The violence she experiences is presented as a complex symptom
of unease between the sexes. This violence is also produced by
Jane and the others who experience the 'black cloud' of sexual
radiation which is already falling. The complexity of these relationships is presented through typical Weldonian invitations to
self-examination and self-accusation as the clones come to a
recognition of 'the sudden bright consciousness of the self as
something defined by others'.[35] By omitting such discussions the
engagement of the viewer is reduced, the action predominates,
the provocatively feminist issues are subsumed by action.

In the novel the clones are representative of 'women ... [who]
were by their very nature supplicants' experiencing 'female desola-
tion, decay and disappointment'.[36] By the end they become
'sisters' without the aid of Carl's manipulation. They locate each
other coincidentally, can relate to each other and ultimately experience the wholeness which enables Joanna to shake off Carl's
control. Gina, the battered wife, decides 'this can't go on', leaves
home, fortuitously having met her 'sister' Julie, who is considering
divorcing Alec who is unable to produce children. Gina and the
children move in with her, and eventually Gina hands over the
children to Julie who is now fulfilled. They too have taken control
over their lives significantly by thwarting biological constraints
and, simultaneously, their husband's control over them through
their bodies.

The decentralisation of specifically female issues is largely
abetted by the change from open discussion in the novel to that
of closed suspense form in the serial. In the novel we are
introduced to the clones in Chapter 2. The serial dramatises their
meeting by mysteriously bringing them together at Carl's
command.

Drama similarly restructures the ending. As chairman of
Britnuc, Carl plans to desensitise the issue of the danger of

nuclear waste by jumping into a cooling pond with girlfriend Bethany at an Open Day. In both versions Carl dies as a result; in the novel because of radioactive contamination, in the serial because of the supernatural intervention of the clones who, seeking revenge and a way to free their mother/sister, cause him to drown. The Lord of the Dance is dead, but not before he has persuaded Joanna to clone him also.

The final image of the serial is of Joanna surrounded by her 'family' of clones and friends enjoying the cosy treat of little Carl's third birthday. Carl is being given a second chance in his new loving environment. The implications of 'the King is dead' are kept out of frame, as is Joanna's temptation to:

> beat him black and blue ... to punish him for what he did to me, for the unlived life he gave me, so many years of it, the guilt he made me feel, the loss he made me endure.[37]

The form's desire for narrative closure resists any continuation of the threat of control through the intervention of its happy-ever-after conclusion which even manages to defuse the implications of the radioactivity threat by removing Carl's demise as ironic punishment into the realm of fantasy.

Where the serialisation of *Cloning* shows accommodation via decentralisation, the film of Weldon's earlier *The Life and Loves of a She-Devil* demonstrates appropriation by genre.

This novel is also about the control of nature and a consequent control of woman. It raises serious issues of identity and, in particular, of gender construction through a model of 'the feminine'. It was televised in Britain and filmed in America. The televised version stays closely to the narrative and utilises suggestive supernatural effects present in the novel. Although the novel has been compared to a 'film noir', the actual film retains few suggestions of the narrative's proximity to this.[38] It ignores most of the subversive aspects of the novel in order to concentrate on a conventional revenge motif which arises out of the heroine's particular experience.

Like *The Cloning of Joanna May*, *The Life and Loves of a She-Devil* interrogates the make-up of female identity, but also situates this within social and cultural demands of femininity. It explores women's willingness to conform to this image through self-mutilation and subsequent loss of identity. It is a blistering examination of one woman's attempt to redress balance by taking over the power so dominant in her husband by literally becoming the object of that husband's desire and approval. By turning herself into the Mary Fisher of his, and of Ruth's, romance-world the statuesque Ruth gives up herself. Ruth has colluded with the powers which insist on demarcation of female identities into categories. The novel provokes suspicion of this categorisation by demonstrating Ruth's apparent willingness to adopt strategies which conform to it. Weldon invites speculation as to the benefits accrued, as the reader recognises that 'it was not so difficult after all; nor she so special'.[39]

In order to become the feminine ideal as embodied by Mary Fisher, Ruth is prepared to undergo very painful and expensive surgery to reduce her size and shape. More importantly, the reader witnesses Ruth's identity shrinking along with her body as she literally becomes her rival. Becoming the feminine ideal of popular culture has removed her self and dehumanised her. This is a significant issue for women, yet the film completely defuses its generic and radical import. Instead, the film focuses on the decline of Mary Fisher's 'beauty', the warning seeming to be that she might find it easy to be transformed into an unglamourous Ruth, with all that that encodes. The film-Ruth never has to undergo anything more humiliating and painful than a perm, and the ending finds her unambiguously in a position of power-dressed control. The reduction of the title to *She-Devil* signals its preoccupation with something straight-forward, far removed from the complex character who grows out of the 'life and loves'.

By redefining the heroine the film redefines women's discourse, neutralising the radical element by positioning the heroine's dilemma within a more acceptable convention, that of thwarted woman. As such, her potential role as interrogator of female experience is subsumed by that of revenger. Any actions, however extreme, are made 'understandable' and, hence, contain-able within this superimposed genre. The film has renegotiated her position and the viewer's point of view has been manipulated into acceptance of the expectations aroused by the genre which deflects engagement outside of it. The film becomes categorised as another domestic drama of jealous, revengeful females. The new office bimbo's delight in similarly wreaking revenge on Bob (the Bobbo of the novel), who had also rejected her, backs up this reception.

Simultaneously, it is easy for the viewer to side with Ruth against Bob because he fits the construct which dictates that he deserves his treatment! The emphasis on the comic outcome of the various revenge acts again ensures that this motif is always central. The viewer has little time to consider what is happening to Ruth who is the force behind this action. By positioning Ruth's role within the revenge motif the film fails to engage the viewer with the wider implications of the construction of the feminine which made her seek revenge in the first place. The film invites participation in this construction rather than rejection of it. The novel-Ruth shows how easy (although painful and expensive) it is to become the desired feminine and by so doing Weldon invites us to consider gender construction itself. The final image in the novel is one of reduction and waste. Ruth has become diminished and the reader is encouraged to feel distaste for what Ruth has done to herself. However, the nagging questions which surface on the pages of the narrative have been conveniently expunged in the film so that the viewer is able to respond to an exaggeration which does not involve herself. The novel refuses this distancing. We are continually reminded of how much Ruth is sacrificing herself to become an artificial construct like Mary Fisher. While the conclusion rockets Ruth into a position of power 'I have all, and he has none. As I was, so he is now', we are left with an image of contraction, 'I am a lady of six foot two, who had tucks taken in her legs. A comic turn, turned serious.' [40]

Given the ambiguity surrounding Ruth's emergence as Mary Fisher, it would be reductive to discuss her as a warning figure; nevertheless, typically, Weldon's discourse does insist on being taken seriously, the implications of Ruth's experience for good and bad demanding to be addressed. She might more effectively be called a commentator on this experience which the reader is then invited to interrogate. The film mediates this function so that her choric effectiveness is destroyed.

Thus the plot is simplified for the film audience which has, perhaps, been attracted to the publicity which promotes it as 'a Hollywood blockbuster comedy', about Mary who is:

> pretty, thin, very sexy and always gets everything she wants including Bob, Ruth Patchett's wayward husband. Ruth's fat, frumpy and mole-ridden. But she's just about had her fill of her cheating husband and his beautiful scheming mistress. So when Bob decides to make arrangements with Mary more permanent, Ruth gets more than mad. She gets evil![41]

A promotional still shows Ruth and Mary fighting over Bob, who looks on smugly. The central issue of gender construction is marginalised into supporting roles of Revenging Angel or She-Devil.

A reduction in the number of characters encourages passive rather than active engagement with the plot,[42] and in *She-Devil*'s case this extends to the removal of the nurturing relationships to which the novel-Ruth exposes herself. The film's subsidiary plots are present solely to support the mechanics of the conciliatory revenge plot. In both formats Ruth works at the Golden Twilight Home in order to wreak vengeance on Mary Fisher. She runs the Vesta Rose agency in order to infiltrate Bob's working life, but we are not shown her emerging identity via her relations with the old man, Carver (through whom Ruth begins her preoccupation with rule breaking); Vickie of Bradwell Park; Father Ferguson who felt 'that something of her had gone into him' for the better; or 'the commune of separatist feminists'. All of these are episodes which enlist sympathy for her search for fulfilment rather than for vengeance. The film devalues the newly inverted terms of the she-devil by positioning her within this genre.

Any sympathy for the heroine's wrong treatment and victim status quickly transforms into support for her attempt at victory on any terms. Bob's transgressions are so huge, yet understandable, that Ruth's punishing is similarly acceptable. At the end, even Bob's discomfort is forgotten. Whereas in the novel Bobbo is lobotomised by his experiences and becomes a slave of Ruth, in the film he is anticipating a return to the security of his obliging, avenged spouse. The convention holds. He has deserved punishment and received it. The issue has been contained.

Ironically, Weldon's Mary Fisher dies of cancer, the body beautiful ultimately refusing to be controlled. This reinforcement of the body issue which is so central to Ruth's decision to accept its prominence is resisted by the film which ends with Mary Fisher continuing to promote gendered deceits through her writing of romances. The film-Ruth meets Mary on her own, unambiguous terms of romance; a closed discourse which the novel can only suggest we resist.

The opening titles show Ruth manoeuvring her way among beauty products and models, which invites the viewer to support her self-projection as a freak. The viewer is situated as a witness to Ruth's 'deformity' and implicitly invited to sympathise with her efforts to conform to the role model of femininity. The sad fact of the novel is that Ruth, seeing that her body militates against her, is prepared to control that body and transform it into something more socially fitting. The waste involved reminds the reader of the acceptance of such mutilation and wasted potential within society's gender images. The film makes it possible not only to ignore the implications behind this deforming construct but also to see Ruth's adoption of this as cause for celebration. The film-Ruth's loss is unambiguously her gain. Her potential for power has been channelled into a designated route, that of equally categorised 'power woman'. The film's final image is of a fully made-up, self-confident and happy woman surrounded by women who, presumably, have also 'found themselves'. Ruth has been made safe, defused by providing her with a new 'satisfying' role in the power struggle. The music supporting the final credits augments this reading, through its nod to feminism in 'You can have him,

I don't want him' and 'I will survive'. The ending effects a
closure on any discussion that the narrative might have
produced. This woman is to be admired unequivocally, which is
a restructuring of Weldon's ambiguous ending, the openness of
which insists upon debate and engagement. The novel presupposes this engagement, the film destroys any need for it, the
viewer merely becoming a witness to actions which have already
been defined as conventional.

The three texts have shown how changes are made in order to
fit them for popular consumption. Vases have become the more
homely tea-sets, conducive to the domesticity of the television
experience or, in *She-Devil's* case, to the 'Hollywood' audience.
Changes in perspective are not necessarily a bad thing. As Winterson's Deuteronomy chapter states, 'the lens can be tinted,
tilted, smashed'.[43] What we have to assess is the damage caused.

Notes and References

1. Phillippa Giles and Vicky Licorish eds *Debut On Two: A
   Guide to Writing for Television* London: BBC 1990 p. 59.
2. For fuller discussion of the theory and practice of TV and
   film see especially Robert Giddings, Keith Selby and Chris
   Wensley *Screening the Novel: The Theory and Practice of
   Literary Dramatization* London: Macmillan 1990; John
   Tulloch *Television Drama: Agency, Audience and Myth*
   London: Routledge 1990; Helen Baehr and Gillian Dyer eds
   Boxed In: Women and Television London: Pandora 1987; Tony
   Bennet et al eds *Popular Television and Film* London: British
   Film Institute in association with the The Open University
   Press 1981.
3. Giddings et al *Screening* 1990 p. 2.
4. David Morley 'Changing Paradigms in Audience Studies',
   Blaubeuren Symposium 1987 quoted in Tulloch *Television
   Drama* 1990 p. 19.
5. John Ellis *Visible Fictions* London: Routledge 1982 p. 167.
6. Geoffrey Wagner *The Novel and the Cinema* Rutherford, New
   Jersey: Farleigh Dickinson University Press 1975 quoted in
   Giddings et al *Screening* 1990 p. 19.
7. Giddings et al *Screening* 1990 p. 22.
8. Ibid. p. 23.
9. Jeanette Winterson *Oranges Are Not the Only Fruit* London:
   Pandora Press 1985, Vintage 1991. Serialised by the BBC,
   1989, starring Emily Aston and Charlotte Coleman as Jess
   and Geraldine McEwan as the mother.
10. Fay Weldon *The Cloning of Joanna May* London: Fontana
    1990. Screened by Granada, 1992, starring Patricia Hodge as
    Joanna and Brian Cox as Carl.

11. Fay Weldon *The Life and Loves of a She-Devil* London: Coronet 1984. Serialised by the BBC, 1986, starring Julie T. Wallace as Ruth, Patricia Hodge as Mary Fisher and Dennis Waterman as Bobbo. Filmed by Orion Pictures, 1990, starring Roseanne Barr as Ruth, Meryl Streep as Mary Fisher and Ed Begley Jr as Bob.
12. Video blurb.
13. Giles and Licorish *Debut* 1990 p. 59.
14. Winterson *Oranges* 1985: the heroine of the novel is called Jeanette, but is Jess in the serial.
15. Winterson *Oranges* Introduction to 1991 Vintage edition p. xiv.
16. Ibid.
17. Giles and Licorish *Debut* 1990 p. 60.
18. Ibid.
19. Ibid.
20. Winterson *Oranges* 1991 p. 106.
21. Ibid. pp. 91–2.
22. Ibid. pp. 164–8.
23. Ibid. Introduction p. xiv.
24. Ibid.
25. Ibid. p. xiii.
26. Ibid. p. xiv.
27. Fay Weldon *The Cloning of Joanna May* 1990, video blurb.
28. Ibid. publisher's publicity material.
29. Ibid. pp. 324–6.
30. Ibid. p. 65.
31. Ibid. p. 103.
32. Ibid. p. 69.
33. Ibid. p. 263.
34. Ibid. p. 264.
35. Ibid. p. 9.
36. Ibid. p. 260.
37. Ibid. p. 348
38. *City Limits* 20 January 1984.
39. Weldon *She-Devil* 1984 p. 240.
40. Ibid.
41. Ibid. Orion Pictures publicity material.
42. Sonia M. Livingstone, *Making Sense of Television: The Psychology of Audience Interpretation* Oxford: Pergamon 1990 Chapter 2 'The Active Viewer'.
43. Winterson *Oranges* 1991 p. 93.

PART TWO

GENDER AND GENRE

CHAPTER 7

Love and Marriage in the Works of Winifred Holtby

Sally Brown

Winifred Holtby (1898–1935) was an extremely prolific writer who, in addition to producing six novels and two volumes of short stories, wrote a considerable number of essays, articles and journalistic pieces, as well as a satirical work *The Astonishing Island*, poetry, letters and criticism. She is probably best remembered as the writer of *South Riding* and as the friend of Vera Brittain, who recorded aspects of their relationship in her moving biography of Holtby *Testament of Friendship*. *South Riding* was reissued by Virago in January 1988 and it is still widely read; her other five novels are also published by Virago. After some years of neglect Holtby's work is currently being re-evaluated both in the field of literature and in the political arena, particularly with regard to her work for feminism and for international peace.

This chapter will range across the extent of Holtby's work, looking in the first instance at her work within the context of the times in which she wrote, then exploring the theme of romantic love as she portrayed it, and finishing with an examination of how marriage is shown to be highly problematic in her fiction, as in contemporary life.

Holtby is a writer who seems to have affected all those with whom she came into contact, politically and intellectually as well as socially. Her work has been alluded to in many works about the period and its literature, although rarely has she been made the central focus of analysis and criticism.

Spinsters and Wives

At a time when many writers, male and female, found the whole arena of sexual politics problematic, Holtby seemed fascinated by the near impossibility of satisfactory relationships between men and women, a theme that is prominent in her fiction as well as in her political writing, and, it seems, in her private life as well. Characters in Holtby's novels, especially women, seem to experience serious difficulties whether they marry or remain single.

In the period between the two world wars much attention

was paid to the changing role of women in society, and in particular to the group dubbed 'surplus women'. The 1921 census indicated a female majority of 1.7 million, compared with a 1911 figure of 1.3 million, and this majority rose to closer to 2 million following the ravages of an epidemic of Spanish flu.[1] Sexologists of the period described the potentially terrible results of the thwarted sexual impulses of women without access to sexual intercourse, which, it was suggested, would lead to the atrophy of women's sexual organs, depression, bitterness and manhating. A male sexologist, A.M. Ludovici, in *Lysistrata or Women's Future and Future Women*,[2] described the phenomenon and linked it to the dangers that feminism posed for marriage, undermining the whole institution by spreading the doctrine that women could manage quite happily without marriage:

> As the number of these women increases every year, and, in their systematic depreciation of the value of life, they are joined and supported by thousands of disillusioned married women who also scoff at marriage and motherhood as the only satisfactory calling for women, swell with imposing rapidity.

Ludovici's critique and that of many other writers was founded on the conviction that only in the proper domestic sphere could women find an appropriate outlet for femininity. Women such as Charlotte Haldane in *Motherhood and its Enemies* (1972)[3] were very concerned at the harmful psychological, emotional and physical effects of virginity, and even feminist writers like Stella Browne and Rebecca West focused principally on the problems of the spinster without access to full heterosexual relationships.

Holtby, in her work of criticism on Virginia Woolf, pointed out the irony of the fact that:

> at the very moment when an artist might have climbed out of the traditional limitations of domestic obligation by claiming to be a human being, she was thrust back into them by the full authority of the psychologist. A woman, she was told, must enjoy the full cycle of sex experience, or she would become riddled with complexes like rotting fruit.[4]

In *The Female Malady, Women, Madness and English Culture 1830–1980* [5] Elaine Showalter describes the way in which hysteria was seen as a particular female sickness, linked with sexual problems such as frustration, at least until the problem of shellshock – leading to similar symptoms in men – was fully recognised in the post-war period. In the chapter 'Feminism and Hysteria – The Daughter's Disease' she comments on the tendency by doctors to label rebellious, unconventional and independent women as hysterical.

In the period in which Holtby was writing, the whole issue of whether or not women should or could marry was being widely re-evaluated and the phenomenon of the unmarried female was seen as a new and potentially disruptive social force. This anxiety about the growth in the number of unmarried women in the post World War One period was compounded by the unease that many (particularly men) felt about the success of the Women's Suffrage movement, which gave an extremely limited franchise to some women in 1918 and led to growing expectations of equal pay, equal opportunities and equal education for women. The phenomenon of the modern woman was one which exercised the minds of many contemporary thinkers and writers who presupposed, rather prematurely, that this new category of independent women within society heralded the collapse of western civilisation. Holtby effectively satirises this anxiety in the chapter 'I Succeed in my Quest for a True Woman' in the *Astonishing Island* [6] 'by having her hero confront a range of stereotypes of modern women. He finds himself totally confused by the categories 'Mother', 'Vamp', 'Modern Girl', 'Gold Digger', a confusion mirrored in the society (a barely disguised England of the 1920s) in which he finds himself.

Certainly this was a period in which the role of women was being more closely and seriously examined than previously; the sexual licence that prevailed in the war years had shocked and excited popular imagination, and there was widespread public discussion of sexual issues. The effective campaigns by women to promote moral reform and continence in men at the end of the nineteenth century and beyond have been well documented.[7] By campaigning at the end of the nineteenth-century against sexual abuse of women and children, and particularly in the action to reform the Contagious Diseases Acts of the 1860s, women gained considerable knowledge of matters that had been taboo until then, as well as experience in public action, and this carried through into the interwar years. Additionally the social climate that looked less harshly on sexual indiscretions committed when soldiers were about to go off and die at the front carried over to some extent into the 1920s and 1930s, although the dual standard for men and women prevailed.

Information on conscious control of reproduction also became more accessible at this time. Although contraception had been widely available in Britain for the upper class at least since the 1870s, it wasn't until the pioneering work of Marie Stopes and her contemporaries of the interwar years that it became readily available to the ordinary working-class women of Britain, as Sheila Rowbotham describes in *A New World for Women: Stella Browne Socialist Feminist*.[8]

All these matters together tended to foreground the whole issue of marriage – its desirability, its structure, its basis and its future in a period of social change – and this tended to be reflected in the novels of the period, not just in those of Holtby but in a range of writers like May Sinclair, Rebecca West and Virginia Woolf, who saw the battleground/playground of marriage as an area of central interest.

Many writers of the period found a central and engrossing focus in the exploration of the minefield of sexual relationships. In serious fiction as well as in romantic novels, writers were examining the ways in which partnerships developed and progressed in the climate of social change. The growing awareness of psychology, with the light this threw on motivation and sexual behaviour, affected the work of writers as diverse as D.H. Lawrence, E.M. Forster and Rebecca West, often with marriage as a central issue.

For Virginia Woolf the sexual politics of relationships was a crucial strand in novels such as To the Lighthouse[9] and Mrs Dalloway.[10] Mrs Ramsay's status in the narrative of To the Lighthouse is established largely through her relationship with her husband, a relationship that is problematic because he requires her to lose her individuality in her acceptance of the female role of wife and mother, though her charisma is so strong that she remains the central persona in the novel long after her death. Clarissa Dalloway exists in a permanent state of siege in her society, protecting her ego from disintegration by a complex pattern of behaviour. She has deliberately chosen to marry Richard Dalloway rather then Peter Walsh because it was possible with Richard to keep a certain distance between them:

> For in marriage a little licence, a little independence there must be between people living together day in day out in the same house, which Richard gave her and she him. Where was he this morning, for instance? Some committee, she never asked what. But with Peter everything had to be shared, everything gone into. And it was intolerable.[11]

Marriage for Clarissa Dalloway threatens ego engulfment, a threat that is exemplified by the loss even of her own name on marriage. To survive, she must withhold herself, withdrawing progressively into a safe, protected world in her own home, living nominally within the institution of marriage but not subscribing whole-heartedly to it.

The realisation that marriage was not without its dangers and problems was by no means a new one in the period in which these writers were working, but other factors threw it into sharp focus. Developments in the field of work for women through the end of the nineteenth century and into the twentieth, for example, gave middle-class women an opportunity to consider alternatives to the role of wife and mother.

In the interwar years attitudes to women working continued to be ambiguous, vacillating between the belief that the proper sphere for the unmarried woman of quality was the domestic environment and the economic necessity for the unsupported spinster to earn her own living. While thousands of women continued to work in the fields of medicine, clerical work, the law, education, the arts, literature and religion at this time,[12] there was always pressure on them to regard themselves as deviant from the 'normative' femininity of women in the family home.

During World War One women had taken over from men many high-profile occupations; they worked as skilled engineers, munitions workers, drivers of buses and cars and as agricultural labourers, thus releasing men for the front, and this was regarded as something of a novelty. Of course, working-class women had always been participants in the workforce in both heavy and light industry as well as in domestic and agricultural work, and this pattern had been only slightly modified by the nineteenth-century Factory Acts which restricted women's and children's work in certain categories such as coal mining.

The novelty of the situation during World War One was that upper- and middle-class women were taken out of the suffocating atmosphere of the drawing room and given opportunities to be socially useful, whether as nursing auxiliaries like Holtby herself, or in productive or servicing occupations. After the war considerable social pressure was placed on these women to withdraw from paid labour in order to enable the returning soldiers to find employment in the steadily worsening work environment of the post-war slump.

In order to persuade women to give up the relative freedom of the workplace and return to the domestic spheres much effort was put into promoting ideas of 'proper' femininity and the incompatibility of this with a professional career. Marriage was promoted as the only really acceptable career for women, and both men and women spoke out in favour of the desirability of women reverting to the role of 'Angel in the house', a role from which women could most properly influence the future of the nation through home and family. The term 'Angel in the house', used as a shorthand expression to suggest ideal Victorian womanhood, is derived from the poem by Coventry Patmore in which the woman in the domestic environment is idealised as a locus of purity and selfhood emanating outwards from the home into society, stabilising and civilising the harsher outside world. Carol Christ in her article 'Victorian Masculinity and the Angel in the House' describes it thus:

> Experiencing at once the breakdown of faith and the dehumanising pressure of the market place, many Victorian writers relocated these values in the home and the woman who was its centre. It was she who could create a sanctuary both from the anxieties of modern life and also those values or relevant to modern business.[13]

In her journalism Holtby argues against this tendency, comparing the situation in Britain with the draconian situation in Germany where women were being compelled by legislation to give up their jobs to husbands and soldiers.[14] In England, as Martha Vicinus indicates,[15] the pressure on women to release jobs was more subtle but was reinforced by low pay and low morale. In her political writing Holtby fought against this pressure, for example, in an article in the *Manchester Guardian*, 23 November 1928.[16] Here she responds to an article by 'a mere man' writing in a Women's Institute journal who has suggested that women should spend less time at Women's Institutes and more time making their husbands' teas. She supports her comments with statistics from the *American University Women's Journal* to suggest that, where the husband is cooperative, a working wife can enhance the life of the family. Without ignoring the problems, she promotes the advantages of such a life:

> But the husband of a professional woman has great fun in the nursery. He often becomes proficient with baths and toys and prams and drying rails. He may even be the first discoverer of a newly cut tooth, the first to hear a newly spoken word.[17]

Arguing against those who would reinforce conventional sex roles she writes:

> At least we know definitely enough where the other 'ideal' leads us. 'We want men who are men and women who are women,' writes Sir Oswald Mosley. He can find them at their quintessence in the Slave markets of Abyssinia, or in the winding alleys of a Chinese city.[18]

Here as elsewhere she makes a direct link between fascism and anti-feminism, as does Woolf in *Three Guineas*.[19] In a climate which considers the employment of women as short term and second best, Holtby champions the course of women who chose to work, not just as a poor alternative to marriage but as a challenging and satisfying way of life in its own right.

Romance and Love

In the interwar years amid the changing patterns of social behaviour, and despite or perhaps because of the period's more questioning attitudes to sexual relationships, romance was in the air. In her account of the woman's novel between the wars[20] Nicola Beauman examines the kind of books middle-class women were borrowing from the circulating libraries at that time. The author of a 'pretty book' of the period supported established versions of romantic relations and did not have the same preoccupation with negotiating new kinds of male/female relationship as did some of the writers of the period like Virginia Woolf and May Sinclair. However, the tight focus on the interaction between man and woman remained.

The essentials of romantic fiction consist of predictable components that follow established patterns, with the reader able to make assumptions about the outcome. Beauman suggests:

> The basic storyline should be boy meeting girl, various seemingly insuperable difficulties coming between them and, finally, the revelation of their true and hitherto suppressed feelings.[21]

It is always assumed in these novels that ultimately the pair will come together in marriage, the kind of narrative closure frequently found in the novels of the nineteenth century. But whereas, for example, the characters in *Jane Eyre* or *Middlemarch* were expected to have undergone some kind of moral development during the overcoming of the difficulties that divided them, in these romantic novels the function of the process was merely to titillate the reader as a kind of novelistic foreplay before the ultimate consummation of the final embrace.

Beauman describes how writers such as Ethel M. Dell, Elinor Glynn, Georgette Heyer and E.M. Hull, while rarely infringing the laws of censorship with overt sexuality, frequently utilise the language and symbolism of sadomasochism in their depiction of male/female interactions.[22] Heroes tend to be strong, silent, brutal, much given to smouldering looks, violent kisses and rough embraces; heroines tend to have bruised lips, fluttering eyes and trembling hearts. The heroines have all the submissiveness and trembling femininity that psychologists like Stekel[23] could have wished for, as this extract from E.M. Hull's *The Sheik* suggests:

> The flaming light of desire burning in his eyes turned her sick and faint. Her body throbbed with the consciousness of a knowledge that appalled her. She understood his purpose with a horror that made each separate nerve in her system shrink against the understanding that had come to her under the consuming fire of his ardent gaze, and in the fierce embrace

that was drawing her shaking limbs closer and closer against the man's own pulsating body.[24]

The cool English heroine of the novel succumbs eventually to the brute who, having kidnapped her, ignores her resistance to his advances, thereby confirming the dangerous doctrine that women secretly long to be swept off their feet (raped?) by strong silent men, no matter how much they protest to the contrary.

It was not just pulp fiction that was preoccupied with romance; writers like Rosamund Lehman, Vera Brittain and Nancy Mitford were also exploring love and its repercussions in their novels, with 'insuperable difficulties' separating their lovers, including wartime deaths, the married status of one or more partners and an unbreakable social code preventing predictable, happy endings.

Beyond literature, other media were also demonstrating an interest in love; the developing medium of the cinema, for example, had a profound effect on the social climate. Many of the films of the 1920s and 1930s took marriage and its alternatives as a subject. Gloria Swanson, appearing in films such as Paramount's *Don't Change Your Husband*, *For Better for Worse* and *Male and Female*, all made in 1919, has been described as: 'a new kind of women, sumptuously gowned and jewelled, the modern girl (usually a victim) indulging in avant garde morality'.[25]

In 1927, the novel of *Anna Karenina* was filmed as *Love* by Metro Goldwyn Meyer, and remade in 1935 as *Anna Karenina*. In 1928 one of the last silent films made by MGM, *Wickedness Preferred*, appeared with a title sequence stating: 'Marriage is like a cafeteria: you take the first thing that looks good and pay for it later.' [26] Actresses like Clara Bow and Greta Garbo projected an image of a new kind of woman, one who was sexually assured and demanding, and exactly the kind of role model the founders of the fictional Christian Cinema Company in Holtby's *Poor Caroline* were hoping to oppose with their work.

The Rudolph Valentino film *The Sheik*, based on E.M. Hull's novel [27] was made in 1921, the same year that the scandal concerning the rape and murder of the appallingly appropriately named actress Virginia Rappe at a Hollywood party shocked society and ruined the career of Fatty Arbuckel who was accused of the crime.[28]

The cinema, then, brought to ever-widening audiences an opportunity to participate vicariously in a dangerous exciting world of vividly portrayed romantic film narratives with strong sexual overtones. Attendance at cinemas gave middle-class women of the 1920s and 1930s an opportunity to indulge in escapist fantasy in the same kind of way that novels did, but on a more grandiose scale. Romantic fictions were widespread in both prose and film, some carrying dangerously sadomasochistic awareness; Holtby's engagement is somewhat unusual here.

Holtby's novels utilise the theme of romantic love on occasions, but she takes from the genre what she wants and modifies it for her own uses, thus frequently subverting it. She made it clear that she expected her writing to be deemed middlebrow rather than highbrow, making it obvious that by doing so she hoped to appeal to a wider audience than would otherwise be possible.

By using a romantic motif she was able to make her readers feel comfortable within the texts. At the same time, by denying them the conventional closure of the 'happy ending', she caused them to question their own assumptions. In her novels the wedding is only a stage in the narrative, not the end.

As Marion Shaw suggests in her article in *Women's Writing: A Challenge to Theory*,[29] Holtby's novels are within the realist tradition of George Eliot and Mrs Gaskell. Shaw points out that while adhering to the 'realist traditions of documentary verisimilitude and external presentation of nineteenth-century fiction', Holtby, with considerable erudition and political sagacity, developed these traditions producing novels which, while remaining formally within the genre, asked readers to question the position of women in society and their own attitudes to romance. This is not brought about in a heavy-handed way: Holtby self-confessedly abjured polemic in favour of a popular approach. Her technique was subtly to undermine assumption about the construction of gender through an accessible and engaging narrative.

In two of her early novels, *Anderby Wold* and *The Land of Green Ginger*,[30] the central female figure, a married woman, has the balance of her established marital pattern disturbed by the introduction into the household of an outsider who serves to point out the problems within the marriage.

In *Anderby Wold*, despite her Yorkshire pragmatism, Mary Robson harbours romantic dreams. The language describing her love moves beyond the lending-library fictions it echoes, however, proving symbolic. Similarly symbolic, with legendary overtones, are the references and names in *The Land of Green Ginger*, which both echoes and questions the romantic plots, characters and language of the popular fiction of the day. Holtby refuses formulaic developments and conventional closure.

The self-delusive possibilities of romantic love are quite frequently shown in Holtby's work. For example in *Poor Caroline* Caroline Denton-Smythe manages to construct the fantasy of a love between herself and the curate Father Mortimer, based on no more than a throw-away line of his: 'Why, you have helped me, Miss Denton-Smythe. You've given me a lovely thing.' 31

Romantic love in Holtby's novels rarely lives up to expectations. In *The Crowded Street*33 what seems like a perfect love match, that between Martin Eliot and Delia, is inevitably destroyed when Connie's calculating attempts to secure the love of Eric by becoming his mistress result in self-hatred and feelings of cheapness when she believes him married, and leads to her loveless marriage to Ben. Muriel's love for Godfrey, encouraged to desperation by her mother, has a single moment of bliss when he kisses her after the air raid at Scarborough. But his neglect of her over the long period from this time until after his engagement to Clare has fallen through gives her time to decide upon her own future, so that ultimately she rejects his proposal in order to retain her hard-won autonomy. It is as if the fragile plant of romance is incapable of survival for long periods of time unsustained.

One is reminded to Holtby's short story 'Lovers' Meeting' in *The Truth is Not Sober* 34 where a long-awaited reunion is marred by the returning wanderer having no recollection of the woman he left behind. The still girl-like Kate, unmarked by the 14 years that have left her contemporaries with 'their faces lined and their bodies slack from child bearing and constant overwork'35 is free to marry a loyal local suitor, freed at last from an impossible dream of what might have been. Thus the ideal of romance is frequently shown to be much better than its actuality.

South Riding 36 Holtby's last novel, published posthumously, develops the problematics of romantic love in interesting directions, making use of an unusual narrative structure and utilising extracts from council minutes to focus on events in public and private arenas. As often happens in her novels, in *South Riding* one's expectations both in terms of narrative development and character progression are regularly challenged, and the reader is required to examine basic assumptions. For example, the novel focuses in the first place on a reporter Lovell Brown, who seems to have a central importance in the novel at this stage but who subsequently emerges as a very minor character. This compares, for example, with the way in *The Land of Green Ginger* the novel opens with the character of Edith Burton who, far from becoming the central focus, dies in Chapter 2.

Another original aspect of *South Riding* is the choice of non-traditional central characters. The reader is not offered a wilting flower of a heroine and a Byronic male hero but is introduced instead to:

a plump sturdy little women, whose rounded features looked as though they had been battered blunt by wear and weather in sixty years or more of hard experience ... She was seventy two years old, a farmer's daughter, and had lived in South Riding all her life.[37]

Anyone opening the novel and expecting to find a story within the romantic tradition might well find her a rather surprising central figure, and the principal character of the novel, Sarah Burton, introduced subsequently, has several unexpected aspects too. Not only is she a prospective headmistress, MA, BLitt, but she has 'astonishing crimson red hair' and ankles 'as slender as a gazelle' [38] and she is thirty-nine years old.

Robert Carne, the man upon whom both women concentrate their affections, is a Lawrentian rather than a traditionally romantic figure, but he too is well past the first flush of youth, and he is a failure both as a farmer and as a local politician. Like Szermai in *The Land of Green Ginger* he has disturbing and distressing/aggressive associations with are tied up with his masculinity.

Much of the characterisation of Carne, however, would not be out of place in a Georgette Heyer novel; like Szermai, he is a big, dark, unhappy looking man, and his face is described as being not unlike a photograph of Mussolini,[39] a detail by which Holtby again makes a link between male oppression and fascism (pace Plath). Like many a conventional hero, he is landed, though not wealthy, associated with horses, strong, silent, kind to animals and married to a mad wife. With Carne, as with Szermai, how-ever, the masculine powerfulness is ambivalent, seen not simply as a desirable symbol of virility but also as a threatening force for evil, since his marital rape certainly has some responsibility for his wife's insanity.[40]

By portraying these two characters in terms of the romantic hero, and then allowing the reader to see their shortcomings, Holtby is perhaps signalling that they represent a dying species. Significantly both men are associated with the setting sun – Szermai is first seen by Joanna at sunset[41] and Carne falls to his death on the cliff top recognising in the blazing sky a reminder of Sarah Burton's 'brave oriflamme of hair'.[42]

In *South Riding* the relationship between Sarah Burton and Robert Carne is complex. In this novel the power of sexual desire is made much more overt, and romantic love is shown far less in terms of wish fulfilment than in terms of a necessary human interaction. Sarah and Carne are drawn to each other despite wide personal and political differences (like Mary Robson and David Rossiter, in *Anderby Wold*) and their attraction for each other has the opportunity to come to fruition only through a chance encounter in a hotel in Manchester.

Even here, however, love is portrayed by Holtby in ambiguous terms: it is clear that Carne has a different viewpoint from Sarah's; for him love is little more than an opportunity to be seized, whereas for her it is a chance to fulfil her secret desires. Sarah's behaviour is uncharacteristically bold for the period, but Holtby uncharacteristically withholds from the characters and the readers the consummation of their passion, as Carne becomes seriously ill.

The reader is left in no doubt at the end of the novel that Sarah Burton has been enriched by the experience of loving Carne, even though he had been killed in a riding accident before the opportunity for a reconciliation. It is interesting to note how often Holtby's romantic hero figures come to a sticky and often brutal end: David Rossiter is murdered; Martin Ellis is killed in the war; Robert Carne falls off a cliff on horseback. This is an interesting reversal of the plots of Victorian novels where the woman frequently pays for her behaviour by untimely death.

It seems, then, that Holtby valorises an idea of romantic love in her writing, holding it up as an idea to be strived for but suggesting that its existence is much rarer than is commonly believed. Nevertheless she seems to have an incurably romantic aspect to her personality; her novels reflect a poignant belief, like that of Tennyson, that it is better to have loved and lost than to have never loved at all. This mirrors to some extent the feelings she had about the man, Bill, with whom she had an intermittent relationship through her own life. Vera Brittain in *Testament of Friendship*[43] quotes a letter of Holtby's in which she says:

> I returned to find a letter from Bill inviting himself down for the day on Thursday. I never asked him. I want and don't want him. I want to work ... I took myself vigorously in hand that evening, and decided that if I couldn't have what I wanted, I would want what I could have. It is undignified and ridiculous to regret or complain, and I'm damned if I won't enjoy everything ... I have written across my heart: 'I will not be dismayed.' And the curious result is that, at the moment I am not. After all, it is living and not being loved which is the vitalising experience. I will give him everything that he is prepared to take, though I think that is very little, and be thankful that at least I have known what it is to love.

She seems to have been prepared to accept the heartache and humiliation that the relationship brought, largely because it seemed to satisfy a need within herself to retain a belief in her own romantic capability. In her novels her heroines share this need, even though the price of romance can for them be literal or metaphorical crippling or death.

Marriage and Millstones

Changing attitudes to marriage in the interwar years led to increased expectation by both men and women which in turn led to a questioning of just how achievable was marital happiness. The ideal Victorian marriage, with its concentration on financial, societal and dynastic concerns, did not encourage high expectations, but psychologists and sexologists increasingly gave prominence to the role of sexual intercourse and the necessity for women to respond actively.

According to contemporary sources [44] there was a decline in the use of prostitutes in the first two decades of the twentieth century, largely because of increased knowledge of and concern about venereal disease brought about by the earlier campaign against the Contagious Diseases Act and the spread of information during World War One.

Freudian psychologists such as Wilhelm Stekel in *Frigidity in Woman in Relation to her Lovelife*[42] estimated that as many as 50 per cent of women suffered from what he described as 'sexual impotence' or 'deficient sexual sensibility' as a result of their repression and, in many cases, homosexual tendencies, which needed treatment to 'improve' attitudes to men. Stekel and others linked women's frigidity with feminism and went to great lengths to suggest the dire physiological and psychological effects of incomplete heterosexuality.

The 'companionate marriage', which could offer love, a mature physical relationship and friendship between men and women, was the ideal towards which couples were encouraged to strive in the 1920s and 1930s. Holtby consistently questions the viability of marriage – she seems uncertain about whether the institution has anything valuable to offer women, and is dubious, too, of its effect on men – yet there is a distinct ambiguity in her attitude, for marriages in her novels are described in terms of how far they deviate from a putative ideal, which presupposes that such an ideal might exist.

In her wide-reaching book *Archetypal Patterns in Women's Fiction*[46] Annis Pratt describes the way in which marriage is portrayed in novels of the nineteenth and twentieth centuries in terms of suffocation, dwarfing and mental illness, citing such examples as the dehumanised, insane wife Antoinette Rochester in Charlotte Brontë's *Jane Eyre* and the suffocating entrapment of Dorothy Brooke in her marriage to the sickly Casaubon in *Middlemarch*: 'In novels of marriage, similar archetypes occur, the authors depicting matrimony as one of the primary tools for dulling a hero's initiative and restraining her maturation.' [47] She posits the view that in the woman's Bildungsroman the wife is coerced into growing down rather than up, moulded into conformism in the same way that aristocratic Chinese women's feet were bound to make them conform to views of ideal feminine beauty. She suggests that the widely heralded sexual emancipation of the 1920s was as likely to free a woman for further enslavement as to encourage sexual freedom, and that an escape into madness was often the only available final resort.

In *The Crowded Street* Muriel's dilemma is entirely due to the fact that she is perceived by herself and others as having only one goal in life, marriage. Ideally this should be to as prosperous and as personable a man as possible, but ultimately any marriage would be better than none. Her sister Connie in desperation uses the sexual freedom that wartime conditions provide to ensnare a man into marriage, initially the socially acceptable Eric, but then in desperation the unspeakable inappropriate Ben, resulting in her pregnancy.

In a desperate outpouring, she blames primarily her mother but ultimately the system that she supports:

> And you wouldn't let us work, or go away or have any other interests, because you were afraid of our spoiling our chances of a good marriage. And if we didn't get partners at dances, we were beastly failures. And if our friends attracted more attention than us, they were sent away. And it was all because of our healthy homely influence, wasn't it, mother? And now that one of us has taken the only means she saw to fulfil your wishes and get married, you aren't sorry, and if I'd been successful, you wouldn't have been angry, would you, mother?[48]

Connie thus exposes the hypocrisy and cant of a society that valorises marriage above all else. In order to maintain a facade of respectability she is forced by her parents to marry Ben, despite her absolute and declared opposition. Ultimately the power of family and society is too much for her, she marries but courts disaster by her rash behaviour and ultimately dies of pneumonia, like many of her novelistic forebears. At the riverside in the rain when she is contemplating suicide she says to Muriel: 'It wasn't as if I hadn't tried other things. I wanted to chicken farm, I wanted to go away and just do anything. But mother wouldn't let me. It was just men, men, men, and make a good match.' [49]

Entrapment and constriction, then, are seen as central elements in Holtby's view of matrimony: but it isn't just women who have their roles predetermined. The short story 'The Wronged Woman' in *Pavements at Anderby* [50] tells the tale of three wasted lives: the woman who entraps a doctor in wartime into marrying her by offering him consolation then letting him believe she is pregnant; the colleague whom he really loves, who also becomes pregnant by him; and the doctor himself who cannot free himself from a loveless marriage, bound as he is by societal norms and conventional expectations.

In *The Crowded Street* Muriel is free to realise her selfhood only when she declines Godfrey Neale's proposal in order to continue her autonomous single existence. Her choice is a strong indication of her developed political consciousness, showing her view that women can and should expect more from life than a stultifying marriage.

Happy marriages are rarely shown by Holtby as being an attainable goal; the prospectively ideal marriage of Delia and Martin Eliot, with each respecting each other's intellectual professional and social needs for space within the union is, Holtby suggests, inevitably destroyed by his death. The outwardly successful marriage of Muriel's parents is disfigured by Mr Hammond's adultery, and the engagement of Godfrey Neale and Clare Duquesne is called off because of the obvious gross disparity between their views of the function of marriage. The cause of this failure is demonstrated primarily as being a reluctance of women to continue to perform in traditionally wifely patterns. Having tried the flamboyant and original Clare, Godfrey then moves on to Muriel, and surprised by her refusal (it has never crossed his mind that she might), it is hinted that he will then move on to the mouselike Phyllis Marshall Gurney who is less likely to assert her own needs:

> As he watched her [Muriel] go, an expression of tenderness, regret and compassion crossed his face. He sighed a little. Perhaps she was right. A wife with ideas? How queer women were! It seemed as though he, who knew himself to be sought after, only wanted what he could never gain. He felt older and a little weary. Certainly it would be good to go where he was wanted, to have his vanity soothed by a simple, loving woman who would accept him as he was.[51]

It is symptomatic that Godfrey Neale sees no need to change himself or reconsider his own demands (he wanted a custodian for his family inheritance as much as a wife) and continues to look for 'a simple loving woman' (without ideas).

Thus traditional marital patterns are seen as potentially restricting and confining for husbands, too. In another of her stories, 'The Perfect Wife' [52] Holtby suggests that perhaps the ideal matrimonial partner is not such a desirable personality as might have been imagined. In the story, two former schoolfriends meet and discuss how far their schoolgirl ambitions have been achieved. Doris has succeeded in becoming a neurologist, and Cathie has become a successful trainer of racehorses as she had planned. They discuss the third member of their group, Mimi, who had declared that her only ambition was to be a perfect wife. Cathie discovers from Doris that Mimi has been such a perfect wife that she has mollycoddled and fussed her husband into a hypochondriac early grave, and at the end of the tale Cathie returns home only just in time to prevent her own ex-husband being perfect-wifed to death by the vampire-like Mimi.

The ultimate marriage in *Mandoa! Mandoa!* [53] between Jean Stanbury and Maurice Durant is portrayed as a particularly down-beat affair. Holtby seems to be suggesting that only marriages based on realistic and fairly low-level expectations can hope to succeed. This is a bleak portrait of the future of marriage as the pragmatic partnership of realistically minded people who trade needs with one another. Romance and passion seem to play no part in this view.

Perhaps Holtby's most extreme condemnation of the institution of marriage is in the novel *South Riding*, where a broad cross-section of marriages are serially anatomised and shown to be destructive, dehumanising and dismal. The central marriage in the novel is the unfortunate union between Robert and Muriel Carne. Both partners are blighted by the results of their elope-ment, and it is hard to say who comes off worst. Muriel Carne is effectively dehumanised, incarcerated in a mental hospital and reduced to a non-life by the loss of everything she holds most dear: her vivacity, her physical attractiveness, her riding, her selfhood. She cannot even recognise Robert. He, too, loses just about everything. Having ruined himself financially to keep her in a private hospital in accordance with his view of her station, he is still unable to redeem his 'crime' in his own eyes which is: 'the one occasion when he had forced himself upon her, taking by violence what her whim refused.' [54]

He never really knew whether or not it was this action that resulted in the conception of their daughter, Midge, and which in turn precipitated Muriel into insanity, but he: 'longed for proof that this ... had not been the final cause of her destruction.' [55] As a result of this, he is totally disempowered by his guilt:

> He knew that women found him attractive, and he liked them.
> These brief and casual encounters had made the bitter tragedy
> of his marriage bearable. They meant nothing to him after they
> were over but a certain flattery, a certain gratitude, a certain
> memory of passing pleasure.[56]

This disempowerment, by which I mean the way in which he has literally and metaphorically been deprived of the capacity to act as he wishes because of the conditioning of the society and environ-ment in which he lives, is demonstrated by his inability to carry

through to coition the encounter with Sarah Burton. Physically he
is prevented from consummation by an angina attack, but the
psychological subtext of the situation is obvious to the reader. He
says in a weakly hilarious manner: 'This is just like one of those
what-d'you-call-its in a moral story book.' [57] He is nevertheless able
to draw from the situation the emotional succour he needs: 'Let me
rest,' he says, 'And don't go.' [58]

Physically, too, he draws strength from Sarah: 'he lay back
limply with his head on her breast ... he still held her hand',[59] and
this is regardless of *her* physical comfort. She was 'pierced with
cold', her hand lifeless with cramp' while he lay dreaming of his
wife. For Sarah it is a devastating experience which almost ruins
her life, while for him it is an embarrassing and humiliating
moment, but after a short while a closed episode.

Holtby's attitude to the apportioning of blame in the devastating results of this marriage is ambiguous; she makes it clear that
his single, brutal act is responsible for Muriel's insanity (at least
in his own eyes), but at the same time she stresses the responsibility Muriel bears for elopement (it is clear that she initiated it
in the first place). Muriel, it is suggested, has been unfaithful to
Carne and volatile, to say the least, before her pregnancy. What is
quite unambiguous, however, is the implication that their marriage is the source of the undoing of both participants.

Other marriages in the novel are also seen in a jaundiced light.
Emma Beddows, a pillar of the community and a most positively
observed character, is disappointed in her marriage to Jim Beddows:

> She had gone to Jim Beddows in love with his brisk efficient
> geniality expecting him to prove a gallant lover and a stalwart
> companion. She found him a man of straw, mean, ungenerous,
> jealous, hugging his little grievances and grudges, rejoicing
> when other men could lose a fortune, but lacking the enter-
> prise himself to make one. Emma's first two babies died at
> seven weeks, and in both cases she was sure they could have
> been saved if her husband's economics had not included the
> prohibition of medical advice. For years she had thought her
> hatred and unhappiness irremediable.[60]

Emma Beddows, however, is shown not to be the kind of woman
who would permit this to ruin her life. Instead, it is implied, she
has put all her energies into her public life, sublimating her
unhappiness into effective public service. Her indomitable character is exemplified by the way in which at 72 she still thinks of
herself as a young woman, and wears purple pansies to enliven
her velvet toque.

Lily Sawden's marriage is, quite literally, the death of her. Her
misguided wifely loyalty to Tom, which makes her conceal her

cancer so that he can go ahead with the plan to run the Nag's Head, means that by the time she consults the doctor it is too late. The failure of communication between them is total. She represses the urge:

> to scream out to him her secret telling him that she had let herself be crucified upon his simple vanity, that if she had stayed in Leeds she could have been spared this agony. It maddened her that he should be so blind, so childish, so complacent of his masculine strength and patience. He thought that he was being so very good to her.[61]

His insensitivity is such that he buys her an Alsatian dog to keep her company; her wilful self-martyrdom is such that she never reveals to him how much she hates the dog, and she does not tell him the depth of her pain and illness until just before she dies, when it is too late to do anything about it.

Annie Holly's death is also directly related to her marriage. Her husband's sexual incontinence, inflicting on her the final pregnancy, forbidden by the doctor, leads to her death in childbirth, and the outcome is the prospective ruin of their daughter Lydia's chances, too: 'maybe it will finish me ... then that'll finish you too. You'll have to quit your grand school and come home to look after the kids.' [62] Their neighbours, the Mitchells, are ruined too by an unwanted conception for which Mrs Mitchell entirely blames her husband. It is the pregnancy that drags them down from their attempts at genteel poverty to the National Assistance Board, and it is the final straw, Mr Mitchell having lost his job, that ruins their life together.

Councillor Huggins, it is suggested, would never have become involved with Bessy Warbuckle, thus leaving him open to blackmail, had his marriage been a success:

> His affair with Bessy Warbuckle had never pleased him. At best it had been futile and shameful fumbling in the dark plantation – not love but a restless appetite; not discovery but a quest for something that he had never found ... It was not possible for a man like Huggins to conduct his personal life perpetually as though it were a public meeting. Nelly was no wife to him. And she wore her mouse-coloured hair imprisoned in a hideous net that was enough to put off any man.[63]

It is his wife's sexual unavailability (symbolised by the hair net, that he later removes) which is seen as being at the root of his indiscreet behaviour, and his problematic marriage is the source of his failure in public life.

It is not simply marriage itself that Holtby suggests is inevitably destructive, but principally the sexual and progenitive functions of the institution. The marriage of Jessie Brimsley and the widowed Barnabus Holly is shown positively (in liberating Lydia Holly and solving the problem with Jessie's son Ned) largely because sexual issues are not centralised in the relationship. As Lydia thinks:

> But this Mrs Brinsley could look after the children. She would release Lydia of a burden. She would be kind to them. She had superfluous energy which mother had lost in her battle against poverty and dirt and nature. Mrs Brinsley would be more fortunate. Her own years for childbearing were over. She would give the family the good humoured indulgence of a granny.[64]

In *South Riding* it is the women, for the most part, who supply the strength and dynamism to keep marriages, and hence society, functioning. In many of Holtby's novels the conventional view of the male/female role is reversed, and men are shown as the weaker sex who depend on their womenfolk to support and direct them.

In *Anderby Wold* the dynamics of the marriage depend entirely upon the strength of character of Mary Robson. As in many nineteenth-century novels, a marriage of convenience has been made between a younger dynamic woman and her older unromantic cousin, John, and the intrusion of an outsider, David Rossiter, disturbs the equilibrium. It is a loveless marriage, contracted for the woman's benefit (she needs John to labour on the farm to pay off the mortgage her father took out) rather than for the man's benefit, as in many conventional marriages of convenience.

His dependence on her is absolute; he relies on her ability to organise their life and make decisions even before the stroke that disables him towards the end of the novel. At the meal in Chapter 2 where the family are gathered to celebrate the final mortgage payment, for example, she is called upon to make a speech of thanks when her husband is overwhelmed by the situation. This she does competently and effectively, reinforcing further the assembled relatives' view of who wears the trousers in the household. A central part of her frustration with her husband is his insularity, his predictability and his total submission to her will: 'Oh I can't stop her. If she wants to do anything she will ...' [65]

Her attempt to arouse him into some kind of reaction by her gift of David Rossiter's radical book on agriculture (which has excited and disturbed her) falls totally flat.[66] After his stroke he abdicates total control to her in all matters to do with the farm, the strike and their life together. She realises that this is all she has to look forward to:

This would be her life, thought Mary. She would always have
John's large and ineffective figure beside her. His 'Very well,
honey, you know best' would greet every decision that she
made. She would always have the long days at Anderby and
the short hours by the sea, and the homeward road winding
before her in the fading light. There would always be the dull
absence of expectation that rewards those who have realised
their ambitions, and, later there would be failing energy and
old age ...[67]

The third member of the triangle is interestingly presented by
Holtby as problematically dependent on Mary also. One might
expect the novelist to heighten the contrast between the
husband and the younger man by making Rossiter the opposite
of John, with a strong community of interest with Mary to
heighten the reader's awareness of the claustrophobic partnership of the marriage. But while David Rossiter is presented as
vital, exciting, romantic and different, once again the power
dynamics of the relationship are portrayed unconventionally.

Their first meeting in the darkness on the road with a lame pony
offers an opportunity for the stranger to offer masculine assistance
in a situation reminiscent of many first male/female encounters in
novels (one thinks of Hardy and Lawrence). However, David's
behaviour could scarcely be described as masterful or potent; significantly his penknife blade is broken and he is knocked to the
ground by the pony when he takes the stone out of the hoof.
Compare this with the first encounters in Women in Love,[68] for
example, where the man on horseback towers above the women on
the road, and the power relationships are established early. The
figure of Robert Carne on horseback in South Riding is much closer
to Lawrentian symbolic portrayal of a manly figure on horseback.

After helping Mary with the horse, David is sick in the road
(hardly heroic behaviour) and she then takes him back to the farm,
despite his assertion that as a capitalist farmer she is his sworn
enemy and he a rabid socialist of a dangerous and most disreputable
type:

> 'You are nothing so romantic' retorted Mary. 'You are quite a
> young boy with a bad cold who has just been sick in the
> middle of the road and you are coming home with me.
> Evidently you are unfit to be wandering about the Wolds by
> yourself. I don't care whether you're a socialist or not. If
> you're rabid, it just shows that you are not capable of looking
> after yourself.' [69]

Their whole relationship is characterised by the quasi-maternal
nature of Mary's reaction. (It is significant that Mary's child-
lessness is one of the reasons why Mary's in-laws are so
unsympathetic to her and so critical of her behaviour.)

David is swept away by her to the farm, dressed in oversized pyjamas that emphasise his smallness, and placed in an enormous bed. In this way he is reduced to an infantile state, and Mary's self-deluding feelings are made quite overt:

> A sudden desire had seized her to kiss this absurd, fragile boy whose mocking wistful eyes watched her from the pillows. Only he might mistake her strictly maternal intentions, not realising, like many young things, how very young he was.[70]

Mary, who craves for a different kind of man from her husband, still feels the need to exert her power over David by involving him in domestic tasks like folding sheets and fetching cotton reels even while he is attempting to discuss the politics of agrarian reform with her.

The only moment in the novel where their physical desire for each other is brought into the open is a single kiss in the hedgerow, interrupted by the untimely arrival of her husband, a moment that is never recaptured in the novel. It is a curiously sexual instant, and one is reminded of the similarly unconvincing moments of ecstasy in George Eliot's novel *Middlemarch*, where Dorothea is attracted by the young sprig Ladislaw after having become disillusioned with her older husband. It seems that Holtby has no desire to fall into the trap of conventional romantic fiction where the stranger/lover is set up in direct opposition to the stolid, boring husband. In *Anderby Wold* women tend to be active and men reactive rather than vice versa (Sarah Bannister, John's sister, also gives her husband a hard time, even telling him when to use his handkerchief).

In *The Land of Green Ginger* there is another triangle, with Teddy, Joanna Leigh's consumptive husband, totally reliant on her physically and emotionally, and the stranger Szermai disrupting the situation with fatal consequences. Teddy has married Joanna without warning her of his consumptive background and she has no knowledge of this until after the birth of their second child. His irresponsibility develops through the novel into childish petulance and self-pity before culminating in his final gruesome moment of masculine assertiveness in the act of raping her. She carries him metaphorically and literally at times throughout the novel, doing all the 'masculine' hard work of the farm as well as attempting to fulfil the female domestic and decorative functions.

Szermai's desire for her is not portrayed by Holtby in the manner of conventional romantic fiction, with a mysterious stranger offering temptation and relief from a monotonous life of drudgery. Instead his approaches are shown to be yet another burden in her already oppressed life:

> Joanna found her irritation increasing. What did he mean by
> being so miserable? Wasn't there misery enough in their house
> already? She wanted him to be inhuman and exciting. She was
> so tired of the pervading misery of men ... She couldn't do
> with him if he were going to be ill. Really she had had more
> than her share of illness. She was so tired of a world domi-
> nated by physical things.[71]

The point at which he kisses her is by no means tender or loving;
it is as if he is demanding of her the comfort that he can never
get from his lost love, as a price that she, a female, must pay.

Later in the novel, as a widow bearing the child which her late
husband's rape has forced upon her and which the village assumes
is Szermai's, she has to endure the amorous declarations of the
curate, another man who assumes that as a woman she has a duty
to assuage the desire that she has provoked: 'Joanna, Joanna.
Forgive me. I had to speak. You drive me mad. You must drive all
men mad. You can't help it.' [72]

Holtby is giving an enormously depressing view of the nature
of male/female relations in this novel, a view relieved only by the
sheer indomitability of Joanna, who manages at the end of the
novel to assert herself by emigrating to start a new life with her
daughters in South Africa. On the ship fellow passengers assume
she is so happy because she is going to meet her husband,
whereas, ironically, her joy comes from her delivery from the
marital shackles and from the prospect of an autonomous life of
her own.

In *The Crowded Street* the dependence of men on women is
not such a central theme as in other novels, and certainly the
relationship between Mr and Mrs Hammond has a more conventional power dynamic. Nevertheless, in the dependence of the
crippled Mr Todd on the vivacious Mrs Todd, in the portrayal of
Connie's husband Ben Todd as a 'big soft idiot' with a 'great
gawky body' who is unable to free himself from his parent's
domination, and even in the way that Godfrey Neale confers his
proposal to Muriel in terms of custodianship of his dreams for
his ancestral home (he sees their marriage in terms of the extent
to which she can support his lifestyle), the novel continues to
show men as reliant on women's strength.

This is shown, too, in *Mandoa! Mandoa!* in the relationship
between Bill Durrant and Jean Stanbury. Jean realises that Bill
has exploited her shamefully, using her as a sounding board for
his schemes, endlessly discussing his problems, and parasitically
draining her strength:

> At four o'clock in the morning he had lurched off into the
> quiet street; he had dropped off, like a bee drunk with honey,
> nourished upon her courage, leaving her exhausted, drained of

sympathy and feeling, enabled only from the sweet chill of night air through the open door, to find energy to crawl into her bed.[73]

Holtby drew upon personal experience in her portrayal of exploitation of women by needy men. To some extent the relationship between Jean and Bill emulates Holtby's own association with the man she names in her letters as Bill, who having once been her acknowledged beau returned damaged from the war unable to commit himself to a permanent relationship. Throughout her life, however, he continued to appear and to write to her intermittently, drawing on her mental and spiritual resources and always demanding a sympathetic ear.

Men, like drones, batten on to women in Holtby's novels, demanding through the tyranny of the weak the service of the strong and thereby surviving on the resources of the traditionally weaker sex. In *Poor Caroline* Holtby challenges even the basic assumption of the financial structure that underpins patriarchy by showing the helplessly overbred Basil St Denis being rescued from near fatal illness by the amazing Madam Gloria Calmier and subsequently allowing her to provide for him financially until the opportunity of making a fortune through the Christian Cinema Company is dreamed up by her.

In one of Holtby's more oppressively dismal short stories, 'The Sun God' in *The Truth is Not Sober*, the parasitic male is equated with a murderer when the repulsive Cyprian Fane, driven by jealously for a girl who is a wonderful diver and who outshines him on the beach, is nursed back to health by her; he wreaks his revenge on her success by marrying her and having six children:

> 'It was only when I heard ten months later Cyprian had actually married her and carried her off with him to the States and they were going to have a child already that I realised how hideously his pride had been wounded and how much he must have hated her.'
> 'But I don't see' I protested.
> 'Well, he stopped her swimming, anyway, didn't he?' asked Morgan.
> And I had to agree that this was true.[74]

This story shows a level of pessimism about the potentiality of male/female relationships that is rarely shown in the novels. Doubt that equal partnerships between the sexes can exist is ubiquitous in her fiction; instead she develops models in which men's relationships with their loved ones is more like the conventional view of the relationship between child and mother. The women seem to be caught in a classical double bind; the matriarchy they share is not one of power but of burden. In the domestic sphere they shoulder the responsibility for the emotional, physical and spiritual well-being of the whole family, while in the public sphere they are deprived of real power or recognition. Holtby knew from her own experiences what it meant to be weighed down with her family's expectation of her role as a dutiful daughter in terms of caring for the infirm and elderly, an expectation that would not have been the same for a man. However successful, a woman could not expect to retreat from her 'feminine' duty, whether married or unmarried, a biological mother or merely a metaphorical one to her family and menfriends.

Holtby's ambiguous attitude to marriage in her novels as in her life finds no ready solution. A generation of women conditioned to believe that matrimony was ultimately their only socially acceptable goal found it difficult to break away from believing in other forms of self-validation. Patricia Duncker in *Strangers and Sisters: An Introduction to Contemporary Feminist Fiction* [75] suggests that little has changed since the time when Holtby was writing: 'Women's love has always meant giving way, giving up, giving in, in fiction and in our lives.' [76] Holtby's subtlety lay in the way in which she wrote in her own times about issues that were to remain current for the next 50 years at least.

As Vera Brittain makes clear in *Testament of Friendship*, Holtby agreed on her deathbed to marry Bill, the man she had loved all her life. This was the consummation of the relationship that formed 'their strange erratic story, constantly broken and as often resumed'.[77]

Their union could obviously never have been achieved, as she must surely have realised she would not live to marry Bill. The knowledge that she had achieved an 'understanding' with him, and the fact that she was able to communicate this to her mother, seems to have set the seal on some kind of self-acceptance that carried her through to her death. Of course it must be remembered that the account we read has been coloured by Vera Brittain's own viewpoint; as a women who has herself chosen the path of marriage she had a vested interest in projecting a rosy view of the potential joys of married life – joys which she wished her friend to share.

Writing in a period of tremendous flux, when women had high hopes of freedom to choose their own way of living and when society seemed more ready to recognise their abilities and needs, Holtby offers the reader no easy solutions. She shows that such freedom is commonly illusory, in that each choice leads to a narrowing of options in other fields.

Her subversion of a conventional format offers an opportunity to address a wide range of readers, many of whom, attracted by the use of familiar subject matter and story lines, are further engaged by the strenuous realism of her technique. She pulls no punches in examining the sexual politics of relations between men and women, retaining considerable scepticism about the possibility of heterosexual bonding, particularly marriage. However, while she avoids the conventional closure of the typical happy ending of romantic fiction, her tone is neither pessimistic nor self-absorbed. She offers the reader a model of womanhood that was appropriate for the spirit of the age, an embodiment of fortitude, resolution, resourcefulness, independence, but above all a recognition of the duty that is both a millstone and a reward in itself, to care for and serve others without losing sight of the need to value oneself. It is a spirit that friends and correspondents described as being characteristic of Holtby herself.

Notes and References

1. Quoted by Nicola Beauman in *A Very Great Profession* London: Virago 1983 p. 41.
2. Quoted by Sheila Jeffreys in *The Spinster and Her Enemies: Feminism and Sexuality 1880–1930* pp. 172–4.
3. Ibid. p. 173.
4. Winifred Holtby *Virginia Woolf* London: Lawrence and Wishart 1932 p. 29.
5. Elaine Showalter *The Female Malady: Woman, Madness and English Culture 1830–1980* London: Virago 1987 Chapter 6.
6. Winifred Holtby *The Astonishing Island* London: Lovatt Dickenson 1933.
7. For example, Jeffreys *The Spinster* 19 Chapters 1, 3 & 4.
8. Sheila Rowbottom *A New World for Women: Stella Browne Social Feminist* London: Pluto Press 1977. F.W. Stella Browne's essay 'Sexual Variety and Variability among Women', p. 87, is most useful here.
9. Virginia Woolf *To the Lighthouse* London: Hogarth Press 1927.
10. Virginia Woolf *Mrs Dalloway* London: Granada 1976 (1925).
11. Ibid. p. 9.
12. Martha Vicinus in *Independent Women: Work and Community for Single Women 1850–1920* London: Virago 1985 has a most useful chapter, 'The Revolt Against Redundancy', that cites figures in support of this.
13. Carol Christ, 'Victorian Masculinity and the Angel in the House' in *A Widening Sphere: Changing Roles of Victorian Women* ed Martha Vicinus, Methuen, London 1980 p. 146.
14. Winifred Holtby's article 'Unemployment and Women who Work' in *Testament of a Generation: The Journalism of Vera Brittain and Winifred Holtby* London: Virago 1985.

15. Vicinus *Independent Women* 1985 p. 287.
16. Holtby 'Counting the Cost' *Testament of a Generation* 1985 p. 54.
17. Ibid. p. 56.
18. Winifred Holtby *Women and a Changing Civilisation* London: John Lane 1934 pp. 192–3, quoted in Vicinus *Independent Women* 1985
19. Virginia Woolf *Three Guineas* London: Hogarth Press 1938.
20. Beauman *A Very Great* 1983.
21. Ibid. p. 178.
22. Ibid. Chapter 7 'Romance'.
23. Wilhelm Stekel, quoted in Jeffreys *The Spinster* p. 169.
24 E.M. Hull *The Sheik* 1919 p. 59 quoted in Beauman *A Very Great* 1983 p. 189.
25. Roy Pickard *The Hollywood Studios* London: Muller 1987 p. 86.
26. Ibid. p. 353.
27. Alan Arnold *Valentino* London: Hutchinson 1952 p. 69.
28. Ibid. p. 88.
29. Marion Shaw 'Feminism and Fiction Between the Wars: Winifred Holtby and Virginia Woolf' in Moria Monteith ed *Women's Writing: A Challenge to Theory* London: Harvester 1986.
30. Winifred Holtby *Anderby Wold* London: Virago 1984 (1923); *The Land of Green Ginger* London: Virago 1984 (1927).
31. Winifred Holtby *Poor Caroline*
32. Ibid. p. 19
33. Winifred Holtby *The Crowded Street* London: Virago 1981 (1924).
34. Holtby *The Truth is not Sober*, London: Collins 1934.
35. Ibid. p. 23.
36. Winifred Holtby *South Riding* London: Collins 1936.
37. Ibid. p. 5.
38. Ibid. p. 25.
39. Ibid. p. 4.
40. Ibid. p. 493.
41. Holtby *The Land* 1984 p. 87.
42. Holtby *South* 1936 p. 495.
43. Vera Brittain *Testament of Friendship* London: Virago 1985.
44. Outlined by Sheila Jeffreys in *The Spinster* p. 169
45. Quoted in Jeffreys *The Spinster* 19 p. 169.
46. Annis Pratt *Archetypal Patterns in Women's Fiction* Bloomington: Indiana University Press 1981.
47. Ibid. p. 41.
48. Holtby *The Crowded* 1981 p. 152.
49. Ibid. p. 199.
50. Winifred Holtby *The Pavements at Anderby* London: Collins 1937 pp. 148–73.
51. Holtby *The Crowded* 1981 p. 271.
52. Winifred Holtby 'The Perfect Wife' in *The Truth is not Sober* 1934 pp. 249–63.

53. Winifred Holtby *Mandoa! Mandoa!* London: Virago 1982 (1933).
54. Holtby *South* 1936 p. 493.
55. Ibid.
56. Ibid. p. 394.
57. Ibid. p. 425.
58. Ibid. p. 426.
59. Ibid. p. 427.
60. Ibid. p. 5.
61. Ibid. p. 249.
62. Ibid. p. 137.
63. Ibid. p. 318.
64. Ibid. p. 558.
65. Holtby *Anderby* 1984 p. 80.
66. Ibid. p. 101.
67. Ibid. p. 287.
68. D.H. Lawrence *Women in Love* London: Martin Secker 1921 (1920)
69. Holtby *Anderby* 1984 p. 115.
70. Ibid. p. 123.
71. Holtby *The Land* 1984 pp. 145–6.
72. Ibid. p. 278.
73. Holtby *Mandoa! Mandoa!* 1982 p. 77.
74. Holtby *The Truth* pp. 147–8.
75. Patricia Duncker *Sisters and Strangers: An Introduction to Contemporary Feminist Fiction* Oxford: Blackwell 1992.
76. Ibid. p. 266.
77. Brittain *Testament* 1985 p. 436.

CHAPTER 8

Croquet and Serial Killers: Feminism and Agatha Christie

Odette l'Henry Evans

As a genre, crime fiction has not yet achieved full academic respectability and is still derided by those exponents of 'pure' literature who argue that since the paradigm for a detective novel is the gradual unveiling of a mysterious occurrence, interest in the text is bound to be ephemeral. Such stories, they say, can attract only the common reader, looking for the excitement and suspense generated as the killer is slowly unmasked, but unable to perceive the difference between a crime writer and a talented novelist.

Nevertheless, for the past century crime fiction has flourished; it is one of the most popular and enduring literary genres. It has influenced and inspired many leading figures of modern literature, from Ernest Hemingway and Albert Camus (who openly acknowledged his debt to J.M. Cain when he wrote *L'Etranger*) to Virginia Woolf or, more recently, Alain Robbe-Grillet.

Readers' loyalties and huge sales figures have shown that this is a field in which women writers have carved an important place for themselves. At the same time, leading academics such as Roland Barthes, Stephen Knight and Richard Bradbury are showing an increasing interest in detective fiction, recognising the importance of a genre which more than any other calls for a rigorously organised narrative structure.

When she died at the age of 85 Agatha Christie had seen her books translated into 157 languages, selling over 350 million copies worldwide. She was admired as a supremely skilful weaver of plots but not as a truly great writer. Nor was she credited with any pronounced psychological insight or interest in exploring the subconscious of her victims or of her murderers.

Plots are tightly constructed, incidental details are painstakingly researched, dialogues reveal characters' inner thoughts, actions are clearly shown and telltale clues are provided – usually in such a casual way that readers, while they certainly cannot argue that they have been misled, often end up by misleading themselves. There is, however, no suggestion of frenzied or sadistic behaviour, no deviant murderer killing for the sake of it. Agatha Christie herself stated on several occasions that she hated violence and despised people who went about slugging each other for no reason.

Does this mean that while admiring the ingenuity of the storyline and the precision of the style we must nevertheless accept that her books are part of 'popular' culture, nothing more than lighthearted, entertaining fiction, the genteel creation of a carefully brought up, modest Victorian lady, fresh from a world of nannies, tea parties and croquet on the lawn? This is a point worth considering, and one that may help towards the reappraisal of an author who should eventually come to be recognised as an important novelist rather than just a crime fiction writer.

Exploration of the human mind takes many forms in Agatha Christie's tales of murder, and it is interesting to note how Hercule Poirot's manner of extracting information is reminiscent of Freud's method of psychoanalytic investigation, in W. Muschg's description of how Freud worked:

> [He] started asking questions, in a desultory manner, virtually anywhere, dealing with apparently unimportant elements. When he has a number of elements in hand, he discards some, digs further here and there and eventually standing at the centre shovels deeper and deeper in a single-minded search.[1]

This is precisely how the little grey cells of the mind of the famous Belgian detective are set into motion and, to illustrate this, it would be tempting to quote in its entirety the scene in Chapter 13 of *The Murder of Roger Ackroyd*. There Poirot, over a bottle of whisky for his guest and hot chocolate for himself, chats seemingly aimlessly with the local doctor James Sheppard, asking random questions, practically making a fool of himself with his naive comments, and then considering and discarding possible motives with the very man he will publicly unmask, in the final pages, as Roger Ackroyd's killer.

Poirot was eventually to become one of the most famous of fictional detectives, played on stage by Charles Laughton and in films by Albert Finney, Peter Ustinov and, more recently, David Suchet. Agatha Christie made use of him often and most felicitously, yet she may well have had a softer spot for her other sleuth, Miss Jane Marple, a character inspired it is said by her own grandmother and portrayed on screen in turn by Margaret Rutherford, Angela Lansbury and Joan Hickson. After all, it must be remembered that she allowed Poirot to get himself killed in *Curtains*[2] while Jane Marple won a reprieve. Despite rumours that she was herself meant to meet her fate in Christie's last book, published posthumously, she survived and, modest as usual, unmasked the villains at the end.

Miss Marple is far less flamboyant than Poirot – quite the

opposite in fact. Small, with snow-white hair, a pink, crinkled face, innocent blue eyes and a piece of half-completed knitting nearby, she does not ask questions but listens and observes quietly. More perceptive than Poirot, she advances slowly but unerringly towards the truth.

Miss Marple proceeds by association of ideas, very much as if, in the words of the neo-Freudian theorist Laplanche, 'what may be called a moment of insight, the resurgence of a forgotten memory, a sudden illumination, unquestionably conscious in the descriptive sense' [3] makes her suddenly understand what causes people to act the way they do.

Not only does Christie show a marked preference for her lady sleuth but she also appears to have a predilection for casting women in the role of murderer. When crimes are committed by male characters, even though they usually try to organise things beforehand, they are often clumsy and fail to react to circumstances. In *The Man in a Brown Suit*, for instance, Sir Eustace Pedley, the 'deep-dyed criminal' feared everywhere as the 'Colonel', manages to fail more often than he succeeds in his murderous endeavours. On a liner, making his way back from South Africa, he tries to throw a young woman, Anne Beddingfeld, overboard, failing to notice the other passenger who has followed her on deck; later he makes careful plans to kill a man in London, arranging an elaborate alibi in the South of France, booking hotels in Cannes and Nice, only to find himself face to face with an acquaintance as he reaches his destination and quite unable to improvise. He is finally unmasked by the same Miss Beddingfeld, assisted by her boyfriend.

Agatha Christie's murderesses are, on the whole, far more subtle and more interestingly depicted. Christie herself was no stranger to death in its most cruel form, having joined the Voluntary Aid Detachment in 1914 and worked in a Red Cross hospital in Torquay. It was there that she met the Belgian refugees who would provide the inspiration for the Poirot of her first novel, *The Mysterious Affair at Styles*, and there also that she learnt to hate violence, suffering and mutilation, making it impossible for her to indulge in writing tales of 'blood and gore'. She drew on her hospital experience when she took up the challenge of her elder sister who dared her to write a good detective story. She knew about various drugs and poisons and would continue to study their effects in detail all her life. Indeed, she unwittingly contributed to real-life crime detection when her description of the symptoms of thallium poisoning in *The Pale Horse* helped a South American doctor to save the life of a man slowly being poisoned by his wife. The same description contributed to the solving of a case in England where a man had mysteriously died after drinking tea.

Christie always insisted that she knew nothing of guns and other firearms and she seldom used them for her crimes. Her victims might be pushed under a car, into a river or out of a window, they might be stabbed with daggers or stilettoes, or hit with a blunt instrument, but more often that not they are poisoned.

Far from being drawn to substances such as arsenic, favoured by most real-life poisoners from Florence Maybrick to Anna Kahn, Christie looked for more unusual drugs. In addition to thallium she used curare, cocaine, nicotine, chloral hydrate, sleeping tablets, pus from a cat's infected ear in order to cause septicaemia, old hat paint containing oxalic acid, as well as phosphorus from vermin paste or foreign matches. Phosphorus was particularly suitable since the symptoms of phosphorus poisoning were much the same as those of the liver complaint from which the victim was already suffering, a fact of which the murderess was well aware, having studied chemistry and helped her father in his laboratory.[4]

Such attention to detail, combined with an obvious ability to write from within the female 'criminal' perspective and to bring to light the reasons behind the act of murder, certainly justify a critical examination of Agatha Christie's literary production (the term is used here deliberately) as part of a corpus of works. These qualities should encourage a psychoanalytical investigation of her character presentation and plots to see whether this could yield further elements related to what is now critically termed feminine writings.[5]

Feminist approaches to literature rest mainly on the theory that the distinctive function of women is observable, either collectively in gender-oriented social relations or individually in their distinctive nature. In point of fact, such critical appraisal, more accurately defined as feminine epistemology,[6] reaches beyond the accepted gender function of love, motherhood, care of home and respect for social values, in order to attempt an exploration of the systemic relations of a 'sex-gender' universe.[7]

As far as Agatha Christie is concerned, children are rarely featured in her stories and, probably because women's traditional role hardly fits in with the craft of murder, a search for the stereotypical attributes is bound to meet with very limited success. There is, however, a particular instance where strong mother love is shown by a murderess: Bella Tanios, in *Dumb Witness*. Passionately devoted to her children and unhappy with a husband who has speculated with her money and lost it all, she twice attempts to kill her wealthy aunt in the hope that her inheritance will give her a chance to provide the children with a proper education. She eventually succeeds in her endeavour and plans her husband's death, which will look like suicide, with a confession that will point to him as her aunt's murderer. When this fails she kills herself, dying in her sleep of what could look like an accidental overdose.

As Poirot explains: 'Was it not the best way? She thought so. There were, you see, the children to consider ...' [8]

A wide variety of motives lead Agatha Christie's characters to commit murder. In the early novels male murderers are almost the norm and are usually motivated by a thirst for power, as in *The Secret Adversary* (1922), where the criminal reveals his motives in a posthumous diary:

> I noticed that ... it was the riff-raff who drifted into crime. Strange that men of brains had never realized its extraordinary opportunity ... The power I dreamed of was absolute! A dictator ... and such power could only be obtained by working outside the law.[9]

It is in the later novels where female criminals are more frequently found and where the motives are more personal and subtle, ranging from the desire, or indeed the need, for money, to revenge, jealousy and unrequited love, the latter proving one of the most powerful themes: 'Hell hath no fury like a woman scorned ...' whispers Bridget, Lord Whitfield's fiancée, as she realises that the older woman previously rejected by him is now intent on killing her.[10]

While qualifiers of sexual differences as posited by Freud in 'The Dissolution of the Oedipus Complex', to the effect that 'anatomy is destiny', may appear blurred at times in Agatha Christie's stories, they can nevertheless be identified in her heroines' attitudes, well mannered, often churchgoers, outwardly respectable and eager to conform to the expectations of their social circle. Their refusal to accept the passive 'feminine' attitude and their assumption of the 'virile' role of murderer remains hidden and is never made explicit until they are unmasked.

In this light, when the accuracy of Christie's observation is fully appreciated, together with her ability to focus on the anomalies and neuroses of the human mind, it becomes possible to assess the extent to which her work represents a feminine form of writing, and to establish a clear pattern of semiotic functions[11] in the stories. Taking as an example the beautiful Marthe Daubreuil, who turns out to be a double murderess in *The Murder on the Links*, a number of elements suggest from the start the range of emotions that assail her. There is first of all, at the subconscious level, the trauma of her heredity:

> A truly beautiful young girl – modest, devout, all that she should be. One pities her, for, though she may know nothing of the past, a man who wants to ask her hand in marriage must necessarily inform himself and then ...[12]

When Hastings meets her at the start of the story he describes her as a 'young goddess', but Poirot, who is with him, remarks: 'I saw only a girl with anxious eyes.' Later in the book, although she is only present for an instant opening the front door and informing her mother that visitors have come to see her, 'her eyes widened with apprehension', and again much later, in the garden, happy to run forward and talk to Poirot, 'despite her acquiescence, her eyes looked troubled and afraid'.[13]

Throughout the book her body language proves equally significant. Early on, 'her left hand was pressed to her side, as though to still the sudden unconquerable agitation of her heart'; later 'her voice sounded rather breathless and her hand stole to her breast' which shows that her voice also provides several referential functions, 'At last, almost in a whisper, she asked ...' and 'There was a hint of bitterness in her low voice ...' [14]

These details are casually given and, as the story unfolds, cleverly interspersed with Marthe's concern that her mother may be implicated and her understandable torment when her fiancé is arrested by the inspector of police. Even Poirot, the super-sleuth, does not begin to suspect her until much later, yet these are all clues. In order to constitute a clue a message must have several functions, not all of them readily perceivable, and the example above gives us an opportunity to identify them. First, a referential function has been given: we know what Marthe looks like and what the inflexions of her voice are; to this is added an emotive function – sadness is expressed. More importantly still, there is a phatic function, or more accurately a phatic intent – although the explanations offered for her sadness seem satisfactory at the time, they will later be shown to be the result of her own criminal acts.[15]

From this brief incursion into McLuhanism,[16] and without going so far as to insist with him that 'the medium is the message', one feels that a semiotic approach could well be attempted here, and would enhance further a feminist reading of Agatha Christie's work, not in the superficial form that some feminist propagandists have favoured[17] – the meek, old-fashioned gentlewoman that she was[18] would thwart any such attempt – but at the deeper level of feminist psychoanalytics, where writing can be seen to explore subconscious motives and reactions, an art in which women have long excelled and which has made for enthralling tales of mystery and detection.

Notes and References

1. Walter Muschg 'Freud Ecrivain' trans. J. Schotte in *La Psychanalyse* 5, 1959 pp. 69–124 (my translation).
2. After Hercule Poirot's 'death', in 1975, a farewell review appeared in *The Times*, while the *New York Times* ran a full obituary on page 1.

3. Jean Laplanche and Serge Leclaire 'The Unconscious' in *French Freud* Yale French Studies 1972 p. 118.
4. See *Tragedy in Three Acts, Dumb Witness, Murder is Easy, Peril at End House,* among others.
5. Julia Kristeva interview in *Tel Quel* no. 59 (1974) rept. in *Polygone,* a collection of Krysteva writings Paris: Seuil 1977.
6. See Nancy Hartsock 'The Feminist Standpoint' in S. Harding and M.B. Hintikka eds *Discovering Reality* Dortrecht-Reidel 1983.
7. Hilary Rose 'Women's Work, Women's Knowledge' in J. Mitchell and A. Oakley eds *What is Feminism?* Oxford: Blackwell 1981
8. Agatha Christie *Dumb Witness* 1969 p. 216. The feminist approach to mother love in literature is interestingly analysed in Nancy Chodorow *The Reproduction of Mothering* Berkeley: California University Press 1978.
9. Agatha Christie *The Secret Adversary* London: Pan Books 1955 (1922) p. 216.
10. Agatha Christie *Murder is Easy* London: Collins 1973 (1939) p. 172.
11. This semiotic approach is best explained in Roland Barthes *S/Z* Paris: Edition du Seuil 1977 and the method of investigating a coherent textual pattern in Kristeva 'The Bounded Text' trans. T. Gora in *Desire in Language* Oxford: Blackwell 1980. See also A.J. Greimas *Sémiotique. Dictionnaire Raisonné de la Théorie du Language* Paris: Hachette 1979.
12. Agatha Christie *The Murder on the Links* (1923) London: Pan Books 1964 p. 56.
13. Ibid. pp. 15, 57, 139.
14. Ibid. pp. 57, 139, 60.
15. Barthes *S/Z* 1977. See also O. l'Henry Evans 'Towards a Semiotic Reading of Mickey Spillane' in *American Crime Fiction* London: Macmillan 1988 pp. 101–14 for an illustration of a detailed semiotic textual study.
16. *The Medium is the Message,* title of H.M. McLuhan's best-known book (1967), is commonly quoted by those sociological critics who follow him in believing that literary works are inescapably conditioned by external circumstances, social assumptions, the media, etc.
17. Mainly those feminist critics engaged in empirical studies of language conventions, such as Sally McConnell-Ginet, Ruth Borker, Nelly Furman. See *Women and Language in Literature and Society* London: Croom Helm 1980.
18. These were the words used by Agatha Christie's literary agent to describe her. Quoted in Virginia Kelly, 'Agatha Christie – Murder by the Book' in *Reader's Digest* January 1977 in connection with the publication of her posthumous novel *Sleeping Murder* in October 1976.

CHAPTER 9

Life on the Street:
Pat Barker's Realist Fictions

Sue Anderson

Since the Victorian era, experimentation in the novel form has been
rife. In the early twentieth century Virginia Woolf was one among
many modernists who rejected the realist novel in favour of 'stream
of consciousness'. Although many twentieth-century women writers
have developed their work experimentally, there has always been a
strong strain of realist writing, capturing the everyday quality of life,
but frequently within the context of a romantic tale.

In the post-modernist era many women novelists have returned
to realism, subverting and changing it into an exciting new form. Pat
Barker is one of the plurality of women writing in their own
individual style but focusing on similar themes. Others favour fantasy, magic, the spiritual. Angela Carter is an exponent of 'magical
realism', inventing women with wings (*Nights at the Circus*); Toni
Morrison includes the spiritual world in her novel *Beloved*; and Fay
Weldon's protagonist, Ruth, changes her shape and identity to
become 'the other woman' in *The Life and Loves of a She-Devil*.

However, Pat Barker has made different choices. With her
excellent ear for dialogue, she uses the realist genre to portray the
lives of ordinary women and men. This is the same skill that Alice
Walker displays, especially in her latest novel *Possessing the Secret
of Joy*. However, like Alice Walker, Pat Barker uses other literary
devices to enhance her fiction, placing what is unbearable before
the reader in a context that allows for assimilation. Fay Weldon
uses the words 'courageous, daring and powerful' when describing
her writing, and these three elements are to be found set within a
realistic framework.

Her forays into the realm of realism are diverse and controversial. She writes about women's lives spanning the generations from
the turn of the century. *Regeneration*[1] (published in 1991) appears
initially to be a departure from this theme but the reader soon
becomes aware of the parallel nature of the life lived by men in
the trenches during World War One and the lives of women
generally. Confinement and submission to authority produce the
same symptoms and qualities in the neurasthenic officers as are
present in the women who live restricted lives. This realisation

reinforces the social criticism aspect of Pat Barker's novels – an authoritarian and uncaring society produces damaged personalities. Her first three novels, *Union Street*,[2] *Blow Your House Down*,[3] and *The Century's Daughter*[4] deal specifically with this topic.

Pat Barker uses realism in all her novels to lure the reader into a false sense of security and then, by crossing the genre boundaries, she defamiliarises and forces the reader to consider the actual content of her novels and to appreciate the powerless position in which women find themselves, entrapped in a patriarchal society. Her novels do not provide a comfortable read; they are subtly didactic but, like all good pedagogues, she allows the reader to reach the point of awareness. Her fourth novel, *The Man Who Wasn't There*,[5] interweaves a sharply edged realism with fantastic and dream-like elements as a twelve-year-old boy, brought up by his mother, searches for self-identity in the absence of a father figure.

In this chapter I will explore a dual definition of 'realist'; the realistic style in which Pat Barker naturalistically describes the events in the lives of women, and the accuracy and truthfulness with which she portrays the major events of their lives – the births, marriages, deaths, abortions and rapes. Emphasising the content of the novels, I will argue that by combining the above elements she produces a fiction that is both enjoyable and didactic.

Life on the streets is portrayed as harsh and cruel for the women concerned. Her first novel, *Union Street*, uses the term in the title and conveys the 'union' that evolves from the women's need for comfort and communality outside the home. The topic of public/private is explored through the juxtaposition of an insecure life in private (behind closed doors) due to violence perpetrated by both men and women, the effects of poverty and social pressure on the inmates of the home and an emotionally secure life created between the women 'on the street', in public, as a means of support and a way of coping with the unsatisfactory 'private' life.

The title of her second novel, *Blow Your House Down*, makes a social comment on the treatment of the lives lived by prostitutes in a society that values permanence and respectability above feeling and insight. In the fairy story we are reminded that solid good sense helps survival: the only little pig to survive was the one who built his house of bricks. Society does not acknowledge the existence of those who live on its periphery, who live such ephemeral lives.

The realistic style takes the reader instantly into a woman's world where the author then proceeds to demythologise and deconstruct the male construct of woman as nurturer, or virgin/whore, which myth is taken apart, particularly in the novel *Blow Your House Down*. In *Union Street* George is confused and disconcerted after his evening with the prostitute Blonde Dinah:

> She looked like Gladys [George's wife] lying there ... She ought not to look like Gladys. He had always believed there were two sorts of women: the decent ones and the rest. He felt they should look different, for how could you tell them apart, how could you remember they were different, if every sag, every wrinkle of their used bodies proclaimed that they were one flesh? [6]

The character Kelly vandalises a middle-class home as part of an expression of anger against a society that has allowed her rape to go unrecorded. She desecrates the bedroom: 'It was a woman's room, a temple to femininity. And the altar was the dressing-table.' [7] Kelly sees it as a sacrificial room where women deny their identity as they conform to a male construct of the female. Since her rape, Kelly herself has denied any expression of her own femininity by cutting her hair into a spiky mess and wearing dirty and unattractive clothing to conceal her gender. This rejection is a direct result of her suffering through being treated as a mere object for sexual gratification. Self-loathing leads her to redefine herself. In *Union Street*, Pat Barker depicts the life of working-class women in a specific northern context, but this does not prevent all women from identifying with some aspect of her novels. Childbirth, menstruation, sex and abortion cross the class boundaries and relate to most women's experiences.

In *Union Street*, the labour pains:

> were harder to ride than those varied and unpredictable pains that come at the beginning of a normal labour. It was like trying to swim in a sea of corrugated iron. There was never any time when you could relax and allow the current to carry you.[8]

Pat Barker's language in this passage is typical of her novels. It has a natural place in the realistic details and is gritty, related to the real world. The text is immediately accessible to women but this same accessibility might, perhaps, account for the fact that men feel excluded from some of her writing. Barker's male characters are frequently marginalised. The only sympathetically depicted men are those who are in some way damaged or alienated by the rest of society; treated as 'other'. Joss is a dwarf (*Union Street*); John Scaife is terminally ill (*Union Street*); Stephen is homosexual (*The Century's Daughter*); and Colin (*The Man Who Wasn't There*) has identity problems and a liking for women's clothes.

Menstruation and sex are both dealt with naturalistically. Kelly's distaste for her sister's habit of keeping her used sanitary towels in the bedroom drawer is described with everyday detail. Kelly expresses what most young girls must feel in a society that regards menstruation as 'unclean'; 'she didn't want to drip foul-smelling brown blood out of her fanny every month.'[9] Smells are important to Kelly; she sniffs the armpits of her mother's jumpers and prefers to wear them herself as she finds the smell comforting. When vandalising the bedroom she pulls the dirty linen out of the basket:

> She could tell whether the pants belonged to a man or a woman with her eyes shut, by the smell alone. She snuffled into armpits and stained crotches, then sniffed her own armpits.[10]

Kelly's mother is unable to comfort her after her rape, and Kelly is shown as sublimating the contact that she desperately needs with her mother by employing her sense of smell to comfort herself. It seems a vaguely distasteful occupation to an adult but Kelly is often described as acting like an instinctive animal; she has 'eyes of a curious naked amber: an animal's eyes'.[11] Without her mother's reassurance Kelly is reverting to basic needs.

The sexual act crosses the boundary of male/female relationships, but again, Pat Barker depicts it from the women's point of view through the characters in her novels. Sex, seen from the women's viewpoint, is not a satisfactory occurrence in their lives and usually leads to pregnancy. Joanne Wilson's story in *Union Street* centres on pregnancy and the necessary marriage that this entailed. Joanne's predicament is treated lightheartedly at first. The tone changes when Joanne tells Ken of her pregnancy. After earlier unsatisfactory lovemaking, Ken stops in the railway tunnel on their way home. He was

> thrusting into her as though he hated her, grinding and screwing and banging hard enough to hurt. She was afraid for the baby and immediately knew what he was trying to do: he was trying to screw it out of her.[12]

Joss, the dwarf, one of the few men depicted as suffering the same fate as women in society, that of the 'other', is loving and caring. His concern and love for Joanne runs deep but they both find themselves unable to express their feelings for each other owing to Joss's deformity. He is the only one who is concerned that Joanne risks making herself unhappy by marrying a man who is so tied up in his own ego that he cannot see the 'problem' of the pregnancy from any point of view but his own. It seems imperative that Joanne marry Ken; it is expected, and Ken also

accepts this. There are no choices for women who are economically dependent upon men.

Sex is treated quite differently in *Regeneration* where, in a
moving account of the relationship between Prior and Sarah,
Sarah's ability to give herself to Prior acts like a rebirth for him.
It is described in religious terms when he lifts Sarah 'until her
whole pelvis became a cup from which he drank.' [13]

Backstreet abortion, the only other choice open to women who
do not want to continue with pregnancy, in this period, is dealt with
graphically in *Union Street*. Pat Barker uses realistic description and
the style of fractured time to force the impact of this horrific event
on the reader. On returning home from the abortion with her
mother Iris, Brenda is sitting on a sagging blue plastic bucket trying
to pee. The solidarity between mother and daughter is expressed
when, through Iris's thoughts, she acknowledges her love for her
daughter: 'Its funny – yesterday I could've killed her. Now if I could
bear the pain for her I would.' [14] The pathetic unwanted new life
lies on the 'floor of the lavatory with the *News of the World* spread
over him.' [15] Iris buries the bundle under some builders' rubble in a
derelict house:

> She hardly thought at all of what she was doing. Her mind
> was bound in by horror. Only her blood seemed to cry out
> against it. This was her own flesh and blood. She was burying
> her own flesh and blood.[16]

This is the baby that Kelly has found earlier in the novel:

> ... she found a baby buried under a heap of broken bricks, a
> baby as red and translucent as a ruby. She looked at him, at
> his sealed eyes and veined head, and put the rubble back
> carefully, brick by brick, guarding this secret as jealously as if
> it had been her own.[17]

Time is explored throughout Pat Barker's novels. In *Union Street* it
is portrayed as cyclical, related to the regularity of the natural cycle
in women's lives. The novel is divided into separate chapters concerned with different women in the street, all linked to each other
through analogous events in subsequent chapters, emphasising the
point that, as Alice says before she takes her final walk of death,
'She had been so many women in her time.' [18] This technique
highlights the many different roles that women play in their lives –
daughter, mother, wife and lover – and all that goes into making up
those roles. The novel itself can be read as one woman's life told via
these various stages or as a series of short stories with a central
theme – womanhood. The link between Kelly and Alice is very
strong. Kelly meets Alice in the park at the start of the book and in
the final chapter they are linked again, this time more closely, by

the joining of hands. The life-giving image of the tree and the joining of hands are just some of the many instances where Pat Barker hovers on the fringe of the spiritual, though she usually undercuts such references, denying the existence of an external controlling, rewarding and punishing force.

In *Union Street* she does this when Alice says 'Is not the life more than meat and the body than raiment? She wasn't quoting. She had lived long enough to make the words her own.' [19] This theme is also explored in *Regeneration* where power is in man's hands alone. Dr Rivers is acting the part of God in making the men anew; a form of rebirth. The imagery used is that of a caterpillar transforming itself into a butterfly:

> Cut a chrysalis open, and you will find a rotting caterpillar. What you will never find is that mythical creature, half cater-pillar, half butterfly, a fit emblem of the human soul, for those whose cast of mind leads them to seek such emblems.[20]

Time is deconstructed in *Blow Your House Down* as the chapters vacillate between the present and the past. In Chapter 15 the narration changes to first person as the reader learns the history of Jean and Carol's lesbian relationship and of Jean's determina-tion to discover and kill Carol's murderer. A similar technique is used in *The Century's Daughter* as the conversations that take place between Lisa and Stephen in the present lead to a retelling of Lisa's life in the past. The variation in timescales requires constant readjustment and helps the reader to view the novel objectively and to consider the societal implications of the lives of the characters represented there. The experience of fractured time is a technique that, in Pat Barker's novels, emphasises the differ-ence between the impersonal, unrelated time of life lived in public, on the streets, and that of private life, lived in the home. Public life on the streets is seen to be a process that forges connections in women's lives, creating a sense of communality and affiliation. It is interesting to relate this to *Regeneration* because it is not until the young officers in the trenches find themselves entrapped in a 'no choice' situation and unsupported by the army commanders (the equivalent of 'fathers') that they also develop a sense of affiliation for their fellow sufferers. Sassoon ends up by returning to France for just this reason. His dead colleagues appear to him in his dreams and accuse him of deserting them, of no longer being one with them. One of the problems with this affiliation in men is the fear that it will be downgraded by suggestions of homosexuality and effeminacy, which is indeed the case. The officers feel doubly threatened.

The subject of war had been touched on before in Barker's work, in her earlier novels, with regard to power and authority.

After the birth of her male child, the mother in *The Century's Daughter* realises that 'they' (a society that tyrannises the weak) 'could take him away and kill him ... They could fill his head with dreams of adventure and glory and make him want to go. Her son was no different from the rest.' 21

Although symbolism and realism do not normally fuse, Pat Barker's use of symbolism deepens and enriches the novel, adding to its accessibility. Her use of symbols is closely connected to women's lives. In *Union Street* women's communality is likened to a flock of starlings chattering, making a sound like women chattering and brushing their hair at once. Individually, women are portrayed as weak and fragile, vulnerable and birdlike even, but collectively they form a centre of power.

Symbolically, Alice is the small bird that Kelly finds near death due to the cold and ice, 'its feathers fluffed out'.22 Kelly is aware of the frailty of the bird – 'she felt the thinness, the lightness of its bones' 23 – in the same way that she appreciates Alice's vulnerability and need to end her life in her own way. Kelly leaves the bird to die rather than put an end to its life. The bird incident parallels Alice's fall on the ice and subsequent stroke24 that ends in her taking her own life. *Blow Your House Down* ends with a reference to birds. The starlings descend upon the city in the evening 'until at last every bird is lodged, and the singing dies away ... they hump black and silent; unnoticed, unless some stranger to the city should happen to look up and be amazed.' 25 Maggie also wants to be 'back with the flock, in no way different from the others.' 26

Pat Barker seems to be saying that the birds/women are patient in their collectiveness and will one day be recognised for the strength they possess. In a society that discriminates against the female gender they can do no more than be passive. It must be left to the women of the future to look up and 'be amazed'. In *Union Street*, Kelly symbolically desecrates the seat of male power, the headmaster's study, at her school, committing an act which echoes her own rape, born out of self-disgust. In her anger she defecates in the corner of his room and wipes the 'satiny turd' over his chair and desk. She writes 'PISS, SHIT, FUCK' on the blackboard and 'Then, scoring the board so hard that the chalk screamed, the worst word she knew: CUNT.' 27 Animal imagery and Kelly's behaviour accurately portray the anger and hurt she feels after being raped. She finds that she is weak and helpless when faced with male power and so she attempts to destroy the symbols of that power. Her eyes are now hard and cold, changed.

Women's eyes abound everywhere, especially in *Blow Your*

House Down and *Union Street*. Their eyes stare out at the rest of society accusingly, all knowingly. The eyes of dead Kath on the poster follow you everywhere: 'In life Kath Robson hated being stared at. Not in death. In death she looks ready to outstare anybody.' [28] Beattie, the landlady has only one made-up eye: 'her one naked eye staring out like the eye of God.' [29] Women are shining a spotlight on the rest of society; they are the oracles that society fails to consult. Pat Barker warns against the explicit self-confidence of society when she quotes from Nietzsche's *Beyond Good and Evil* in the epigraph to *Blow Your House Down*:

> Whoever fights monsters should see to it that in the process he does not become a monster. And when you look long into an abyss the abyss also looks into you.

Kath stares accusingly at the rest of society that has mistreated her and colluded in her murder. Similarly, after her rape Kelly's eyes are described as being 'Cool. Amused. Hostile. Controlled.' [30] They affront people, who turned away from her gaze. In adversity women are portrayed as feeling superior to men: 'She knew she had the power.' [31]

Realistic settings are also symbolic. The women in the novels work in factories, on conveyor belts. The analogy cannot be missed – their lives are endless and monotonous, interrupted by the events of birth and death, and their main source of joy comes from close female friendships. In *Union Street* the workplace is a bakery where Jean, an ex-employee, used to spit in the cake mixture. When questioned by Kelly as to her reasons she replies 'Because I couldn't reach to piss in it ... It had years of my life that place.' [32] Explanation permeates their lives. Women are paid meagre wages for very long hours and in *Blow Your House Down*, where the bakery becomes a chicken factory, many of the women turn to prostitution to earn enough money to bring up their children. There is a close parallel drawn between these two forms of work: the chicken factory's mindless monotony is similar to that of prostitution, and women are treated as battery animals in both jobs. The chickens are described as headless (without a brain), and women are referred to in metaphors using chicken imagery because they are just as exploited, used, vulnerable, degraded. Maureen's decision to work from home makes her 'feel like a bloody battery hen.' [33] The murderer attempts to fill the dead Kath full of feathers, 'like stuffing a chicken ... the effect he wanted ... a ridiculous little white frill between her legs.' [34] Killing the chickens is a job 'for the men'.[35] The social comment is voiced by Maggie, who is not a prostitute yet who has been attacked one night walking down a quiet street:

across her mind's eye moved a line of faces, all women, young, old, fat, thin, smiling, serious. She knew who they were: she'd seen them in the papers ... but then it had been just a story, something that had happened to somebody else ... But now it was real because it had happened to her. The image faded and was replaced by a line of chickens waiting to be killed. In each eye the same passive uncompromising terror.[36]

Maggie becomes aware of the parallel and realises that she cannot go back to work at the chicken factory. Women are used and then discarded by those in power both in the workplace and at home; men use women, and degrade them, but so does their condition of employment.

Settings are significant. The wasteland described in *The Century's Daughter* is a landscape scarred by the demolished houses where 'long scars ran through the grass';[37] it is the wasteland of the women's lives that Lisa Goddard (*Union Street*) looks over after the birth of her baby daughter – there is little hope even for future generations of women. Her daughter contains eggs: she will continue the cycle of childbirth and suffering. An analogy is made again to T.S. Eliot's *The Wasteland* in *Regeneration*. The women from the munitions factory are talking during their tea break, discussing Lizzie's husband who is coming home on leave:

Lizzie's yellow face showed two bright spots of colour ... Do you know what happened on August 4th 1914? ... I'll tell you what happened. Peace broke out. The only little bit of peace I've ever had. No, I don't want him back. I don't want him back on leave. I don't want him back when it's over. As far as I'm concerned the Kaiser can keep him.[38]

The conversation then pointedly returns to false teeth and 'Time, ladies', a reminder of age. It is men who make the women's lives on the streets harsh and cruel, and these women feel more at home in their own community even in a deadening job, than with husbands who treat them as objects.

While using a realistic narrative Pat Barker also subverts the realist nature of her novels. She often crosses the boundaries from one genre to another. *Union Street* is simultaneously a mixture of social novel, regional novel and Bildungsroman; it can also be read as a series of short stories. Emphasis is placed on the influence of social and economic conditions on characters and events, but the novels offer no implicit or explicit programme of social reform. Of them all, *The Century's Daughter* is more of a social novel in its overt criticism of the unfairness of a society that tyrannises the weak.

Although aspects of the regional novel are present in Barker's first four novels where settings, speech, local structure and customs describe a northern town, as does the use of dialect, she moves away from the deprived lower classes in *Regeneration*, in which she combines fact and fiction in a form of pseudo-realism that recreates the relationships between Dr Rivers and his officer patients.

At the start of this chapter I set out to explore Pat Barker's realistic style through discussing the accuracy and truthfulness of the content. In my opinion she succeeds in skilfully combining realism and various techniques of localised symbolism in a manner that produces very readable novels of high quality. Through the various devices of symbolism, fractured time, demythologising and genre subversion, women's strengths are displayed in terms of toughness, durability and ability to survive. Alice (*Union Street*) leads a tough life and yet she survives into old age and shows her lifelong determination in implementing her decision to die when, where and how she wants:

> Getting her stockings on was a struggle. It was hard to bend and still harder to straighten up again. This body that seemed to have less and less to do with her, demanded more attention now than ever it had done in youth ...[39]

Liza (*The Century's Daughter*) has also live a hard, strong life. She refuses to leave the house that she loves even when the men are demolishing the other houses all around her. When Liza is beaten up by the robbers who break into her home looking for money and leave her for dead, she crawls across the floor to collect her life's memories together to place them in her special metal box:

> When she'd found everything, even the buttons from a dress she'd been fond of, she pulled a blanket from the bed ... She did not now believe they would find her alive. This didn't worry her: for many years she'd been attached to life by no more than one or two easily unravelled threads. But she owed it to the person who found her to make herself as little unsightly as possible.[40]

These two women have survived the vicissitudes of life. The need for women to survive and to keep in contact with each other so that the new generation can draw strength from the old is imaged in the scene at the end of *Union Street* when Kelly and Alice meet on the park bench that Alice has chosen as her place to die:

> The girl held out her hand. The withered hand and the strong young hand met and joined. There was silence. Then it was time for them both to go.[41]

Pat Barker contrasts the warmth and care the women feel for each other with the male construct of women as the ones who are warm and caring about men. It is clear that men appreciate a similar warmth and care for their own gender only when they find themselves out on their own in a cruel world where they must survive as best they can.

The harsh, gritty everyday life is one of suffering and deprivation for Pat Barker's women who are locked into a cycle of dull, repetitive work, loveless relationships and poverty. There is a relentlessness about this which is mitigated only by the sense of community and sharing portrayed throughout the novels, and in the celebration both of stoicism, and of the hope of new life, of regeneration. It is with the *images* of regeneration and stoic individuality among others that her realism is tempered, and some little hope suggested.

Notes and References

1. Pat Barker *Regeneration* London: Viking 1991.
2. Pat Barker *Union Street* London: Virago 1982.
3. Pat Barker *Blow Your House Down* London: Virago 1984.
4. Pat Barker *The Century's Daughter* London: Virago 1986.
5. Pat Barker *The Man Who Wasn't There* London: Penguin 1990.
6. Barker *Union Street* 1982 p. 30
7. Ibid. p. 53.
8. Ibid. p. 128.
9. Ibid. p. 3.
10. Ibid. p. 53.
11. Ibid. p. 46.
12. Ibid. p. 100.
13. Barker *Regeneration* 1991 p. 130.
14. Barker *Union Street* 1982 p. 214.
15. Ibid. p. 215.
16. Ibid. p. 216.
17. Ibid. p. 62.
18. Ibid. p. 263.
19. Ibid. p. 67.
20. Barker *Regeneration* 1991 p. 184.
21. Barker *The Century's* 1986 p. 82.
22. Barker *Union Street* 1982 p. 63.
23. Ibid. p. 64.
24. Ibid. p. 245.
25. Barker *Blow* 1984 p. 170
26. Ibid. p. 166.
27. Barker *Union Street* 1982 p. 56.
28. Ibid. p. 71.
29. Ibid. p. 124.
30. Ibid. p. 47.
31. Ibid. p. 49.

32. Ibid. p. 61.
33. Barker *Blow* 1984 p. 125.
34. Ibid. p. 65.
35. Ibid. p. 34.
36. Barker *Union Street* 1982 pp. 155–6.
37. Barker *The Century's* 1986 p. 284.
38. Barker *Regeneration* 1991 p. 110.
39. Barker *Union Street* 1982 p. 261.
40. Barker *The Century's* 1986 p. 270.
41. Barker *Union Street* 1982 p. 265.

CHAPTER 10

Radical Taoism: Ursula K. Le Guin's Science Fiction

Bruce Woodcock

Feminism, Science Fiction and Mysticism

Over the last two decades a number of significant feminist writers have turned to science fiction as a vehicle for exploring issues of gender and power. In their fictional practice writers like Doris Lessing, Joanna Russ, Marge Piercy, Margaret Atwood and others have taken a populist form that has traditionally been seen as a male preserve and transformed it into one that engages women as writers and readers politically and imaginatively. Equally, feminist theorists and cultural commentators have explored the validity and contradictions involved in such a project. Of particular interest are the problems involved in adapting a male-dominated tradition which in its most popular forms has been generally associated with male stereotypes. Sarah Lefanu, Jenny Wolmark and many others[1] have considered the ways in which women writers have appropriated this fictional terrain to uncover issues which might be less easily addressed through conventional fiction. In doing so they have questioned whether in fact we can draw such distinctions between popular 'light' literary forms and 'serious' ones. Science fiction has allowed feminist writers to produce some of their most investigative work, which has nevertheless remained eminently readable and imaginatively stimulating.

Yet science fiction is also a form associated with tendencies towards utopianism, escapism and mysticism. The particular connection between mysticism and science fiction raises an intriguing combination of critical issues, not least because contemporary with the development of feminist science fiction there has been a strand of feminism which has focused its attention on issues to do with spirituality in the broadest sense. Since the 1970s significant elements of feminism in America and Britain have turned towards mystical, spiritual or archetypal ways of conceiving the world or dealing with issues of gender. This movement is represented in terms of its theorists by writers such as Mary Daly among many others.[2] Some of this work has fallen under the influence of Jung, whose theories of gender and sexual archetypes have seemed to some writers to offer a more benign or negotiable psychoanalytic space for reconstructing masculinity and femininity than that offered by Freud, despite there being many acknowledged problems with Jung.[3] Other traditions, including theories of the Goddess have also been influential.[4]

The incorporation of such traditions into some versions of feminism raises issues which remain fundamental to any assessment of a feminist 'politics', since one argument put against such feminist mysticism has been precisely that it is an abdication of a 'politics'.[5] Such arguments have been countered in practice by those who believe that a feminist politics demands an integrated holistic view. This was perhaps best epitomised in the 1980s by the Greenham women, in whom the convergence of feminist spirituality and feminist politics was emblematised in images of women outside Cruise missile bases with bolt-cutters for the fences singing their anthem, 'You can't kill the Spirit, She is like a mountain, Old and strong, She goes on and on and on.'

In the case of Ursula Le Guin the traditions of Taoism have enabled her to create a science fiction in which a feminist engagement with mysticism appears to work with, rather than against, her political concerns for the present and possible future power relations between the sexes. This chapter seeks to explore the degree to which this apparent negotiation of a radical gender politics and mysticism is achieved in examples from her earlier, more explicitly Taoist work, in particular *The Left Hand of Darkness*, and some of the contradictions that arise. Le Guin provides an intriguing case study of a writer using a popular fictional form for the investigation of significant political and philosophical issues. She also offers an instructive example for critics from the left who ask what possible relationship there can be between traditions like Taoism and radical politics.[6]

Gender Issue

I will be considering the nature of Le Guin's Taoism later in the chapter, but to begin with I want to focus the discussion on the issue of gender politics.

One obvious reason for anxiety about feminist mysticism lies in the argument that it encourages not only an apolitical stance but also a binary essentialist view of gender division. Sarah Lefanu has given a fairly stringent critique of this element in Le Guin's work. She has argued that Le Guin's utopian outlook enforces a binary view of gender which fosters a 'denial of conflict' and is far from subversive.[7] Paradoxically, Lefanu argues, this is part of her appeal for women readers as well as men readers. Discussing *The Left Hand of Darkness*, Lefanu argues that:

> The problematics of sexual desire are, quite simply, eliminated. The book offers a retreat from conflict ... it speaks to liberal rather than misogynistic male readers, to readers who feel at ease with the kind of feminism that seeks to remove conflict and difference.[8]

She compares Le Guin unfavourably with what is for her the more radical work of Joanna Russ, 'the single most important woman writer of science fiction':[9] 'the revolutionary nature of her writing is to be found, as Toril Moi says, in her deconstruction of "the death-dealing binary oppositions of masculinity and femininity" ';[10] 'For Joanna Russ's view is not a holistic one: her concern is not to construct a "whole" or consistent self, but instead to deconstruct, to pick apart, to open up.' [11] Lefanu concludes her critique by arguing that:

> of the writers looked at in the second half of this book, Ursula Le Guin is the least radical in her approach to sexual politics. Sexuality is, in her work, too integral a part of a philosophy of binary systems [i.e. presumably Taoism] that leads, ineluctably, to stasis. This is related, I think, to her search for the whole person, for Mrs Brown, her idealistic hope that, there, symmetry or balance can be found ... her conception of her beloved outer space and her inner lands is too closely related to parameters set by mainstream narrative modes to explore to the full the explosive potential of science fiction.[12]

This seems to suggest that Le Guin's radicalism falls victim not simply to her own mystical bent but also to the dominant patriarchal orientation of science fiction as a genre – as if Le Guin's narrative skills were trapped within the closed certainties of dominant science fiction conventions. But if we look more closely at *The Left Hand of Darkness* we find this is far from being so.

One of Sarah Lefanu's most apparently trenchant criticisms of Le Guin's work stems from her observation that 'Le Guin's "people" are always men.' [13] In the case of *The Left Hand of Darkness*, despite the androgynous nature of the Gethenian inhabitants of the planet Winter, according to Lefanu, they never appear as women; and she quotes Le Guin herself admitting that 'the central failure in this area comes up in the frequent criticism I receive, that the Gethenians seem like *men*, instead of men-women.' [14] This is compounded for Lefanu by 'the use throughout of the generic "he" '.[15] This too is a criticism Le Guin has herself taken on board in her reflections on one of her earlier essays on gender, accepting that 'This is a real flaw in the book' and 'I think women were justified in asking more courage of me and a more rigorous thinking-through of implications.' [16] But, despite Le Guin's own self-criticism of this text, these arguments miss a fundamental point. And this point derives from the fact that, far from being a victim of the genre, *The Left Hand of Darkness* creates a complex narrative effect whose dynamic is precisely to problematise questions of gender.

Take the opening section of the novel. This is presented as a report written by Genly Ai on a mission to the planet Winter to encourage the bisexual Gethenians to join the Ekumenical alliance. Ai is a male from Earth; and, as Lefanu correctly points out, he is 'apparently, a trained anthropological observer, but his preconceptions of and prejudices towards women are positively prehistorical'.[17] And *that*, quite simply, *is* the point, but it is one for which Lefanu fails to give Le Guin's text full credit or see the textual implications of. The Gethenians are all described as 'male' because Ai's own male perception cannot imagine or cope with anything else. We are given a biased and partial male narrative view point which itself enforces a gendered categorisation on the bisexual Gethenians. Moreover, it is one which, far from denying conflict, opens out a far-reaching investigation of gender issues.

Throughout the opening section of the novel the narrative presents Ai's incomprehension and resistance to an ungendered identity, and his remorseless inability to avoid gender categorisation. Thus the very use of the male pronoun by Ai is signalled as early as the third page, while Ai describes his conversation with the bisexual Gethenian, Estraven, 'the man – *man* I must say, having said *he* and *his*.' [18] Throughout the next few pages what is stressed is Ai's continuing inability to comprehend the psychology of the Gethenians despite the fact that he's been an envoy on the planet for some two years, his inability to 'master the protocol', his lack of 'experiential feel'.[19] The limits of the description and classification of behaviour are a continuing exposé of the limitations of Ai's own male perception: he remains unable 'to see the people of the planet through their own eyes'. Instead his efforts take the form of 'self-consciously seeing a Gethenian first as a man, then as a woman, forcing him into those categories so irrelevant to his nature and so essential to my own.' [20]

So, in his dealings with Estraven in this opening section, Ai misreads Estraven's actions as examples of 'effeminate deviousness'.[21] Ai doesn't trust him,[22] sees him as 'faithless',[23] and suspects him of manipulation, of using his own mission and himself as 'pawns in his power-game'[24] Ai admits that Estraven was 'too incalculable', but feels 'Trust him or not, I might still get some use out of him.' [25] The language here is not simply that of an Earthly political Machiavell; it also borders on the language of male sexual politics, and this is an aspect that Ai's text reveals in itself. He admits to having thought of Estraven's behaviour as 'womanly, all charm and tact and lack of substance, specious and adroit', and it was for this reason that he disliked and distrusted him – because Ai simultaneously found it impossible to think of Estraven 'as a woman ... and yet whenever I thought of him as a man, I felt a sense of falseness, of imposture: in him, or in my own attitude toward him'.[26]

This argument applies not just to the opening section: it can be extended to the whole of the book. Ai's main narrative takes up nine of the 20 chapters. But it is clear from the structure and from explicit indications in the text that the rest of the narrative, including the records of Karhidish law and, most importantly, the sections from Estraven's journal, are presented as having been transcribed within Ai's report.[27] This is crucial, since it determines the overall narrative viewpoint of the text. In other words, we see everything through Ai's eyes and hear everything in his language. All the usages of gender specific pronouns and nouns ('he', 'king', etc.) are being presented as Ai's mistranslation of concepts he cannot understand or which cannot be adequately represented in his manmade language.

Thus the binary gender division enforced in this book is a product not of Le Guin's own limitations: it is the very object of investigation in the form of her deliberately chosen partial male narrator, Ai, who cannot do other than enforce a binary opposition on ungendered people who defy his criteria and experience. We learn in Chapter 7 that the very first investigator of the first Ekumenical landing on Gethen, Ong Tot Oppong, had warned future visitors against doing what 'a bisexual naturally does' – that is, 'to cast [a Gethenian] in the role of Man or Woman' and then assume a role corresponding to the conventional expectations of 'the patterned or possible interactions between persons of the same or the opposite sex'. Ong stresses that Gethenians 'cannot play the game. They do not see one another as men or women. This is almost impossible for our imagination to accept.' [28]

The fascinating thing about this statement and the whole chapter is that, as we realise in its final paragraph, Ong Tot Oppong was a woman, 'the only voice of a woman in the book' as Le Guin herself has pointed out.[29] Yet despite her provisos, Ong too finds the conceptualisation of the Gethenians problematic linguistically: the pronoun 'it' is inadequate since 'They are not neuters. They are potentials or integrals. Lacking the Karhidish "human pronoun" used for persons in somer, I must say "he".' [30]

Despite this directive, at the opening of the novel Ai has none of Ong's awareness, precisely because he is male. Lefanu argues that, like all Le Guin's 'male heroes with their crises of identity, caught in the stranglehold of liberal individualism', Ai acts 'as a dead weight' at the centre of the novel.[31] But that is to miss the complex function of this male voice as a linguistically and ideologically biased narrator, a narrative device which generates a self-exposé of patriarchal assumptions and relations. This is the book's 'political unconscious', because in her self-criticism of the book quoted earlier [reference 16], Le Guin also apparently misses it. It is as if she too could not see the actual workings of her own text and was assuming a limitation in this text by virtue of its apparently unavoidable entrapment in patriarchally gendered language, just as her own creation Ong Tot Oppong does despite her own directive that when you meet a Gethenian 'you cannot and must not ... cast *him* in the role of Man or Woman' [my emphasis].

The almost marginal voice of Ong (merely a five-sided chapter) is thus most representative of the contradictions in Le Guin's own position at the time of writing. What she wrote is nevertheless remarkable for its anticipation of central issues – for its awareness of the gender-enforcement effected through language, and perhaps even more for its exploration of the limits of *masculinity* and of male sexual perception. This particularly must be taken as historically and culturally specific to Le Guin's own writing of the novel. Her writing of this book was contemporaneous not only with the rise of the feminist movement; it also anticipated the rise of concern for the problems of masculinity and male power among feminists and men influenced by feminism during the next two decades.

The delimiting effects of Ai's masculinity on his perceptions are exposed explicitly through his own admission at various points in the novel. In Chapter 5 he describes 'the biological shock I suffered as a human male among human beings who were, five-sixths of the time, hermaphrodite neuters'.[32] More tellingly, during his journey with Estraven, he admits that the source of his refusal to contemplate friendship with Estraven is because he is 'locked in my virility'.[33] Why? Because of what he later calls 'the more competitive elements of my masculine self-respect', which Estraven lacks and which therefore do not 'complicate his pride'.[34] Perceptively, Le Guin's book offers us an insight into the origins of such masculine complications, the origins of aggressive-defensive masculinity itself – sexual fear. During their journey across the ice, Ai finally sees 'what I had always been afraid to see, and had pretended not to see in him: that he was a woman as well as a man'. His 'fear' is replaced by an 'acceptance of him as he was' which he had not been prepared to give previously: as he admits, 'I had not wanted to give my trust, my friendship to a man who was a woman, a woman who was a man.'[35]

Cleverly, the novel has Ai present his narrative of these events from the point of view he had as they happened, without the benefit of his later experiences with, and insight into, Estraven and his/her motives. Thus one direction that the novel offers for the reader's exploration is the growing awareness of its male narrator Ai to issues of sexual politics: he undergoes something of a 'crisis in masculinity', with which he finally comes to terms, and this for 1969 was quite an advanced proposition, given that the focus on masculinity and the male response to feminism has been a phenomenon of the 1980s.

By the end of the novel, as Douglas Barbour puts it, 'Ai finally comes to accept and love Estraven as a whole person',[36] and that is the point at which Ai explains to Estraven the yin-yang symbol of the Tao. Intriguingly then, it is precisely in relation to the personal tensions between these two characters and the political machinations in which they are caught up that Le Guin chooses to introduce a third element – Taoism. Is this a mystical defusing of what has so far been seen to be a questioning and critical text?

Radical Taoism

The mission to Gethen is on behalf of the Ekumen, an alliance of planets which approaches possible new members on the basis of a personal relationship offered by one lone representative, in this case Ai. Ai stresses this aspect of his mission a number of times throughout the book, but what he fails to do, until the journey with Estraven, is fully practice his own politics. He does present an honest and gullible persona, who easily becomes the victim of political machinations in both Gethen nations he visits, Karhide and Orgota; but as he comes to realise on the ice, he has been unable actually to accept the only individual person who truly trusts him and believes his story – Estraven. In accepting Estraven and forming a friendship with him, the text suggests, Ai is achieving a truer version of his political mission at the personal level. After Estraven has been shot Ai realises that he must fulfil what he died for, for friendship's sake rather than principle.[37]

The sense of this is to stress what became the crucial feminist slogan 'the personal is political'. But Le Guin does not leave it there. She insists on a further awareness which negotiates the dialectic between personal and political – that is, an attention to the overall process within which these two terms are caught up. The 'personal-is-political-is-personal' proposition still remains formulated within the limits of those two terms. As a result, as with any formulation of revolutionary activity, it is liable to the effects of a backward and forwards action–reaction influence which tips the balance one way and then the other. The only way to avoid getting caught up in the kind of revolutionary action–reaction chain of events so familiar from past historical examples is to introduce an awareness of the ongoing *process* at work, the dialectical process of which such oppositions are the building blocks. To put it in the terms offered in the novel by Estraven: to oppose the political with the personal is to maintain it – 'To oppose something is to maintain it ... you must go somewhere else; you must have another goal; then you walk a different road.' 38

For Le Guin in 1969 the only vehicle available to her through which to express this sense of process, this other road, was the mystical, Taoism. That she should have wished to involve her political awareness with a mystical one is readily explained since, as she says in an essay, 'Taoism got to me earlier than modern feminism did.' 39 It is perhaps not surprising that Le Guin should have made this connection between radicalism, feminism and Taoism given her historical and cultural placing. Her major early work was being written in the context of two fundamental influences, the emerging of eastern mysticism as an influence in the 1950s and 1960s and the simultaneous emergence of the contemporary feminist movement. The emergence of eastern influences was in fact being laid much earlier: it first came through in the early twentieth century with figures like Yeats and Pound and Fenellosa. By the 1930s a figure such as Alan Watts was undergoing a transformation from Anglican to Buddhist-Taoist, and in his early writings Watts gets as close as anyone to catching in language a sense of that elusive 'here-and-now' approach to life which characterises both Taoism and Zen, with his view that spirituality is 'creative spontaneous living'.40 By the 1950s with *The Way of Zen* he had become a seminal influence for the transmission of Zen and Taoism into contemporary cultural movements such as the Beats and the Hippies. Le Guin's admission that Taoism got to her before feminism is, then, historically about right since it was such movements which encouraged the dissemination of eastern mysticism in the 1960s, and these prefigured feminism.

More specifically, Le Guin's view of Taoism seems to have been shaped by one particularly influential work from the 1950s, generally acknowledged to be one of the landmarks of modern scholarship, the extraordinary 15-volume *Science and Civilisation in China* by Sir Joseph Needham.41

Needham is a biochemist, now in his nineties working in Cambridge. His multivolume history of Chinese science and civilisation is seen as the definitive work not just by western scholars but by Chinese scholars too. Needham is also a life-long left-winger. Taoism is often considered simply as a set of values, an outlook, a practice. But Needham saw the political context of Taoism as crucial to any understanding of it. Needham's treatment is extensive and his evidence overwhelmingly convincing.

In his account, Taoism is born as a critique of the dominant feudalism of the Chou dynasty, and all its recommendations for the quiet life are to be seen as semi-utopian visions of a lost semi-communistic lifestyle before the advent of feudalism.[42] Needham's account explains why the *yin* principle, the yielding feminine principle, is the starting point for Taoism by pointing out that before feudalism in China, there would have existed a matrilineal tribal organisation with no aggressive notion of private property in which work and ownership were seen as in common.[43] He presents the Taoists as analogous with the Levellers, Diggers and Ranters of the seventeenth century in Britain, a religio-political phenomenon. He also presents them as proto-empiricists, whose insistence on emptying the mind was a specific answer to the Confucian insistence on values, a false knowledge of social distinctions which cluttered awareness with preconceptions and prejudices which needed purging.[44]

He finds 15 chapters of the *Tao Te Ching* to have 'a clear political significance',[45] attacking acquisitiveness, private property,[46] exploitation of the peasantry and common people by feudal lords;[47] and he sees them as advocating instead the virtues of common life and natural liberty,[48] advocating the commonsense wisdom of the common people who have the 'knack' of living intuitively,[49] and looking back to a lost social harmony when balanced relationships echoed the balanced harmony of the cosmos.[50] The Taoists, he says, had 'the poetical expression of a cooperative collectivist society', such as had existed 'in the primitive collectivism of the villages before the full differentiation of lords, priests and warriors in bronze-age proto-feudalism'; and which 'was to exist again (though the Taoists could not know that millennia must elapse before humanity would return to their ideals)'. The lingering elements of Taoism in China have, he argues, been 'Conducting a socialist holding action for two thousand years.'[51]

Perhaps Needham's view of the Taoists as proto-Maoists now seems naive, and is to be explained by the context within which *he* was writing during the 1940s and 1950s. But he puts a fascinating case for seeing mysticism as potentially playing the role of a progressive social force when he argues: 'When a certain body of rationalist thought has become irrevocably tied to a rigid and outdated system of society, and has become associated with the social controls and sanctions which it imposes, then mysticism may become revolutionary.'[52]

Some people may want to disagree with Needham's reading of Taoism, though from the evidence it would be very difficult to do. Nevertheless, even if he were quite *wrong* in his assessments, we would still have an intriguing case. There is no doubt that in part at least Ursula Le Guin bases her view of Taoism directly on Needham's account. Needham's second volume, dealing with Taoism, appeared in 1956, and was reprinted continuously through the 1960s. I have no exact date for when Le Guin read the book; but in her reply to the *Ursula Le Guin Special Issue* of *Science Fiction Studies* (1976), she takes issue with some of the critics who have given appraisals of her Taoism and says:

> May I make one remark about the Tao? In one or two of these pieces ... and all too often elsewhere, I find the critic apparently persuaded that Yin and Yang are *opposites*, *between* which lies the straight, but safe, Way. This is all wrong. There is some contamination from Manichaeanism/Christianity, or Marxist dialectics, or something. I really do not dare try to explain about the T'ai chi t'u, I will get wandering off ... but I recommend reading Joseph Needham (NB: a Marxist), or Wilhelm's Introduction to the *I Ching*, or Holmes's *Parting of the Ways*. The central image/idea of Taoism is an important thing to be clear about, certainly not because it's a central theme in my work. It's a central theme, period.[53]

And any reading of her *own* views of Taoism will notice the way in which she invariably links it to a form of politics usually described as anarchism, a word Needham also uses.[54]

In part, she sees Taoism as akin to anarchism in its political form. In her novel *The Dispossessed*, she presents us with a political community founded on the life and ideas of the woman revolutionary, Odo; and she has described the philosophy behind the idea like this:

> Odonianism is anarchism. Not the bomb-in-the-pocket stuff, which is terrorism, whatever name it tries to dignify itself with; not the social-Darwinist 'libertarianism' of the far right; but anarchism, as prefigured in early Taoist thought, and expounded by Shelley and Kropotkin, Goldman and Goodman. Anarchism's principal target is the authoritarian state (capitalist or socialist); its principal moral-practical theme is cooperation (solidarity, mutual aid). It is the most idealistic, and to me the most interesting, of all political theories.[55]

Elsewhere she has elaborated:

> The major utopic element in my novel *The Dispossessed* is a variety of pacifist anarchism, which is about as yin as a political ideology can get. Anarchism rejects the identification of civilisation with the state, and the identification of power with coercion; against the inherent violence of the 'hot' society it asserts the value of such antisocial behaviour as the general refusal of women to bear arms in war ... In these areas anarchism and Taoism converge in both matter and manner.[56]

The links with the philosophies of political anarchism are clearly marked in *The Dispossessed*. At one point a character asks 'Listen, wasn't it Odo who said that where there's property there's theft?', and is given a quote from Odo in reply: '"To make a thief, make an owner; to create crime, create laws."' [57] Such arguments are clearly related to the ideas of Kropotkin.[58] Elsewhere, we can see her overt use of Taoism in various texts: in the novel *City of Illusions* (1967),[59] the Old Canon of wisdom used by Falk is based on the *Tao Te Ching*. In *The Lathe of Heaven* (1972),[60] chapters are prefixed by an epigram from Lao Tzǔ or Chuang Tzǔ, while the title is taken from Chuang Tzǔ.

The reason Taoism offered her a possible model is partly because it is made of three distinct terms rather than two: the *yin* and the *yang* are the parts that make up the whole process, the *tao*.[61] As Ai explained to Estraven, the apparent binary divisions which make up the tao are in fact not separable: all apparent binary opposites, light and dark, male and female, are 'Both and one.' [62] The *tao* is a way of stressing process as something holistic over and above the particularities and parts, but at the same time it is not other-wordly or transcendental: it is made up in fact *only* of the particularities and parts, caught up in the natural, spontaneous process of energy transformation which is the present moment. The freedom achievable through Taoist awareness as through Zen is partly one of acceptance of the moment and non-attachment to any one of its components. Using Chuang Tzǔ as his text, Alan Watts put it in a way which chimes well with Le Guin's views:

> If you never lose hold on this eternal Now, you find yourself in harmony with life ... The realization of this brings the most unbelievable freedom of spirit, releasing energies of the soul hitherto undreamed of. Loss and gain become things of no account because you have nothing to gain and nothing to lose; you can stake your life without turning a hair, and at every point you find yourself free to go left or right, backwards or forwards, just as you choose. For you yourself have become the eternal Path, and carrying it with you you can never depart from it whichever way you turn. This is called responsible irresponsibility, for the sage is a law-abiding vagabond.[63]

To put it another way, for Le Guin, Taoism was a metaphor for the awareness of overall process which allows political–personal formulation to escape the delimiting nature of each part of the equation. And if the proposal that there might be an overlap between political philosophy/practice and the views explored in Taoism seems farfetched, it is worth remembering that such hard-headed materialists as Engels and Lenin both variously presented views of dialectical philosophy which smack of much the same sense of process and change that Le Guin's text explores.[64]

The way *The Left Hand of Darkness* expresses this is, fittingly, positive and negative. Negatively, having arrived in Mishnory after his failure in Karhide, Ai explains his mission to the Orgotians with little conviction. He defines the Ekumen not as a government, but as 'an attempt to reunify the mystical with the political'. He admits that this is mostly a failure, 'but its failure has done more good for humanity so far than the successes of its predecessors'.[65] Positively, Ai reformulates his project to Estraven on the ice in the middle of their journey, having experienced his own sense of acceptance at being part of a process. He explains that the Ekumen send their primary envoys singly because although they cannot change the world alone they can 'be changed by it'. Such a strategy depends on creating a relationship which is 'not impersonal and not only political: it is individual, it is personal, it is both more and less than political'. It is not political 'but mystical':

> In a certain sense the Ekumen is not a body politic, but a body mystic. It considers beginnings to be extremely important. Beginnings and means. Its doctrine is just the reverse of the doctrine that the end justifies the means.[66]

What Le Guin's text is doing here is offering an awareness that 'you are *what* you do *and how* you do it', one that has become crucial for all political activity deriving from or influenced by feminism. This stress on attention to the process of change rather than the goals or ends of change is a subversive questioning of conventional left models of revolutionary action; and it is achieved through her appropriation of the model offered by Taoism. 'The way that can be spoken is not the true way': to prescribe a path is to deny the process; fix your final goals and you kill the revolution, or become Stalin enforcing them. The Taoist emphasis on change as a process seems to appeal to Le Guin precisely because it offers a model for social change as well as personal and natural change. It is not offered as an asocial timeless transcendental truth which elevates awareness to some ethereal mystical plane. Quite the reverse: it is, for her, a paradigm of the here-and-now business of change between individuals and groups.

The Left Hand of Darkness, then, is a novel which simultaneously offers a critique of masculinity and a critique of the political process. What Le Guin was offering in this book was a forethinking awareness of the difficulties which lay ahead and a suggestion for a model which might allow at least a different way of looking at the issues involved, in a fictional form which is all the more involving for being an explicitly popular form. It is here that we can see something of the answer in Le Guin's case to the question of what possible relationship there can be between her fictional practice, Taoism and radical politics.

That relationship has in fact between anticipated in other radical writers. The revolutionary mystic William Blake is one obvious example of a creative writer in whose work radicalism and mysticism are inextricably part and parcel of a total critique of the social, psychological, historical and cosmic levels of experience. On a less grandiose scale and perhaps more intriguing for that, Bertolt Brecht was an ardent reader of Lao Tzŭ, whose *Tao Te Ching* still forms the basic text for Taoist thought.[67] Throughout her development, Le Guin has recurrently chosen to integrate the popular science fictional form with an investigation of gender issues, political issues and mystical issues. Similarly she challenges the over-ready categorisation of what constitutes the 'political' by offering a negotiation of traditions which are often seen as antagonistic, radical politics and radically concrete mysticism. She takes on these negotiations of form and content in ways which open doors rather than close them, and this is in keeping with her view of the feminist project as 'demystification'.[68] Le Guin has noted her own tendencies to be 'an extremely moral writer. I am always grinding axes and making points.'[69] Yet her best fiction avoids being prescriptive because, as she has put it, 'If utopia is a place that does not exist, then surely (as Lao Tzŭ would say) the way to get there is by the way that is not a way.'[70] It is precisely this kind of radical challenge which Le Guin's Taoist-feminism science fiction presents for its readers.

Notes and References

1. See Sarah Lefanu *In the Chinks of the World Machine: Feminism and Science Fiction* London: The Women's Press, 1988 which includes an excellent bibliography, and Lucie Armilt ed *Where No Man Has Gone Before: Women and Science Fiction* London: Routledge 1991.
2. Mary Daly *Gyn/Ecology* The Women's Press 1979. A gloss on my use of the word 'mysticism' is appropriate. I am employing the term in the double sense indicated by the *Oxford English Dictionary*:

   1. The opinions, mental tendencies, or habits of thought and feelings, characteristic of mystics; mystical doctrines or spirit; belief in the possibility of union with the Divine nature by means of ecstatic contemplation; reliance on spiritual intuition or exalted feeling as the means of acquiring knowledge of mysteries inaccessible to intellectual apprehension.

   2. As a term of reproach. a. from the hostile point of view, mysticism implies self-delusion or dreamy confusion

of thought; hence the term is often applied loosely to any religious belief to which these evil qualities are imputed. b. Sometimes applied to philosophical or scientific theories alleged to involve the assumption of occult qualities or mysterious agencies of which no rational account can be given.
There are obviously different mysticisms to be discriminated and different elements within each of them. I would consider certain elements of Taoism (including the works of Lao Tzŭ, Chuang Tzŭ and Lieh-tzŭ) to share at least two aspects of definition 1; while I would consider other aspects of later Taoism (including its pursuit of alchemy and magic) as belonging to definition 2. My investigation in this essay is partly to consider which of these definitions is more appropriate to Le Guin's usage of Taoism.

3. For a positive attempt to reconcile feminism and Jung see D.S. Wehr *Jung and Feminism* London: Routledge 1988. A critique of Jung and feminism can be found in Lucy Goodison *Moving Heaven and Earth* London: The Women's Press 1991.

4. Some examples include Nor Hall *The Moon and the Virgin: Reflections on the Archetypal Feminine* New York: Harper & Row 1980; Charlene Spretnak ed *The Politics of Women's Spirituality* New York: Anchor Press/Doubleday 1982; Hallie Iglehart *Womanspirit: A Guide to Women's Wisdom* San Francisco: Harper & Row 1983; Jean Shioda Bolen *Goddesses in Everywoman: A New Psychology of Women* Harper & Row 1985; Brenda Mallon *Women Dreaming* Fontana 1987; Jennifer Barker Woolger and Roger J. Woolger *The Goddess Within* Rider 1990.

5. Examples of feminists critical of the feminist deployment of myth for example include Angela Carter's scathing critique:
    If women allow themselves to be consoled for the culturally determined lack of access to the modes of intellectual debate by the invocation of hypothetical great goddesses, they are simply flattering themselves into submission ... All mythic versions of women, from the myth of the redeeming purity of the virgin to that of the healing reconciling mother, are consolatory nonsenses; and consolatory nonsenses seems to me a fair definition of myth (*The Sadeian Women* London: Virago 1979 p. 5);
    and Elizabeth Janeway *Powers of the Weak* New York: Knopf 1980 ('Myth, Legend and Ritual ... function to maintain a status quo' p. 147).

6. It is a question I pose as a man on the left for whom Marxism and feminism have been decisive shaping influences in terms of political awareness and activity, but who at the same time has always found that the traditions of Zen and Taoism speak to me of equally significant areas of experience, and who practices a Taoist art in the form of T'ai Chi.

A number of other critics have previously mapped out the influence of Taoism on Le Guin's writing, though the link-up with her feminism has not been dealt with as fully. Examples of work which looks at the Taoism include particularly the essays of Douglas Barbour, specifically 'The Lather of Heaven: Taoist Dream' *Algol*, 21 November 1973 pp. 22–4; 'Wholeness and Balance in the Hainish Novels of Ursula K. Le Guin' *Science Fiction Studies* 1, 1974 pp. 164–73; 'On Ursula Le Guin's *A Wizard of Earthsea*' *Riverside Quarterly*, 6, pp. 119–23; and 'Wholeness and Balance: An Addendum' *Science Fiction Studies*, 3, November 1975 pp. 238–49. The other main example relevant to this piece is John H. Crow and Richard D. Erlich 'Words of Binding: Patterns of Integration in the Earthsea Trilogy' in Joseph D. Olander and Martin Harry Greenberg eds. *Ursula K. Le Guin* New York: Taplinger 1979 pp. 200–24. Crow and Erlich again raise some issues relevant to my argument, particularly with reference to the possible links for Le Guin between Taoism and anarchism, but again they overlook any relationship with her feminism.

7. Lefanu *In The Chinks* 1988 p. 139.
8. Ibid. p. 142.
9. Ibid. p. 172.
10. Ibid. p. 175.
11. Ibid. p. 191.
12. Ibid. pp. 145–6.
13. Ibid. p. 136.
14. Ibid. p. 138.
15. Ibid.
16. 'Is Gender Necessary?' 1976 'Redux' 1988 in Ursula K. Le Guin *The Language of the Night: Essays on Fantasy and Science Fiction* edited with an introduction by Susan Wood, revised edition edited by Ursula K. Le Guin London: The Women's Press 1989 p. 146.
17. Lefanu *In The Chinks* 1988 p. 137.
18. Ursula K. Le Guin *The Left Hand of Darkness* Granada 1977 p. 110.
19. Le Guin *The Left* 1977 p. 19.
20. Ibid. p. 16.
21. Ibid. p. 17.
22. Ibid. p. 16.
23. Ibid. p. 17.
24. Ibid. p. 19.
25. Ibid. p. 18.
26. Ibid. p. 16.
27. Indications that the whole novel is to be seen as having been transcribed by Ai can be inferred from the references on pages 142, 191 and 201 to Ai's possession and transcription of Estraven's notebooks.
28. Le Guin *The Left* 1977 pp. 69–70.

29. Le Guin 'Redux' 1988 p. 146.
30. Le Guin *The Left* 1977 p. 70.
31. Lefanu *In the Chinks* 1988 p. 137.
32. Le Guin *The Left* 1977 p. 39.
33. Ibid. p. 145
34. Ibid.
35. Ibid. p. 167.
36. Barbour 'Wholeness and Balance' 1974 p. 166.
37. Le Guin *The Left* 1977 p. 194.
38. Ibid. p. 106.
39. Le Guin *The Language* 1989 pp. 118–9. For Le Guin's place in relation to the history of contemporary feminist movements, see Susan Bassnett 'Remaking the Old World' in Armitt *Where No Man* 1991 pp. 56–61. In her essay 'Response to the Le Guin Issue' *Science Fiction Studies* no. 8 vol. 3 pp. 43–6, Le Guin refers to a book on Taoism which obviously made an impact on her in the late 1950s or early 1960s, Holmes Welch's *The Parting of the Ways: Lao Tzŭ and the Taoist Movement* Boston: Beacon Press 1957; while in her essay 'The Stalin in the Soul' (1973–7) she states 'I was a feminist in 1968', and then adds a footnote dated 1989 with the gloss 'Well, I was beginning to be one, anyhow.' (Le Guin *The Language* 1989 p. 193.)
40. John Snelling and Dennis T. Sibley with Mark Watts *The Early Writings of Alan Watts* London: Century 1987 pp. 234, 237.
41. See Joseph Needham *Science and Civilisation in China* vol. 2 'History of Scientific Thought' Cambridge: Cambridge University Press 1980.
42. Needham *Science* 1980 p. 86.
43. Ibid. p. 105.
44. Ibid. pp. 87–9, 107.
45. Ibid. p. 100.
46. Ibid. pp. 102, 111.
47. Ibid. p. 112.
48. Ibid. pp. 106, 108.
49. Ibid. pp. 120, 122–3.
50. Ibid. pp. 104, 106.
51. Ibid. pp. 59–60.
52. Ibid. p. 97.
53. Ursula K. Le Guin 'A Response to the Le Guin Issue' *Science Fiction Studies* II, 1976 p. 157.
54. Needham *Science* 1980 p. 70.
55. Ursula K. Le Guin introduction to 'The Day before the Revolution' from *The Wind's Twelve Quarters* London: Gollancz 1976, p. 285.
56. Ursula K. Le Guin 'A Non-Euclidean View of California' in *Dancing at the Edge of the World* New York: Grove 1989 p. 93.
57. Ursula K. Le Guin *The Dispossessed* Granada 1979 p. 120.

58. It is worth remarking that while *The Dispossessed* is more overtly political than *The Left Hand of Darkness*, it is less overtly Taoist. There are certainly clear elements of the book that could be related to Taoist thought. The Odonian critique of egoising or Shevek's emphasis on an empty-handed approach to life are clearly reminiscent of elements to be found in Chuang Tzu: 'If a man can roam in the world with emptied self, who can interfere with him?' But Le Guin transfers much of the mystical weight of the book from a Taoist register into a scientific one. She uses the awareness which has become more widespread since she wrote the book, that post-quantum physics has elements which are analogous with a Taoist outlook (e.g. Fritjof Capra *The Tao of Physics* Fontana 1981, and Gary Zukav *The Dancing Wu Lei Masters* Fontana 1984). So Shevek the scientist, who is seeking to resolve simultaneity and sequentialism, becomes the vehicles for exploring a mystical awareness of the anarchist politics of the Odonians, both as it relates to human relationships with his partner Takver and as it relates to his awareness of a connectedness with the cosmos. A crucial example might be Chapter 9 of the book in which Shevek undergoes both a mystical revelation as he uncovers the final elements of his general theory and a political initiation as he takes part in the workers' strike on Urras. In his moment of scientific enlightenment, Shevek achieves an insight into the laws of the universe which leaves him 'dispossessed' of self in Chuang Tzu's sense, aware of belonging to an organic whole: 'He knew he was part of it, not it of him. he was in its keeping' (p. 234). In his speech to the mass demonstration he presents a political credo which is essentially identical with his scientific-mystical vision, a sense of unity and wholeness predicated upon an awareness of shared 'dispossession', an awareness which forms a basis for collective action: 'We know that there is no help for us but from one another, that no hand will save us if we do not reach out our hand. And the hand that you reach out is empty, as mine is. You have nothing. You possess nothing. You own nothing. You are free. All you have is what you are, and what you give.' (p. 249). This juxtaposition of scientific and political enlightenment achieves a simultaneous presentation of a materialist, political and mystical understanding rooted in the here-and-now.

59. Ursula K. Le Guin *City of Illusions* (1967) Granada 1980;

60. Ursula K. Le Guin *The Lathe of Heaven* (1972) Grafton 1988.

61. See Lao Tzŭ *Tao Te Ching* trans. Richard Wilhelm, Arkana 1987; A.C. Graham *Chuang Tzŭ: The Inner Chapters* Unwin 1989; A.C. Graham trans. *The Book of Lieh-tzŭ* New York: Columbia University Press 1990; Alan Watts *Tao: The Watercourse Way* Penguin 1986.

62. Le Guin *The Left* 1977 p. 180.
63. Watts *Tao* 1986 p. 247.
64. Marx and Engels's historical materialism has a quality which
    connects it immediately with the fundamental outlook of
    Taoism, the dialectic. In Taoism, dialectic is built into a
    fundamental view of life itself, yin and yang making up the
    Tao. The emphasis in on a flowing process of change, and
    that has overlaps with Engels's view of the Marxist dialectic:

> This dialectical philosophy dissolves all conceptions of
> final absolute truth and of absolute states of humanity
> corresponding to it. For it nothing is final, absolute, sacred.
> It reveals the transitory character of everything and in
> everything; nothing can endure before it except the uninter-
> rupted process of becoming and of passing away, of endless
> ascendancy from the lower to the higher. And dialectical
> philosophy itself is nothing more than the mere reflection
> of this process in the thinking brain. It has, of course, also
> a conservative side; it recognises that definite stages of
> knowledge and society are justified for their time and
> circumstances; but only so far. The conservatism of this
> mode of outlook is relative; its revolutionary character is
> absolute – the only absolute dialectical philosophy admits.

More unexpected is the case of that hard-headed materialist,
Lenin. At one point Lenin argues that the course of human
development should be seen as following 'not ... a straight
line, but a curve, which endlessly approximates a series of
circles, a spiral', a view whose overlaps with modern chaos
theory are particularly intriguing in the context of my argument given the way Le Guin uses science in *The Dispossessed*. Lenin elaborated his views further in this manner:

> In our time the idea of development, of evolution, has
> almost completely penetrated social consciousness, only in
> other ways, and not through Hegelian philosophy. Still, this
> idea, as formulated by Marx and Engels on the basis of
> Hegel's philosophy, is far more comprehensive and far
> richer in content than the current idea of evolution is. A
> development that repeats, as it were, stages that have
> already been passed but repeats them in a different way, on
> a higher basis ('the negation of negation'), a development,
> so to speak, that proceeds in spirals, not in a straight line; a
> development by leaps, catastrophes, and revolutions;
> 'breaks in continuity'; the transformation of quantity into
> quality; inner impulses towards development, imparted by
> the contradiction and conflict of the various forces and
> tendencies acting on a given body, or within a given
> phenomenon, or within a given society; the interdepend-
> ence and the closest and indissoluble connection between
> all aspects of any phenomenon (history constantly revealing
> ever new aspects), a connection that provides a uniform,
> and universal process of motion, one that follows definite

laws – these are some of the features of dialectics as a doctrine of development that is richer than the conventional one.

Both extracts quoted in Peter Brooker *Bertolt Brecht – Dialectics, Poetry, Politics* Croom Helm 1989 pp. 29, 40.

65. Le Guin *The Left* 1977 p. 96.
66. Ibid. p. 175.
67. The story of Lao Tzu's writing of the *Tao Te Ching* forms the basis for one of Brecht's best ballads – see Bertolt Brecht *Poems 1913–56* ed. John Willett and Ralph Manheim, Methuen 1976 p. 314 and notes.
68. 'Doing Two Things in Opposite Direction: Ursula Le Guin Talks to Colin Greenland' *Interzone* no. 45, March 1991 p. 61.
69. Le Guin *The Language* 1989 p. 107.
70. Ursula K. Le Guin 'A Non-Euclidean View of California' in *Dancing at the Edge of the World* New York: Grove 1989 p. 93.

Bibliography

Primary Texts

Alther, Lisa *Kinflicks* Harmondsworth: Penguin 1977.
    Original Sins Harmondsworth: Penguin 1981.
Barker, Pat *Union Street* London: Virago 1982.
    Blow Your House Down London: Virago 1984.
    The Century's Daughter London: Virago 1986.
    The Man Who Wasn't There London: Penguin 1990.
    Regeneration London: Viking 1991.
Brittain, Vera *Testament of Friendship* London: Virago 1985.
Brown, Rita Mae *Rubyfruit Jungle* London: Bantam Books 1983.
Carter, Angela *The Magic Toyshop* London: Virago 1967.
    The Bloody Chamber London: King Penguin 1977.
    The Passion of New Eve London: Virago 1978.
    The Sadeian Woman London: Virago 1979.
    Nights at the Circus London: Chatto and Windus 1984.
    Black Venus London: Chatto and Windus 1987.
    Wise Children London: Chatto and Windus 1991.
Christie, Agatha *Murder is Easy* London: Collins 1973 (1939).
    Dumb Witness London: Collins 1969 (1949).
    A Murder is Announced London: Fontana 1963 (1950).
    The Secret Adversary London: Bodley Head 1955 (1922).
    The Murder on the Links London: Bodley Head 1964 (1923).
Hall, Radclyffe *The Well of Loneliness* London: Virago 1982.
    The Unlit Lamp London: Jonathan Cape 1934.
    Miss Ogilvy Finds Herself London: Hammond 1959.
Holtby, Winifred *Virginia Woolf* London; Lawrence and Wishart 1932.
    The Astonishing Island London; Lovatt Dickenson 1933.
    Anderby Wold London: Virago 1984 (1923).
    The Land of Green Ginger London; Virago 1984 (1927).
    The Crowded Street London: Virago 1981 (1924).
    The Truth is not Sober London Collins 1934.
    South Riding London: Collins 1936.
    The Pavements at Anderby London: Collins 1937.
    Manoa! Manoa! London: Virago 1982 (1933).
Jong, Erica *Fear of Flying* London: Granada 1974.
    How to Save Your Own Life London: Granada 1978.
Lawrence, D.H. *Lady Chatterley's Lover* Harmondsworth: Penguin 1961.
Lessing, Doris *The Golden Notebook* New York: Bantam 1973.
Le Guin, Ursula *The Language of the Night: Essays on Fantasy and Science Fiction* ed Susan Wood New York: Petigree 1979.
    Dancing at the Edge of the World New York: Grove 1989.

The Dispossessed London: Granada 1979.
The Left Hand of Darkness London: Granada 1977.
The Lathe of Heaven London: Grafton 1988.
City of Illusions London: Granada 1980.
Maitland, Sara *Three Times Table* London: Virago 1991.
Morrison, Toni *Song of Solomon* London: Triad Grafton 1980.
Beloved London: Chatto and Windus and The Women's Press 1988.
Roberts, Michèle *In the Red Kitchen* London: Methuen 1990.
Rhys, Jean *Wide Sargasso Sea* London: André Deutsch 1966.
Good Morning Midnight Harmondsworth: Penguin 1969.
Voyage in the Dark Harmondsworth: Penguin 1969.
After Leaving Mr Mackenzie Harmondsworth: Penguin 1971.
Quartet Harmondsworth: Penguin 1973.
Smile Please Harmondsworth: Penguin 1983.
Letters Harmondsworth: Penguin 1985.
Tales of the Wide Caribbean London: Heinemann 1987.
Robins, Pauline *Lady Chatterley's Daughter* London: Consul Books 1961.
Sulman, Alix Kate *Memoirs of an Ex Prom Queen* Chicago: Cassandra 1985 (1972).
Stefan, Verena *Shedding* London: The Women's Press 1979 (1975).
Tennant, Emma *Wild Nights, Women Beware Women* London
Faustine London: Faber 1992.
Walker, Alice *The Color Purple* London: The Women's Press 1984.
The Temple of My Familiar New York and London: Harcourt Brace Jovanovitch and The Women's Press 1990.
Possessing the Secret of Joy London: Jonathan Cape 1992.
Weldon, Fay *The Life and Loves of a She-Devil* London: Hodder and Stoughton 1983.
Growing Rich London: Harper Collins 1992.
Winterson, Jeanette *Oranges Are Not the Only Fruit* London: Pandora 1985.
Wilson, Elizabeth *Only Halfway to Paradise* London: Tavistock 1980.
Woolf, Virginia *To the Lighthouse* London: Hogarth Press 1927.
Mrs Dalloway London: Hogarth Press 1925.
Three Guineas London: Hogarth Press 1938.

Secondary Texts:

Abbott, Sidney and Love, Barbara *Sappho was a Right-on Woman* New York: Stein and Day 1985.
Abel, Elizabeth, Marianne Hirsch and Elizabeth Langland eds. *The Voyage In: Fictions of Female Development* London: University of New England Press 1983.
Adelman, Marcy ed *Long Time Passing: Lives of Older Lesbians* Boston: Alyson Publications 1986.
Baker Miller, Jean *Towards a New Psychology of Women* London: Pelican 1976.

Bakhtin, M. *The Problems of Dostoyevsky's Poetry* Manchester: Manchester University Press 1984.

Beauman, Nicola *A Very Great Profession* London: Virago 1983.

Belsey, Catherine and Moore, Jane eds. *The Feminist Reader: Essays in Gender and the Politics of Literary Criticism* London: Macmillan 1989.

Chodorow, Nancy *The Reproduction of Mothering* Berkeley: University of California 1978.

Cixous, Hélène 'The Laugh of the Medusa' in *L'Arc* 61, 1975 trans.

Cranny-Francis, Anne *Feminist Fiction* Cambridge Polytechnic 1991.

Daly, Mary *Gyn/Ecology* London: The Women's Press 1979.

Dollimore, Jonathan 'The Dominant and the Deviant: A Violent Dialectic' *Critical Quarterly* 28 1/2, 1986.

Duncker, Patricia *Sisters and Strangers: An Introduction to Contemporary Feminist Fiction* Oxford: Blackwell 1992.

Ehrenreich, Barbara and English, Deirdre *For her Own Good: 150 Years of Experts' Advice to Women* London: Pluto Press 1979.

Faderman, Lillian *Odd Girls and Twilight Lovers: A History of Lesbian Lives in the Twentieth Century* Harmondsworth: Penguin 1992.

Faludi, Susan *Backlash: The Undeclared War against Women* London: Chatto and Windus 1992.

Felski, Rita *Beyond Feminist Aesthetics* London: Hutchinson Radius 1989.

Freedman, Estelle B., Gelpi, Barbara C., Johnson, Susan L. and Weston Kathleen M. eds. *The Lesbian Issue: Essays from Signs* Chicago: University of Chicago Press 1982.

Freud, Sigmund *On Sexuality* Pelican Freud Library vol. 7 Harmondsworth: Penguin.

Friedan, Betty *The Feminine Mystique* (1963) Harmondsworth: Penguin 1982.

Gallop, Jane *Feminism and Psychoanalysis* London: Macmillan 1982.

Gilligan, Carol *In a Different Voice* Cambridge, Mass: Harvard University Press 1982.

Grahn, Judy *The Work of a Common Woman* London: Onlywomen Press 1985.

Greene, Gayle *Changing the Story: Feminist Fiction and the Tradition* Ann Arbor: University of Michigan Press 1991.

Griffin, Gabriele *Outwrite: Lesbianism and Popular Culture* London: Pluto Press 1993.

Jackson, Rosemary *Fantasy: The Literature of Subversion* London: Methuen New Accents 1981.

James, L. *Jean Rhys* London: Longman 1978.

Kitzinger, Celia *The Social Construction of Lesbianism* London: Sage 1987.

Lefanu, Sarah, *In the Chinks of the World Machine: Feminism and Science Fiction* London: The Women's Press 1988.

Marcuse, Herbert *Eros and Civilisation* London: Abacus 1972.

Millett, Kate *Sexual Politics* London: Virago 1977.

Marks, E. and de Courtivron, E. *New French Feminisms* Brighton: Harvester 1980.

The Newly Born Woman. (La Jeune Nee) trans. Betty Wing Manchester: Manchester University Press 1986.

Monteith, Moira *Women's Writing: A Challenge to Theory* London: Harvester 1986.

Munt, Sally ed. *New Lesbian Criticism* London: Harvester Wheatsheaf 1992.

Newton, Judith and Deborah Rosenfeldt eds. *Feminist Criticism and Social Change* London: Methuen 1985.

Radford, Jean *The Progress of Romance* London: Routledge and Kegan Paul 1986.

Radway, Janice 'Women Read the Romance' *Feminist Studies* 9: 1 1985.

Rolph, C.H. *The Trial of Lady Chatterley's Lover* London: Penguin 1961.

Russ, Joanna *On Strike Against God* Trumansberg, New York: Crossing Press 1980.

Showalter, Elaine *The Female Malady: Woman, Madness and English Culture 1830–1980* London: Virago 1987.

Turkle, Sherry *Psychoanalytic Politics* London: Lowe and Brydone 1979.

Vicinus, Martha *Independent Women: Work and Community for Single Women 1850–1920* London: Virago 1985.

A Widening Sphere: Changing Roles of Victorian Women ed. London: Methuen 1980.

Waugh, Patricia *Feminine Fictions: Revisiting the Postmodern* London: Routledge 1989.

Yorke, Liz *Impertinent Voices* London: Routledge 1991.

Index

Published by Pluto Press

Outwrite
Popular/Rising Lesbian Texts

GABRIELE GRIFFIN

Until recently, studies of lesbian literature have tended to focus on a few 'canonised' texts and authors – Gertrude Stein and Audrè Lorde, for example. **Outwrite**, however, takes as its theme lesbian texts that are either popular (i.e. enjoyed by a wide lesbian and heterosexual audience) or that utilise a popular form (such as the thriller or romance) or a popular medium (cinema or television).

The contributors address such key issues as representations of lesbian sex, how lesbian pulp fiction has been received, and how lesbians encode their stories. Works discussed range from Lorde's *Zami* and Ishmat Chugton's *The Quilt* to Katherine Forrester's *Murder at the Nightwood Bar*, Ann Bannon's Beebo Brinker series, and films such as *Desert Hearts* and *The Killing of Sister George*.

Contributors:

Sonya Andermahr, Barbara Brady, Penny Florence, Gabriele Griffin, Nicki Hastie, Jenny and Celia Kitzinger, Paulina Palmer, and Carol Ann Uszhurat.

ISBNs hardback: 0 7453 0687 X   softback: 0 7453 0688 8

Order from your local bookseller or contact the publisher on
081 348 2724.

Pluto Press 345 Archway Road, London N6 5AA

Published by Pluto Press

Bringing It All Back Home
Class, Gender and Power in the Household Today

HARRIET FRAAD, STEPHEN RESNICK and RICHARD WOLFF

Bringing It All Back Home offers precisely what social critics
have been calling for: an analysis of relationships between
men and women that benefits from the rich traditions of
Feminism and Marxism, and yet is free from the economic,
political and other determinisms that have been so
ubiquitous in those traditions.

Drawing on new Feminist and Marxist theories, the authors
connect the relationships of class, gender and power inside
modern households. The resulting new theory establishes
the intimate arena of the household as a centrally important
object of contemporary social analysis. Weaving their
analysis from the basics of economics, cultural studies and
psychoanalysis, the authors range across abstract social
theory and concrete analyses of topics such as the current
crisis in household life and the anorexia epidemic among
young women.

Harriet Fraad is a practising psychoanalytic psychotherapist
in Connecticut.

Stephen Resnick and **Richard Wolff** are both Professors of
Economics at the University of Massachusetts.

ISBNs hardback: 0 7453 0707 8   softback: 0 7453 0708 6

Order from your local bookseller or contact the publisher on
081 348 2724.

Pluto Press 345 Archway Road, London N6 5AA

Published by Pluto Press

Changing Our Lives
Women In/to Women's Studies

GABRIELE GRIFFIN

☐ *Ideal for anyone entering Women's Studies courses.*

Women's Studies is now an established course subject in many universities and colleges. This history of the development of Women's Studies offers both lay readers and those specialising in the subject a unique overview of the discipline.

Gabriele Griffin covers the establishment of Women's Studies as a discipline; its relation to feminism and to liberation movements; a discussion of its institutional status; its contents and methodologies with special emphasis on the personal–political dimension and an outline of the issues raised by students on Women's Studies courses.

A feature of the book is a series of interviews providing an integrated personal narrative of the interviewees' experiences of Women's Studies.

Gabriele Griffin teaches English and Women's Studies at Nene College, Northampton.

ISBNs hardback: 0 7453 0752 3   softback: 0 7453 0753 1

Order from your local bookseller or contact the publisher on
081 348 2724.

Pluto Press 345 Archway Road, London N6 5AA

Published by Pluto Press

Hidden From History
A Pluto Classic

SHEILA ROWBOTHAM

In this Classic study of women in Britain from the Puritan revolution of the 1930s, Sheila Rowbotham shows how class and sex, work and the family, personal life and social pressures, have shaped and hindered women's struggles for equality.

'In an era of phoney specialisation, I admire Sheila Rowbotham's directness. Women should be grateful for a book of this kind, which fills our inadequate record of the past.' Eva Figes, New Statesman

ISBN softback: 0 904383 56 3

Writing Women
Contemporary Women Novelists

OLGA KENYON

A celebration of the strengths and diversities of feminists writing worldwide. A stimulating survey of the work of women novelists writing today – from Maya Angelou and Alice Walker to Angela Carter, Elaine Feinstein and Alison Lurie.

ISBN softback 0 7453 0564 4

Order from your local bookseller or contact the publisher on 081 348 2724.

Pluto Press 345 Archway Road, London N6 5AA

OPEN LETTERS
WOMEN'S BOOKCLUB

The only specialist bookclub offering discounted new books on women's issues aimed specifically at an academic and scholarly audience. We deliver to your door at a fraction of bookshop prices.

❑ Three catalogues a year offering over sixty discounted new titles by leading academic writers.

❑ All titles carefully selected from publishers large and small.

❑ The ideal way to keep up to date with current debates in art, cultural studies, gender studies, health, history, literary studies, media studies, sexual theory, sociology, philosophy, politics and religion.

Unlike most ordinary bookclubs, Open Letters also provides a valuable information exchange service through Open Letters Noticeboard, giving members a convenient way of learning about forthcoming conferences, exhibitions, summer schools, new courses, works in progress and feminist networks.

Student rate available – ring us on 081 348 2724 (or write or fax on 081 348 9133) NOW for current membership details and special offers.

OPEN LETTERS BOOKCLUB

345 Archway Road, London N6 5AA